Anne & Betty
United By The Struggle

Anne Scargill and Betty Cook
with Ian Clayton

route

Published by Route
info@route-online.com
www.route-online.com

ISBN : 9798328125048

First Published in 2020
This edition 2024

Anne Scargill and Betty Cook assert their moral
right to be identified as the authors of this book

Photos
Photographs are from Anne and Betty's personal collection.
The image of Betty on crutches and of the soup kitchen women
are by Raissa Page and are under copyright, held within the
Richard Burton Archives, Swansea University.

Cover Design:
Scott Luís Masson at SLM Illustration

Typeset in Bembo by Route

All rights reserved
No reproduction of this text without written permission

To my sister Joan, who I miss every day.

To my sons
Michael, the bird who never flew
Donny, who paid the true price of coal
Glyn, I wasn't always there when I should have been.
.

Foreword
Maxine Peake

I remember it well. Driving over to Barnsley from Salford on a clear, sunny day in 2013. I pulled into the driveway of a bungalow. The garden was in bloom, everything looked neat and tidy, well kept. I was feeling anxious. I was here to meet Anne Scargill, Betty Cook, Dot Kelly, Elaine Evans and Lesley Lomas. These women were friends and comrades involved in the occupation of Parkside Colliery, Lancashire, in 1993, during the last wave of pit closures. I was here to interview them for a radio play I was hoping to write about their experiences. I think I was anxious because I imagined that spending five nights and four days down a mine must have taken its toll, and I was going to ask them to return to a dark and difficult place from their past. I was also nervous as Anne was the ex-wife of the infamous NUM president Arthur Scargill, so I had prepared myself for a rigorous interrogation into my political motives. Anne was from Barnsley after all; those Yorkies are as tough as the stone they were carved from.

As soon as the front door was flung wide open and Anne and Betty's faces came beaming out at me, my reservations melted away. I was planning on staying for a couple of hours maximum to record the women talking about their time down the Parkside pit. There was a spread laid on in the kitchen that would have rivalled any wedding reception. Barm cakes or bread cakes (depending on your allegiances) stretched as far as the eye could see. Five hours later, and approximately the same amount of bread based products consumed, I emerged into a South Yorkshire early evening inspired and entertained. The warmth and passion of Anne, Betty and the women was tangible. Their humour was side-splitting; it later became evident that this was a tried-and-tested survival technique. As Anne says, 'If you don't laugh, you'll cry.'

The camaraderie between the women was heart-warming and inspiring. It was evident through this initial meeting that there was a special bond between Anne and Betty – the best of best friends. Their loyalty to an industry that has caused them both immense personal pain still ran red-hot through their veins, despite their experiences at the hands of a ruthless patriarchy that in many ways they fought with, for and against. Betty especially has suffered so much personal loss, so much grief, but she has so much fight. These two women, whom I now feel honoured to call friends, channelled that energy. They didn't cave in as I'm sure I might. They protested, they got educated, they opened themselves to a new world of grassroots politics, not just locally but nationally and globally. They extended their passion, compassion and activism out to the world. To this day they are still the heartbeat of a community that, after the miners' strike of 1984/85, had its veins ripped out by a hateful and vengeful Tory government.

Anne and Betty are a constant inspiration to me. They are two beacons of hope that show that we are all capable of affecting change, tackling life head-on and having a bloody good laugh along the way. I salute you both, my heroes.

Preface
Ian Clayton

I first came across Anne Scargill and Betty Cook on a march. I only saw them, I was too shy to introduce myself. I met them properly for the first time when I was asked to deliver the annual Davy Jones memorial lecture at the National Union of Mineworkers office in Barnsley. Davy was one of the miners killed on the picket line during the strike of 1984/85. His father was in the audience so I was nervous about speaking that day. The big hall at the NUM is a room full of atmosphere and history, the sort of place where the walls, lined with silk banners, speak to you. I gripped the lectern with both hands. Anne and Betty sat on the front row and smiled encouragement. When I finished speaking they made a big fuss of me.

Some time after that, I was with Anne and Betty again at the unveiling of a piece of art work that commemorates the terrible disaster at Oaks pit where 361 men and boys lost their lives in an underground explosion in December 1866. They mentioned to me that they were hoping to write a book about their lives and their involvement with Women Against Pit Closures.

Last year, I went over to Anne's daughter Margaret's house and we planned how we might tackle the idea of writing a book. I wasn't sure how I could do it with a dual narrative, but agreed to give it a try because I knew that Anne and Betty would have plenty to say about lives lived in struggle: the struggle to be heard as women in a tough working-class community; the struggle to support their men folk in the fight for jobs and a future in an industry that was being deliberately wound down; and the struggle to protect their communities and tackle the social problems that came as a direct result of Thatcher and her government's policies.

Anne and Betty remind me of those women I called 'Aunty' when I was a boy – they weren't my real aunties, but I stood there while they spat on their hankies and wiped muck off my face or flattened my hair. We started to work together at Anne's house first.

Sometimes it took an hour for me to commit pen to paper; as soon as I got to Anne's house I was told 'Take off your coat if you're stopping' and asked how many sugars I wanted in my tea. This happened every week before I sat down. Then Anne would tell me that she had bought some nice cheese and tomatoes for lunch, or she'd say that she was going round to the fish shop for a change. Betty brought buns for afters. They looked after me.

Over the weeks I couldn't help but be impressed by the spirit and stamina of these two women and the way they always wanted to be doing things. They told me about their plans for attending conferences in America and Ireland, announced 'You can come if you want', then went straight from that to telling me that I could help them carry their banner at the With Banners Held High festival and at Durham Miners' Gala. I tried my hardest to make them concentrate on telling stories about their lives and involvement in protest. Anne and Betty are not the easiest of people to do that with, they would much rather be 'doing' than 'saying'.

I said to Anne one day, 'Did you ever keep a diary or a journal during the strike?'

'Nay lad,' she laughed, 'I was too busy making apple pie and custard for the lads when they came back from picketing and tormenting bobbies to be writing stuff down.'

Betty was a bit more reflective, she told me that she had written poetry during the strike and had started to write a bit about her life. She handed me a very moving piece of writing about the early years of her marriage. I suggested to them that the time was ripe for them to tell their story because history is mostly written by those in charge, but sometimes the best history comes from the places and stories that are often neglected. I said, 'After all, history is just what people have said and done and everybody should be able to write that.' Betty thought for a bit. She said she agreed with me, but she thought there was a bit more.

'I think history is about what they say and do to us and how we organise ourselves to fight back.'

Anne nodded and said, 'That's right.'

The penny dropped for me that day. I already knew that Anne and

Betty are kind people who want to do good in their community, that they're proud of where they come from and have a great sense of its history. More than that though, they possess an homespun wisdom that comes from experience, sticking together and standing up; an instinctive knowledge of doing what's right in all sorts of situations. They certainly don't like being told what to do and both of them mistrust authority when they think it's not being fair. They have an absolute commitment to dissent.

We met at Anne's house when we talked about childhood, growing up and married life. When we got to talking about the miners' strike and their part in it, the two women suggested we should meet in a little office they have at the NUM. In that office they hang their banners and keep press cuttings and photographs, reminders of the struggle they helped to co-ordinate. I noticed that a lot had been written about Anne Scargill and Betty Cook over the years in books, papers and journals, much of it by well-educated women who see the two as shining lights of the working-class women's movement. I suggested one day that what they were doing in writing their own story was important because for the first time people would be able to read something that was directly from their point of view rather than on their behalf. Anne laughed at me.

'Well we ought to know, we were there, weren't we love.'

This is a book of stories and gathered thoughts by two women who were very much there, in the thick of it. I still think that Anne and Betty are far happier to be on picket lines and protest marches than writing stories about them, but I'm glad they decided to get some of their experiences written down. When we discussed what they should call their book, Betty tried to find ideas around women being strong, Anne suggested, 'We didn't have much but we had some fun.' In the end we settled for *United By The Struggle* because having met during the strike and then continuing to stand up for what they think is right, we thought it captured the essence of that.

'As long as it says inside that we never gave in,' said Anne, 'I don't give a bugger what it says on t'cover.'

Anne and Betty continue not to give in. They are working-class heroines of the finest order. These are their stories in their voices.

We are women, we are strong
We are fighting for our lives
Side by side with our men
Who work the nation's mines
United by the struggle
United by the past
And it's here we go, here we go
For the women of the working class

'Women of the Working Class' by Mal Finch

An Angel With Clogs On
Anne

I was brought up in the heart of the Barnsley coalfield with my mam, dad and sister Joan in a terraced row in Barugh Green. There was a pub called the Phoenix at one end of the row and a Co-op at the other. My dad was Elliott Harper, a coalminer from a big family of colliers in Gawber. My mother was Harriet Hardy from Skelmanthorpe, near Huddersfield. Her dad and brothers worked at the mill. She was twenty-six when she met my dad at the cinema in Skelmanthorpe. He had ridden over on his motorbike. They got married in 1935 and had two sons. The first was stillborn. They named him Elliott after my dad. The second was called Ken. He lived to be ten months old but died of meningitis when an epidemic swept the Barnsley area. I was born on 12th October 1941. My sister Joan came eight years later.

My dad had worked at many different pits before ending up at Woolley Colliery where he became chairman of the union branch. He was a staunch union man and had been involved in a fair few strikes, including the general strike of 1926. He never forgave the blacklegs who had scabbed and he cursed their names when he was that way out. There was one in particular, his name was Mick Smith. If he walked past our house and my dad happened to be looking out he'd say, 'Si thee, there's a scab sneaking past our window.'

Everything in our house was connected to coal mining. We burnt coal for warmth, cooking, and to heat our water for washing. The soap we used was marked 'PHB' which stood for Pit Head Baths. It was yellow and had a distinctive smell. We dried ourselves on striped towels that came from the pit – anybody who has ever lived in a pit village can tell a pit towel when they see one. My dad brought home rolls of rubber belt which he used to sole shoes with, line the back of his van, and protect the paths on his allotment. He also brought home corrugated metal sheets which he flattened out to make wheelbarrows. I'm sure a lot of his shovels and other tools were purloined from the pit as well.

My dad liked his pint of beer. At the weekend he would be helped home from the pub to our house and then shoved through the door. My sister Joan and me guided him upstairs and put the pee bucket next to his bed. My mam would curse him for being a drunken bugger who pissed away their money. The truth was that Dad was incredibly hard working and it was Mam who held the purse strings and ran the house with a rod of iron. He tipped-up all of his money to her and she gave him back what she thought he needed for his beer and tobacco. She was very shrewd with money, tight enough to nip a currant in two.

As a young woman, Mam worked as a cook for Dr Bell. She thought he was the bee's knees; she liked people with a bit of authority behind them. She wasn't the best mother in the world but she was a good cook and excellent baker. She made her own bread every day. I can see her now going barmy because she had put some bread out to cool without a net on and the birds had pecked at her loaves. If she wasn't baking, she'd be tidying. She was house proud and kept everything spotless.

On Saturdays she would do her shopping. She'd call for a 'Raines pie' at the bottom of Eldon Arcade then bring home delicacies such as pig bag, tripe and cow heel – which our Joan and me loved with plenty of vinegar and salt and pepper on. She also called in Woolworths for a large bag of pic'n'mix. My mam and Joan loved a 'bag of spice' as we called sweets round here. We had a roast dinner every Sunday. Mam collected the juice from the meat tin and poured it into a dish to make mucky-fat and bread for Sunday tea and for Dad's snap the following few days.

Our toilet, which we shared with our neighbour, was at the bottom of the yard. I used to be frightened to go down to it. I'd be there with a flickering candle shouting to my mother, 'Are you still at t'door Mam?' Then every few steps, 'Are you still there?' We got bathed in the set pot. My dad made a solid plank that slotted in across the top of the pot for me and our Joan to sit on while our mother washed us in the same water that she had used for boiling the whites.

If ever we fell off the plank, we'd be dancing in the red hot water at the bottom of the iron boiler. After she washed us she used the water again to swill the flags outside our back door. Nothing got wasted with my mother.

I had as many good hidings then as I had good dinners. I was a bugger though and our mother was handy with the stick. She had a thin, flexible branch to hit us with. I called it the 'swisher'. Many is the time I have broken the swisher and thrown it in a bin when she wasn't looking, only for her to get another one. My dad used to hit us with the flat of his hand. When my dad hit me I'd go running off to Aunty Florence's house. She was a lovely woman and very kind to me and our Joan. She'd also lost a daughter to meningitis. Her husband, Uncle Nush, suffered with pneumoconiosis and couldn't get out of his chair. He'd be sitting there with his wireless by his side and he'd say, 'Come here old cock, what have they done to thee now?' My Aunty Florence would chastise my dad, 'You want to give up hitting them kids over t'head.'

Across the road from us there was a football field. There wasn't a lot of girls my age where we lived so I had to play with the lads. I used to rush to get my jobs done so that I could get to the fields. One day I ran straight across the road without looking both ways and a bloke coming up on a motorbike knocked me down. I jumped up and carried on running to the field. When I looked down I could see that my legs were bleeding. The bloke from the motorbike came across and one of the lads, John Smith, said to him 'She only lives over there' and pointed to our house. The bloke picked me up and carried me home. My dad went mad, shoved me straight upstairs and gave me a good hiding for getting knocked down. I don't think he meant to hurt me; I know now that he was probably shocked and didn't want me to be running on roads, but at the time it upset me and I sat on my bed picking grit out of my knees. In spite of the good hidings, my dad was a good man, a loveable rogue. He had the bobbies at the door from time to time, but I think everybody in Barugh Green liked him.

Every now and again my mam would say to him, 'Their hair wants cutting.' That was the signal for Dad to get his scissors out to

Elliot and Harriet Harper.

Anne on her tricycle pedalling up to the Co-op in Barugh Green.

Outside Gawber church. Joan holding hands with Anne and Paul Ashton.

Joan and Anne with Father Christmas at Butterfield and Massies, circa 1953.

cut our hair. She wouldn't let him cut it in the house so we went outside in the yard. The wind always seemed to be blowing down the backs and that meant he never got our hair straight. We used to ask him if he could put the stool somewhere where the wind wasn't blowing. He'd laugh and say, 'There's only a fortnight between a good haircut and a bad one, get sat down.'

My dad loved me and my sister Joan but he found it hard to disguise his disappointment that we weren't the sons he'd lost. He often said to me, 'I wish you'd been a lad.' My mam said it as well, in fact my mam said it more than my dad. This left us always wanting to prove ourselves – well me anyhow, our Joan used to go and spend time with a family up the street. In many ways I was a lad.

Most of my cousins were boys and I used to get their hand-me-down clogs. My dad had some old cobbler's lasts which he used to mend our family's and most of the neighbours' shoes. Dad took the irons off my hand-me-downs and put rubbers on. One Christmas I was picked to be an angel in the nativity play, I suppose because I had blonde curly hair. I was in my clogs in that play. All the kids called me 'the angel with clogs on' after that.

Pulled From One To The Other
Betty

I have snapshots in my memory from when I was young. I have a balloon on a string. My mother is taking me to Bentley from Doncaster on a tram. Everybody on the tram wants to know where I've got my balloon from. It was wartime and you didn't get things like that then. I can go back further. I'm standing in my cot, gripping the wooden bars and looking up at my mother's face. She is leaning over and showing me a pottery ornament. On one side is a Chinese figure and when you turn it over, it's a face. The ornament is chipped, as it was when it was presented to my mum by Mrs Clarissa Jane Benson and her husband George, a wealthy mill owner of Shibden Croft near Halifax. Mum was in service to the Bensons. They were generous at giving things away that were used and they didn't want anymore.

Catherine, my mother, was thirty when she married my dad, Basil, a collier at Bentley pit. When my mum decided to leave the Bensons to get married they tried to keep hold of her. I have a letter they wrote from a cruise ship, it tells her that she is making a mistake and the marriage won't work. Mrs Benson's parents gave my parents a silver-plate tea service as a wedding present. It had been used, but I suppose they thought it was good enough for servants.

Mum still went over to the Bensons to help out even after she was married and had me. She took me with her. At the time, a lot of coalminers' daughters from South Elmsall went to work in the mills over Halifax way. They went on a bus put on by the mill owners. Mum and I travelled on the bus with them. It was a long journey and it was always cold so I cuddled up to Mum. Shibden Croft stood back from the main road. They had a telephone, the first I had seen, on a table in a porch that smelled musty.

The Bensons moved to an old stone farmhouse in Barkisland that was filled with wooden spinning-wheels and cabinets full of miniature ornaments. I went with Mum during school holidays and spent my days there with the animals; they had turkeys and pigs. I was an only child and a lonely child.

Mrs Benson was different to the other women I knew; she had short, cropped hair, drove her own car and played golf. I'm not sure that she liked me, in fact I'd go as far as to say she resented me. She'd had a son called Peter who died in childhood. Her husband became infertile after a bout of mumps and she couldn't have any more children. When my mother married against the will of her employer, then had a daughter, I think it bothered Mrs Benson.

My dad left Bentley pit and went to work at Frickley pit in South Elmsall. He lodged with Grandad and Grandma Armstrong – they weren't my real grandparents, they were the parents of Aunt Dolly, who wasn't my real aunt either. Dolly had also worked for the Bensons and somehow her family had become entwined with mine. Something happened while my dad was away in lodgings. I'm not sure to this day what it was. One of my relatives said to me years after, 'Your dad was naughty!' I have a vivid memory from childhood of an almighty row. I was sitting in front of the fire. Mum and Dad were shouting at the top of their voices at one another. My mother had given me a boiled egg. I ate my egg as I listened to the blazing row, a frightened girl. I finished the egg and not knowing what to do next I started to nibble at the membrane inside the shell.

From that day on it seemed like the argument never ended. They would shout at each other over everything and anything. I loved them both but I was continually pulled from one to the other. My mother was in the kitchen one day getting a wash. She had bolted the kitchen door because they had been rowing again. My dad talked through the door to her, trying to persuade her to open it, but she wouldn't give in. In the end, my dad turned to me and said, 'Come on, I'll take you to Doncaster and buy you a new bonnet.' I went with him. My mother never let me forget that. She was beside herself because she thought that I had chosen him over her.

Shortly afterwards there was a big meeting at the Armstrong's house in South Elmsall.

'There's only one thing for it. You will all have to come and live in our Joe's attic,' Grandma Armstrong said.

Joe was 'Uncle Joe', a son of Grandma Armstrong.
Joe's wife tried to object.

'I don't think Joe will agree to that.'

'He'll agree alright!' said Grandma Armstrong. So that was decided upon.

Joe's wife, 'Aunt' Enid, had three young children at the time; a pair of twins in a pram and another one. They lived in a pit house at the bottom of Broad Lane. Downstairs was a front room, a kitchen, a bathroom and a little pantry. There were two bedrooms upstairs and an attic room above. Aunt Enid craved a three-bedroom house at the top of the street where the deputies and overmen lived, but Joe refused to move because the rent was dearer. We lived in their attic for six months or so. We all used the same bathtub. When I got into it I always smelled the same thing – Dettol disinfectant. My mother was frightened I might catch something off them.

One day Mum took me to a house where there was a woman laid in bed poorly. The woman had another house on Moorhouse View that belonged to her. The poorly woman agreed to rent us her house fully furnished so we moved from the attic. This was during the war. The house had a large kitchen which we more or less lived in. We never used the front room because all of the furniture that belonged to the house was stored in there. It was the same upstairs; furniture that belonged to the house was stored in a spare bedroom.

My mother gave me a mousetrap to play with and a piece of turnip to set it off. I did it once too often and trapped my fingers. The next-door neighbour had three boys who I played with. We had picnics. The boys brought bread and sugar sandwiches. I thought they were delicious and swapped my sandwiches for some of theirs. My mother was horrified when she found out. 'Don't you dare eat sugar sandwiches!' She thought it beneath us to be eating such a thing.

I got my first pet at Moorhouse View. She was a cat we called Bubbles. At the time Mum used to stand me in a bowl of soapy water to wash me and the cat used to come and lick the bubbles.

At Westfield Lane Infants I was on my own all the time. I didn't have any friends. The teacher used to give us pictures to copy. She seemed to always give me a frog. I hated frogs and couldn't draw them. When I got to Broad Lane Juniors I started to find friends, but some of the teachers were awful. There was one called Mrs Smeaton. She'd give out the pencils and rulers and have us drawing measured lines; she always wanted us to measure things. I did mine wrong. She dragged my cardigan off my back and told me I didn't need it on. It was wintertime and freezing. She rattled my knuckles with the ruler and made me go and stand in the playground without my cardigan on. To this day I can't measure properly.

The headteacher at Broad Lane was Miss Spinks, a tall woman with a kind face. She had a beautiful way with her. She often read to the whole school and seemed to make time to see anyone who was having problems. Class sizes at that school were large, so quite often the brighter children were left unsupervised to get on with their work in the corridor outside the classroom. I was in the top group for composition and one day I sat in the corridor and got a funny feeling in my stomach that I couldn't do my work. I wanted to show it to someone and ask for help. I walked down the corridor and knocked on Miss Spinks's door.

'I can't do it,' I said to her.

'Yes you can,' Miss Spinks said. 'Come and sit in my room for a while.'

My mum always sent me with an apple or pear. When I got my apple out my classmates would come up to me and ask, 'Will you save me the core?' A lot of the kids wore shoes without stockings. I can't bear the thought of that still.

Just after the war they served boiled ham for school lunch. Nobody knew what it was, I had to ask one of the dinner ladies. I once heard my mum say to my dad, 'I wish we could get a bit of boiled ham.' I took two pages out of my exercise book, wrapped up the ham and took it home.

We had moved to a new house at Broad Lane, South Elmsall. It was beautifully decorated when we moved in but Mum insisted that it would have to be all done again after one of the new neighbours told her that the man who lived their previously had TB. The house became a hotbed of wall scraping, ceiling washing and paintwork scrubbing. Materials were hard to come by because of the war. The walls were distempered, as was the fashion then. Distemper was like a

Catherine and Basil Danks wedding photo, 1937.

Grandma Gertrude Danks.

Betty's first baby photo, 1938.

mixture of white chalk and glue, a bugger to put on and worse to get off. They stippled it while it was still wet with a piece of net curtain. There was a small gang of lads in Broad Lane. Their favourite pastime was lighting a fire to roast jacket potatoes. The lads said I could share their fire as long as I brought them cigarettes. My dad was a heavy smoker so I would pinch a couple of cigs out of his packet of Passing Cloud every time I went to the fire. He never noticed because he was continuously smoking, or at least if he did he never said anything. Mum didn't smoke and he would never suspect me at that age. Dad loved nature. He took me on nature walks on the Warde-Aldam estate. He pointed to a certain type of flower that he called 'Lords and Ladies' and he showed me where to find violets and spiders' nests with eggs in.

Mum had a thing about cleaning. Every room in the house in its turn had to be emptied out. My worst job was shaking the feathers out of the mattresses so that she could wash the covers. The feathers would be flying about all over. On Friday nights Mum and I cleaned the brass and copper. We marched around the house banging the brass plates together like cymbals and sang:

> Oh! My name is McNamara
> I'm the leader of the band
> And though we're few in number
> We're the best band in the land.

Mum used to buy a flagon of cider to have with our Sunday dinner. I used to wonder why I felt light-headed on Sunday afternoons. I didn't know that it was alcoholic and I don't think Mum did either. Another thing she gave to me to drink was Mather's black beer from Huddersfield. It was full of vitamins and said to be a good tonic. When I told her I didn't like the taste she said, 'Put some lemonade in it, it'll do you good.' It's a good job I did because I found out much later that it is a very strong beer.

Twice a year she took me to Leeds on the train for new clothes. We went to C&A and a shop that sold copies of clothes that film stars wore. One year at Whitsuntide my dad bought me a green dress with frills on it like one of Shirley Temple's.

Nantling
Anne

My dad was full of ideas for making a bit of money. He wanted to go to Australia and set himself up in business but my mother held him back and told him not to be so daft. He wanted to reach out and try new things. She didn't like change, she wanted everything to stay the same – either that or in her control. She could be cold and nasty the way she talked, which left my dad a bit sloughened, but he didn't seem to care about getting his own way, he just carried on regardless.

Dad had a smallholding where he kept pigs and hens and grew tomatoes and vegetables. He used to sell his vegetables to the Co-op at the end of the row. He cured his own hams and had them hung up on hooks over the staircase. We went to bed on a night under hanging pieces of meat and came down in the morning to the same. Sometimes a mother pig would have a bigger litter than she had teats for. My dad would bring the little ones into the house wrapped in a blanket and put them on the warm hearth. I'd feed them with a 'titty' bottle. Everybody laughed at me because I took the little pigs out like dogs on a lead.

By law you were only allowed to keep a limited amount of pigs so he sold the extra meat he had on the black market. When it came to the time for slaughtering I used to have to go with him. He thought that nobody would suspect he was taking pigs to slaughter if he had his little girl with him. A bloke called Alf Walker had an abattoir at the back of his house. I used to sit in the corner and hear them shooting. The squealing was horrendous. Then they would start slitting with their knives. They saved the blood that ran out for black pudding.

A local bobby staked my dad out for months and finally caught him. Dad tried to bribe the bobby by offering him ham. The bobby wouldn't accept it and summonsed him. It went to court. The magistrate let Dad off because he bought pork off my dad himself.

Not long after, Dad saw the local bobby on patrol on a day when it was teeming with rain. He invited him into the house to get dried off in front of a good fire. While the bobby sat there steaming, my dad fetched him some hot food and a drink of tea. The bobby never bothered him after that and often stood talking with my dad – kallin' as we called it – when he was on his rounds past our front door.

My dad was one of the hardest workers I ever knew. He worked regular nights, catching the ten to nine pit bus to Woolley and coming home on the half past six bus the following morning. He would come in, have a cup of tea and a sandwich and then he was straight out into the field to feed the pigs and water the vegetables. He called his routine 'my jobs afore I sleep'. There's been many a time that I've been down the garden looking for him and I've found him asleep in his wheelbarrow in the greenhouse. I'd wake him up and walk back to the house with him.

As if he didn't have enough on he decided to become a part-time chimney sweep. It started when my mam couldn't get anybody to sweep our chimney. He bought some brushes and swept our chimney himself. Then folk started asking him to do theirs. He bought some good brushes and a little hoover to suck up the soot. I went with him on his round from the age of about nine. We did the chimneys on the big houses along Huddersfield Road. He'd be inside screwing his brushes together and I had to go outside and watch the chimney, then come in and tell him when the brush popped out of the pot.

My dad did loads of things on the side to make extra money, not all of which were strictly legal. He went coal picking one day with two of his mates and took his pony from the smallholding to load the coal sacks onto. They were disturbed by the local bobbies and all three men made a run for it leaving the pony with the coal. The sergeant was a wily one, he smacked the pony on the arse and followed it home. My dad had got washed and changed by the time it got there but couldn't get out of being stitched up by his own horse.

Another of his jobs was selling sticks. He used to saw the fallen trees from the local woodland. He had built his own circular saw complete with motor and housing that sounded like a jumbo jet taking off. That saw would have cut through concrete it was so big.

Once he'd cut the wood, Joan and me had to chop it into lengths to fit the average fire grate. It was really hard work and made my shoulder and hand hurt. He used to say 'hard work won't kill thi'. He got permission to do some forestry clearance and was given the plans of which trees to cull. He loaded up the trees and took them home. It was only when he had sawn up all the trees that he realised he had read the plans wrong. The ringed trees on the drawing were the route for the new nature trail. He went back under cover of darkness and painted other trees to make a new trail which he claimed was a better walk anyway.

He had a scheme for selling Christmas trees. In the week before Christmas, he would black up with coal dust on his face and then take the van to the woods to chop the trees down. He looked like the Milk Tray man as he delivered trees to the households who had pre-ordered them, cash in hand.

My mam used to say 'There he goes again with his nantling' – an old Yorkshire dialect word for pottering about in a shed or garden. My dad could make anything. He made a lot of bikes out of scrap. One Christmas Eve he said to me, 'I think I've just seen Father Christmas at the bottom of Longley Street. If you be good and get straight off to sleep he might have a bit of something for you.' Next morning there was a green tricycle. Christmas was always the busiest time and Dad had been so occupied with his pork that he hadn't had the chance to paint my bike until the middle of the night. I couldn't touch it because the paint was still wet. I had to wait for two days for my tricycle.

I loved that tricycle and I spent hours pedalling to the Co-op and back. I'd go up the pavement, turn round against the shop and come back, turn round at our front door and go back again. There was a man called Mr Senior that lived in the village who had a camera and was keen on taking photographs. He was always up and down with his camera round his neck. One day my mam came out and said, 'Mr Senior's taking photographs and he wants to take one of you on your bike.' I started to cry and scream. I thought that taking photographs meant taking you away. I had a picture of myself in my mind, I was pinned to a board somewhere. Mr Senior must have waited until I pedalled off, because there is a photograph of me from behind pedalling up to the Co-op. It remains one of very few photographs of me as a child.

Dad liked to make barrows; he made one that was so large it was a two-man job to use it. He made all the animal huts, his dog kennels were legendary. He wasn't the most subtle of craftsmen, most of his creations were held together by six-inch nails. He had a green Bedford van that I first learnt to drive in. He kept that van going for years. It had a sofa in the back for the kids to sit on. The sofa wasn't fastened down so it used to slide all over when we went round corners.

As Dad got older he got a hut. It was like an Aladdin's cave filled with the stuff he had pinched from the pit. The local kids liked to see him in his hut and they'd even knock on the back door and say to my mam, 'Is Mr Harper coming out?' He'd have them coming round with bits of wood and he'd mend their trolleys and show them how to make bird boxes. One lad used to come who was a bit girlish. Dad gave him a hammer and some nails, but no matter how hard the lad tried he couldn't get on with tools. He kept coming though and in the end Dad said, 'I think thy had better get in that kitchen with Harriet, she'll show thee how to bake.' The lad turned out to be a lovely baker and got a job at Fosters Bakery in Mapplewell. After that he ended up running a boarding house at Blackpool.

My mam was a very hard worker too, and a handy woman. They used to send for her when folk died. Mr Godard kept a flat board in his lavatory that was reserved for 'laying out' corpses. Mam used to wash them down and prepare them. A part of the preparing was to remove their false teeth. My dad didn't have any teeth, he'd lost them all when he was a young man, and from time to time he would keep the teeth if they fit him. Sometimes he would file them down to make them fit. If my mother chastised him he would just shrug his shoulders and say, 'Well they're no good to them anymore are they? I might as well put them to some use.'

The house we lived in was rented. The whole row was owned by a man called Den Pickering. Every Monday he came in person for the rent. If we weren't in, we left the money out with the rent book on the table. Mam found out that Den was selling up. She went to her savings and bought her own house. Not only that, she also bought a house at the end of the row where a bloke called Wilfred lived. Wilfred's mam and dad had died, he didn't have anybody else, so he lived there on his own. My mother let him carry on there and charged him rent. She was a cute bugger.

Grandma Gertrude
Betty

I believe I had a happy childhood, but there was a lot of tension in the family. I didn't really feel part of my mum's side. I had a cousin called Sandra at West Melton. We got on, but she seemed to be treated better than me. Whenever Grandad came back from what the family called 'his convalescent holiday' he would bring back two presents, one for me and one for Sandra. She always had the first pick and I was given the one she didn't want. We were both bridesmaids at our Aunty Charlotte's wedding. They wanted us to wear velvet bonnets. One of the bonnets was lovely, the other was plainer. Of course Sandra ended up with the nicer one.

I got on a lot better with my paternal grandparents. They were divorced; Grandad lived at Nottingham and Grandma lived at Bradford. I was under strict instruction never to tell anybody that they had parted. My mother hated the very word divorce. She thought that once vows were made they shouldn't be broken.

On my birthday there would be a knock on the back door, Grandad would come in with a five pound note in his hand and give me a hug. He would then take me to Doncaster to choose my present. His ex-wife, my grandma, Gertrude Danks, lived above a fish and chip shop that she owned near the cathedral at Bradford. She owned three altogether and went round to collect the rent from the other two. She carried rolls of money around with her and threw it about like confetti. She took me shopping one day in a taxi. When we got into the city centre, she insisted that the taxi driver wait to take us back. He followed us about like a lap dog, I felt embarrassed for him. Grandma paid for everything in cash and handed it to the taxi driver as we went round.

Mum didn't like Grandma. She said that she was a spendthrift who lived above her station in life. She called her Granny Grunt. I was allowed to visit her from time to time. She liked the theatre and took me to the Alhambra. We always had seats in a box. This gave mum another reason to be appalled. When I told her how exciting it was to see the show from the box, the displeasure was written on her face.

'She's spoiling you. She is bringing you up in a manner that you won't be accustomed to.'

Grandma had a daughter called Myrtle who ran a boarding house at Skegness. We stayed there occasionally and travelled on the train first class. One time I got a drop of bleach on my dress. Grandma decided we needed to replace it. She knew a woman who ran a children's clothes shop and asked her to bring a selection of dresses in my size to the boarding house. I couldn't make my mind up between two pretty ones. Grandma didn't blink an eye, she just said, 'Right we'll take these two thank you.' Whenever she went to buy shoes she wouldn't look at any that cost less than five pounds; this was when five pounds was a week's wage for a collier. This annoyed mum even more, because she was trying to keep a family on less than her mother-in-law was spending on shoes.

Grandma's fish shops were successful but she spent everything she earned and eventually went bankrupt. I have clear memories of visiting her solicitor near Forster Square. It didn't deter her. She bought a corner shop in my dad's name and carried on regardless. I was proud but mystified when I saw Dad's name over the door as I went in.

A message came to my dad at the pit one day saying that his mother had collapsed. She was in hospital with a suspected stroke. Dad took time off work to help her. Grandma recovered but was unable to carry on with the shop so they sold it. Much to Mum's dismay, Dad arranged for Grandma to move in with us and he converted the front room into a bedsit for her. I loved having her with us, but Mum couldn't wait to be shut of her.

Grandma decided she wanted to get married again and found someone. She then moved to live at Hemsworth. I was forbidden to see her after that. I saw her by accident once on the bus on my way home from school. Grandma had been visiting friends and was thrilled to see me. As she got off, she pressed a half crown piece into my hand.

My mum started to take lodgers in for the extra money. Two of them were young lasses who worked in a railway signal box. They sometimes let me go with them and showed me how to pull the levers. Another was a night sister at the maternity hospital down the road. She used to ask my mum to go to the chemist to fetch a bottle of methylated spirits for her feet. One day I came home from school to find the doors locked. I knocked hard on the front door. The lodger came and pulled the door open. She was in a dishevelled state and very angry. She shouted and screamed in my face for waking her. I don't know if I smiled, but she lunged at me and slapped me across the face. It was the first time anyone had ever hit me. That was the end of her. Dad turned her out as soon as Mum told him. Later Mum found out that she hadn't just been rubbing her feet with the meths, she had been drinking it. She was a severe alcoholic. She had been drinking spirit out of the lamps on the hospital ward as well. Because she was a sister at the hospital, Mum thought her to be respectable and had taken pity on her at first as she was on her own. It turned out that she wasn't just on her own, she was lonely.

Our last lodger was another young woman in her twenties. When she arrived she announced that her husband was in the forces. She hadn't been with us long when she came downstairs with a letter and announced that her husband was coming home on leave and would it be alright if he stayed. Mum allowed it. The man arrived late one night, he was quite a character. He told dozens of entertaining stories about his experiences. He even said that after disembarking the train at Moorthorpe station he had walked to our house down the lines because he knew we lived by the railway. Mum discovered that this man wasn't the lodger's husband at all, just a fancy man. After that there were no more lodgers, my mother put her foot down.

Dad didn't like me talking to boys. If I walked down Broad Lane into South Elmsall and I saw some boys coming up the other way, I had to cross over. I ended up zig-zagging my way down that lane because there would be boys on the pavement whichever side I was on. My dad wouldn't let me go to dances. Once when we had friends staying he relented and let me go with them to one at Moorthorpe Institute. I was stood at the side watching everybody dancing when my dad came for me; he picked me up so early that I didn't even get the chance to have a dance. The only other one I went to was at Westfield Lane School. It was a pit deputies' dance and my dad was the master of ceremonies. He didn't mind me going then because he could see me.

When I was a little bit older they started having a dance on a Monday night at South Elmsall fire station. It wasn't rock'n'roll times yet, they were still doing the St Bernard's Waltz, the Military Two-step and the Veleta. I longed to go. I told my dad that my friend's cat had kittens and I wanted to visit them. He knew I loved animals, so let me out. I took my stockings and suspenders and make-up in a bag and put them on in the toilets at the fire station. I still had to be home by half past nine. They kept kittens by their mother for eight weeks then, which meant that I had eight weeks of dancing before I had to find another friend who had a cat. There were a lot of cats who had kittens in South Elmsall that year.

Sunshine Corner
Anne

My school was across from where we lived. I didn't like it much. We used to have a bottle of milk in the morning and a little nap on a camp bed in the afternoon. There was a lad in our class who shit himself every time he laid down, poor bugger. In the end they told him to sit at his desk and put his head in his hands and it cured him. One morning I wouldn't go to school. My dad ran me all the way there with his slipper. I tried to hide behind a telegraph pole but he ended up braying me all the way into the classroom.

I did like a couple of the teachers. I loved one called Mrs Longmoor. I liked to listen to her reading. She had a book called *Chang* about a little jungle boy in Siam who finds a white elephant. It was a lovely story and I couldn't wait for the next episode. There was Mrs Green who taught maths, I liked her, so I ended up liking maths.

I must have still been at infant school when I went on my first Miners' Gala day. They took it in turns to have them in Barnsley, Doncaster, Rotherham and Wakefield. When it was in Barnsley, everybody set off on the parade from the church fields, past Sackville Street, Victoria Street, Church Street, then through the town and up Racecommon Road to the top of Locke Park. Our little legs were going like bees' wings because we couldn't keep up. I loved looking up at the big silk banners, they were like moving paintings pushed on wheels on a metal frame. The frame had a bar across about two feet above the road which the little kids sat on to swing their legs. Even though I was just a bairn I could tell that the brass bands, the noise, the people marching and the banners blowing in the breeze were important, that it meant something.

One day a big circus-like tent called Sunshine Corner came to the field opposite our house. My mother took me across to see it. I'd be about ten or eleven at the time. They gave out sweets and lollipops and everybody sang:

> Sunshine Corner oh it's very fine
> It's for children under ninety-nine
> All our welcome, seats are given free
> Sunshine Corner it's the place for me.

Sunshine Corner was an evangelical mission that toured working-class districts. They had a service for the children first – a bit of a sermon but mostly singing – and then a service for the parents. I loved being with everybody singing, it felt as though we were all together. After that, Mam started going to St Thomas's Church at Gawber. She took me with her and we walked up the hill every Sunday. Eventually we were both confirmed.

St Thomas's Church put on summer day trips. One summer we went to Whitby. The bus we travelled on couldn't get up all the hills on the moors so we had to keep getting off and walk behind it. I joined the choir where I met a lad called Paul Ashton. He became my first boyfriend. He came twice a week from Gawber on his bicycle to see me. I don't think he ever came into our house, he'd just knock on the door and wait there till I came out and then we'd go and sit on a wall talking. We were childhood sweethearts.

We got our first television for the coronation, a big one on a stand. One night when my dad had gone to work, my sister Joan and me were sitting with our mother watching a programme about christenings. Our Joan went for some water, sprinkled it on Mam and reckoned to make a sign of a cross. My mam went berserk, jumped out of her chair and threw her shoe at Joan. It bounced off a wall and cut her eye open underneath. Next morning I got up early to meet my dad coming home from the night shift at the bus stop. I wanted to explain to him what had happened. My dad had lost an eye in an accident himself. As a boy he had been given a knife to scrape off some old wallpaper. He slipped and stuck it in his eye. He thought he would get into trouble so he pulled the knife out and carried on scraping. His eye became infected and he had to have it removed. He wore a glass eye. Ever since that he didn't like to know about folk hurting their eyes. All hell was let loose when he got in.

My dad used to pay so much a week into a local miners' health scheme in case we were poorly. Every Friday he gave me some money out of his wage and I went on the bus into Barnsley to take it to the doctor's surgery on Royal Street near the post office. We couldn't afford a dentist, so I'd tie string round the tooth that hurt, fasten it to the oven door and slam it shut. There was no end to the ailments I picked up as a child. I had a tapeworm that they said I caught off some meat that wasn't right. Then I got scabies. I used to bring all sorts of mangy dogs home so I might have caught it off one of them. The doctor said I had to go to Barnsley Baths and sit in a special bath every three days. After the bath they smeared yellow cream all over me. My mam was ashamed because she thought that the neighbours would think we had a mucky house. She said, 'I'm not taking her, Elliott.' She wouldn't go on the bus with me so my dad had to take me.

Dad had a brother called Bernard who played football at centre-half. He started out at Gawber Sunday School team and then played for Barugh Green and West Ward. Barnsley came for him to sign professional. He joined them in 1931 and spent nearly his entire career there. Uncle Bernard was a big, strong, fit man. He was a PT instructor and one of his jobs during the war was to train the recruits. He looked after my dad whenever he got into fights and helped him find his glass eye if it got knocked out. He lived on Queens Drive when he played for Barnsley. He had a parrot in a cage, but they used to let it fly about the house as well. I was frightened to death of it and it seemed to know that. It used to dive at me. I can't do with birds fluttering about near me still to this day because of that parrot. Uncle Bernard always promised me his Barnsley football jersey when he retired but I never got it. I think it went to one of my cousins, a lad.

During the war Uncle Bernard played as a guest for Leeds United and was selected for England against Scotland in a friendly. He ended up as player-manager at Scunthorpe United for a time, just after the war. When he retired from football he and his wife, my Aunty Betty, took The Wheatsheaf pub at Sherburn in Elmet. I used to go over there and stay; it was opposite a bacon factory and next to a railway line. I got friendly with a girl whose dad worked in a signal box. I loved it there and never wanted to come home. One day Aunty Betty took me to one side and said, 'Why don't you come and live with us?' Aunty Betty had lost her only child, June, to meningitis when she was 14. I think she wanted to have a daughter around. At first I said yes and then I thought about our Joan. Though I was only about twelve at the time I knew our Joan was struggling at home. My mother was always at her, she wouldn't let me be either, but I was a bit tougher. Our poor Joan was nervous and didn't know what to do. I asked Aunt Betty, 'Why don't you take our Joan instead?' I think Betty knew that I was wise beyond my years. In the end neither I nor Joan went because our mother must have put her foot down.

Girls' School
Betty

My mother and father's ambition for me was that I would get the best education I could and go on to gain a university place; they were always mentioning 'cap and gown'. This was unusual for a girl in a pit village. We knew of only one girl with a degree from where we lived, she had a degree in music and my mother enthused about her.

I went to sit for my scholarship exam at Westfield Lane School in South Elmsall. I sat at a little desk and watched a trickle of water going by my feet. One of the girls behind me had become anxious and was frightened to put her hand up to go to the toilet. When the results came through I was on a family holiday in County Antrim, Northern Ireland. One of our relatives sent a telegram to let us know I had passed the scholarship to go to grammar school. When we got home a neighbour told us that I was one of the youngest girls to pass. My dad saw that as a feather in his own cap.

I was pleased that I had passed, though it had been expected of me. I actually came out on the first list. At the time, there were two lists for scholarship children. If you got onto the first list it meant you had a choice of which grammar school you went to. My choice was either Hemsworth Grammar or Pontefract Girls' High School. Hemsworth was much closer to home but it was Co-Ed and my dad wouldn't have wanted me mixing. Pontefract High School was ten miles away on a rickety old service bus, but was just for girls, so that's where I went. I started there in September 1949, the youngest girl in my year. A few of us went from South Elmsall, we waited at the bus stop opposite David Haigh's pawn shop. We were dropped near to The Crescent Cinema at the town end in Pontefract, the boys walked one way up the hill to the King's School and we made our way in the opposite direction to Parkside by way of a sweet shop. Sweets were still rationed then so we all shared. Some of us had money and no coupons and others had coupons left and no money. There wasn't a lot of choice, it was mainly aniseed balls.

The Girls' High School was next to Pontefract Park. It was well known for the brown uniform – the locals called it 'brown knickers school'. On the way home the old bus was always full. Some of the conductors would let ordinary fare-paying passengers on and make us wait for the next bus if it got full. I had to explain to my dad that I hadn't been dawdling. I think he thought I was meeting boys, so one day he went with me to the bus. The conductor shouted, 'Fare payers first,' and my dad said, 'Hey, they've paid their fares already!' Sometimes we had to sit on one another's knees. They called it the Ideal Bus Company but it was far from ideal. A girl sat on my knee one day, leant her head on the window and the window fell out.

I had three very close friends who I travelled to school with: Phyllis, known to all as Phyl, from Ackworth; and Marjorie and Yvonne from Upton. When we were fifteen we parted. Your parents had to sign a form to say you could leave high school at fifteen. Their parents signed but my mum and dad insisted that I stay on until I was sixteen to do my school leavers' certificate. In the meantime, Phyl and Marjorie got jobs as trainee nurses at the Marguerite Hepton Hospital at Thorp Arch. I was determined to follow my friends into nursing. Ever since I'd been a little girl I had wanted to be a nurse. My dad was a volunteer in the St John's Ambulance and one of the sisters at Warde-Aldam Hospital was a friend of his. When I dressed up to play, I put on a nurse's uniform and each time I visited hospital as a child I went in my uniform. The staff used to say, 'Our little nurse is here again.'

I pleaded with Mum to let me leave school and start nurse training with my friends. She said that if I stayed on for one more year she promised I could leave then. I completed the school leavers' certificate. It was expected of the girls who did that to go on to sixth form to do A-levels. The A-levels were introduced while I was at Pontefract Girls' High School to replace the old Higher School Certificate. The headteacher at Pontefract was a Scottish lady called Miss McDermott. She was small in stature but determined in nature. She would address the school regularly with a firm message: 'This is a school for refined young ladies. And when you leave this school you will be a refined young lady.' She had me in her office when she heard that I wanted to leave.

'You are not leaving Elizabeth, you will go on to the sixth form, complete your A-levels and then go to teacher training college.'

She gave me a letter to take to Mum inviting her to a meeting. On the bus on the way to school I begged her not to change her mind about letting me leave at sixteen.

'Please don't make me stay Mum, you promised I could be a nurse.'

We got off the bus and as we walked to the school, Mum turned to me.

'Look! I promised you could leave and I'll keep that promise.'

Miss McDermott tried everything to change my mind and my mother's. I was worried because my mother could be very controlling. Mum stuck to her guns with Miss McDermott, and on this occasion she kept her promise.

Arthur
Anne

I left Darton Girls' Secondary Modern at Christmas in 1956, when I was fifteen. In the weeks leading up to it my mam used to say, 'There's only so many more weeks and then you can get a job.' I told her that I wanted to be a hairdresser.

'No!' she said, 'I want some money coming in.'

In those days you had to pay for a hairdresser to train you.

There was a bus stop opposite our house and my mam was always talking to people who were waiting for the bus; she'd even invite them into the front room if it was raining. One day, Mam got talking to a woman called Nancy who acted as a recruitment officer for Brook Motors. Everybody who got a job there was interviewed by Nancy. My mam told her about me. A week before I left school, I went to see her and asked her if I could have a job. I didn't know what job I would do, you didn't then, you got what you were given.

The Monday morning after I left school I was sitting on a chair alongside thirty other people on a shop floor winding wire for electric motors. The motors we wound in Barnsley were then sent to Huddersfield for putting into machines. I had no idea what the motors or machines did or were for, I was just a fifteen-year-old girl looking forward to five o'clock when I clocked out and then eight when I might get invited to a dance.

I gave my mother my wage every Friday and she gave me about two bob back, which I used to go dancing with. I'd go to a dance at the Drill Hall and in the wintertime the swimming pool at Town End baths was covered and made into a dance hall. When rock'n'roll started there was a Sunday night dance at a place called George's near the Catholic church. Skiffle was on the go then and I loved that song Lonnie Donegan sang called 'Rock Island Line'.

When Brook Motors went on to short-time working because they didn't have enough in the order book, we ended up without a full week's work. My mam said, 'I've heard somebody is leaving the Co-op, so there will be a job going if you want it.' I took a job at the Co-op at the end of our row and stayed there for about eighteen months until work at Brook's picked up and I went back.

I used to come home for my dinner at noon and one day I saw a young man standing by the back door. He turned round when he heard me coming down the yard.

'I'm looking for Elliott Harper,' he said.

Dad was usually asleep upstairs because of his regular nights.

'It's my dad, I'll go and see if he's up.'

'Tell him that Arthur Scargill is here to see him.'

And that was when I first set eyes on Arthur Scargill.

That day Arthur told my dad that there was a lot of anger at Woolley Colliery about a certain man called Elijah Benn. Elijah had a warm office on the pit top and a lot of power. He was branch treasurer for the union and spoke on behalf of the men, but at the same time he was extremely friendly with the bosses. He also had a contract for delivering coal to the colliers' houses. At the time coalminers got several loads of concessionary coal per year. The coal was free but the delivery – or leading as it was called – had to be paid for. Elijah was the man they had to pay for the service. He also had a lot of influence over who got the pick of the best pit houses. If you were in with Elijah you might get a nice house, if you weren't you might end up with a shithole. A lot of men and their families got fed up with Elijah but didn't know what to do.

After that first meeting with my dad, Arthur came round to our house three or four times. He saw that there was corruption within the union branch and he got together with my dad and my Uncle Bob to challenge the set up. Arthur used to talk to me when he visited. If truth be known I think he was a lot more interested in me than he was my dad. I was eighteen at the time and I was learning to drive in the big old green van of my dad's. Arthur had a little white Ford and he said to me, 'Why don't you let me teach you to drive in my car?' Arthur was a good instructor and he soon had me driving. He liked to talk to me about politics and the union. I didn't know too much about such things then, apart from what I'd heard my dad talking about.

Arthur had started at the pit when he was 15. He worked on what they called 'the screens'; this was where the coal was sorted out from the stone and muck. Arthur told me that on his first day he had been led down some steel steps to a place full of noise and filth. The people who worked there were mainly young boys and elderly men coming toward retirement; men who had once worked on the coalface but were no longer fit enough for that physical work. A lot of people with learning difficulties worked there too, and disabled men missing limbs. Arthur said he thought he had been sent to Dante's Inferno.

Arthur had organised his first industrial action by the time he was 17. At Christmastime, the older men were let off their shift early but the lads were held back and made to finish theirs. Arthur declared that this was unfair and went to see a bloke called Lomas who wore a greasy trilby and smoked a pipe. Arthur said that the lads were going to go home at the same time as the men.

'I can't give you permission to do that,' Lomas told Arthur.

All the young lads were ready for caving in.

'If he says we can't knock off early we'd better stop where we are.'

'No,' said Arthur, 'he didn't say that. He said he can't give us permission, so we will finish with the older blokes and see what happens.'

On the day the lads came out of the pit at the same time as the others, nothing was said. Arthur claimed that as his first victory. Not long after, Lomas pulled Arthur up.

'I'm going to tell you something young Scargill, you know you would be better off in Russia.'

After the to-do over the Christmas working practices, Arthur gained a lot of grassroots support amongst the men and wanted to stand for the union committee, but when it came to the voting he couldn't seem to get anywhere. He realised that ballot-rigging for union positions at Woolley was rife. The union were manipulating the outcome of votes by having two sets of voting papers printed: one set to be given to the men and another set already filled in with the choice of the current officials. Arthur's friend and colleague Goff Sunderland devised a system to put a stop to this. He made sure that every ballot paper handed out to the men was stamped, and that only stamped ballots were then included in the count. When Jock McBride retired as secretary of the union branch and Goff, who was the current delegate, decided he would like Jock's job as it played more to his strengths, it meant that the delegate's job was now vacant. Arthur put up against a man who represented the fitters and electricians. He won by 100 votes.

Arthur was kind and patient when he was showing me anything, but there were other times when he could be overbearing and controlling. He worked regular nights and he didn't like me going out with people I had known before I met him. Up to then I'd enjoyed going rock'n'rolling with the lasses. When Arthur started taking me on dates he asked me if I liked jazz music; he was a fan of trad-jazz and he was keen to introduce me to it. The first concert he took me to was at Sheffield City Hall where we went to see The Big Chris Barber Band. I loved it. I saw Acker Bilk not long after. Trad-jazz was all the go at the time. Humphrey Lyttelton came to Sheffield and Ken Colyer did as well and so did some of the Americans like Sonny Terry and Brownie McGhee, and Big Bill Broonzy. I'm also fairly sure we went to the City Hall to see The Temperance Seven. I liked their song 'Pasadena'.

One night when we were driving home from a concert, Arthur told me that he was a member of the Young Communist League and that in a few week's time he would be debating with a man called Harold Oldfield at a meeting in Barnsley on the subject of 'Socialism vs. Capitalism'. Harold Oldfield sold pie and peas on Barnsley market, he was also the secretary of the Young Conservatives. Arthur asked me if I'd like to go with him. At the meeting I noticed how knowledgeable Arthur was about things. He was only young, but he was well read. He got that off his dad Harold. He was well tutored as well. He used to go and see Bert Ramelson and other well-known communists at Leeds. Bert was secretary of the Leeds branch of the Communist Party and worked a lot with the miners' union. He lived at the Quarry Hill flats. He was born in Ukraine and said he could remember the Russian revolution taking place. He got wounded in the Spanish Civil War and had a death sentence put on his head by Franco. He was captured by the Germans in the Second World War but escaped to fight with the Italian resistance. All the younger end looked up to Bert and admired his courage.

The communists had a big group in South Yorkshire. Frank Watters was a well-known activist and was another big influence on Arthur. Frank had a good eye for an opportunity. He had a full-time job with the Communist Party and they couldn't pay him much so if ever you saw him it was because he wanted taking somewhere or he was short of money. If he came to your house and there were three loaves laid out cooling on the kitchen table, he would want one to take home. I got on well with his wife Freda, she was an extremely intelligent woman who had read more books than any woman I'd met. She was also a great speaker for women's rights and had been a member of the Communist Party since she worked as a bus conductor in Leeds just after the war. I never bothered much with politics at the time though, I let Arthur get on with it. After that first meeting at Barnsley I'm not sure I went to another.

A Kiss And A Cuddle
Betty

I left Pontefract Girls' High School in the summer of 1954. There were only two hospitals in Great Britain where you could train in orthopaedics from the age of 16. One was in Wales and the other was the Marguerite Hepton Hospital at Thorp Arch. The hospital had been opened before the First World War, a long time before the NHS, when health relied on charity. It was the gift of a Harrogate businessman called Arthur Hepton. He lived in a lovely old country house outside of the village. He was so overjoyed when his daughter Marguerite recovered from tuberculosis that he donated his house and grounds as a children's hospital. Marguerite eventually became the hospital secretary and was known for her kindness and love for poorly children. The hospital was at first an isolation hospital for children suffering from TB, but over the years it came to specialise in children's orthopaedics. The Lane Fox family supported it, as did the Smith family of brewers at Tadcaster. A lot of kids suffering complications from the outbreaks of polio just after the war were treated there.

I was interviewed by Matron Downs who had been in charge of the hospital since the 1930s. She was a stout woman, what you might call a matronly type. She was strict and didn't suffer fools gladly, but my friends told me that she could be friendly and supportive when she wanted to be. My old school friend Phyl prepared me for the interview.

'She will probably ask you what religion you are,' she said. 'If she does, tell her that you're a Methodist.'

On the day of the interview Matron Downs asked me 'Why do you want to be a nurse?' and 'What qualifications have you got?' the usual sort of questions in a job interview. I thought that I had answered her questions well. Then she said, 'What religion are you?' I smiled and said, 'Methodist!' She looked me up and down and then smiled back and I knew at that point that I had been accepted. I started my nurse training the following week.

I hadn't been training long when my dad took seriously ill. He was in Ackton Hospital at Featherstone. The staff there made a telephone call to Matron Downs and told her that I ought to go over to Ackton Hospital immediately. I didn't get to know why, but I assume it must have been touch and go with him. Matron Downs was an understanding person but once she had made her mind up about anything you couldn't alter her opinion. She told them in no uncertain terms that I had been on the night shift and that I needed my sleep. She said that she would wake me in the afternoon when she thought I had rested enough. I went over to Featherstone on the bus and I stayed there for a few days until he was showing signs of improvement.

There were four wards for children at Thorp Arch; one for babies, one for small boys, one for older boys and one for girls. The older boys were not much younger than us trainee nurses and they used to act about with us. One day, one of the boys said, 'The ghosts are walking tonight!' and decided that it would be the ghost of Marguerite Hepton that would be walking. The lads thought it would be a good laugh if the nurses were to dress up as ghosts. We agreed it would be great fun. There was a back door to the ward and we put sheets and pillow cases over ourselves and floated in. One of the girls had false front teeth and she took them out. We were barely into the ward when most of the girls ran back out again and left me and a lass called Bowes behind. The matron had come onto the ward at the other end and stood there in her nightdress, dressing gown, curlers and hairnet.

'Who are you?' she shouted.

'I'm Danks,' I answered.

'And I'm Bowes.'

In those days trainee nurses only ever used their surnames.

'Right then,' said Matron. 'Danks and Bowes, my office, first thing tomorrow morning, now get to bed!'

We were terrified that we would be sacked. The other girls who had run off before Matron came hatched a plan. They decided that we should all share the blame because she couldn't sack everybody.

Next morning we all trooped into the office. Matron was livid. What made matters worse, she said, is that Marguerite Hepton was still very much alive. She had already decided on our punishment. She knew that all the nurses had been invited to a dance at HMS Ceres, a Royal Navy training base at Wetherby. She told us that she had phoned the officer in charge there to say we wouldn't be coming.

I didn't get much pay, just £5 a month and I had to pay for my own books, shoes, stockings and make-up out of that. The hospital paid for our rooms and food. Mum was thoughtful enough to post me the odd parcel with a tin of biscuits in and when I went home on days off she gave me ten shillings to cover my bus fares and something for myself. It took four buses from Thorp Arch to South Elmsall. Mum and Dad were both proud of me becoming a trainee nurse.

Our uniforms had to be spotless. We wore a square white hat and a lilac dress with a starched white pinafore over. The bib was pinned to the dress with safety pins. We had our own rooms at the nurses' home and we all got on well. We often borrowed clothes from our mates who were working when we were off and wanted to go out. We went dancing at Wetherby Town Hall, which was always full of young navy lads. After the dance we'd let them walk us to a bus stop that had a ladies toilet right next to it. We'd all go in to the toilet and, just as the bus came, we'd run out and jump on the bus and be off before they realised we were escaping.

We weren't always allowed a pass but sneaked out anyway with our dancing shoes in our bags. The night sister once caught us. She said, 'I know you have been out dancing so don't tell lies.' We wondered how she knew. Then we realised as we went out that Matron Downs had mirrors positioned all over the wall of her sitting room. She could see if any of the nurses were coming up the drive late. The night sister had looked in one of the mirrors and seen us holding our dancing shoes behind our backs.

I had a boyfriend at Upton who I wasn't too fond of. I thought that I had left him behind when I came to nurse training. He was persistent though and every couple of weeks he would turn up unannounced having pedalled the twenty-five miles to Thorp Arch on his pushbike. On a day off I'd let him take me to the pictures if

Betty in uniform as trainee nurse at Marguerite Hepton Hospital, 1954.

there was nothing better to do. I used him I suppose. He was more serious. I think he loved me. I needed to find a way to tell him that I didn't want to see him anymore. We were sitting one day on the grass at the side of the hospital drive. I was being horrible to him. I was fed up because yet again he had come on his daft bike without letting me know. For some reason he pulled a worm up out of the grass and dropped it down the back of my blouse. That was that. I told him in no uncertain terms to get off home and never come again. My friend Marjorie, who had by then left nurse training and gone back home to live, was in his circle of friends. She told me that he was heartbroken and carried my photograph about with him all the time. One day I received a letter. I opened the envelope and inside was a photograph of this young man on the deck of a ship. The letter came to me all the way from Australia.

The boy I really fell in love with was a joiner called Colin from Bramham, a village near Wetherby. His dad was the greenkeeper at the local golf club and his older brother was going out with my friend Phyl. I was 17 and he was just a few months younger than me. He was handsome, clean, well-dressed and had a wonderful sense of humour. I will go as far as to say it was love at first sight on my behalf. He took me dancing and on long walks in the countryside. I spent a lot of my spare time at his family house. It was the time of the Teddy boys, but he wasn't into that, he was a bit old fashioned. He didn't like women to wear trousers. I went out with him one night in my new drainpipe trousers. He told me not to wear them again. I wore my drainpipes the next time just to tease him. I was determined that a boy wouldn't tell me what I could and couldn't wear. We were walking down the side of a hedgerow. He pretended to pull my trousers off and then threw me straight over the hedge. It was only done for fun, just two kids fooling around. A kiss and a cuddle in the back row at the pictures was about as far as it went.

After the first year at Thorp Arch I was sent to Pinderfields Hospital at Wakefield to do my final year of training. We wore butterfly caps there, which I loved. I came back when I could in order to see Colin. One night I turned up late at the Wetherby Town Hall dance. I caught him doing the Tennessee Waltz with a nurse who

I had known well. This nurse had a reputation for fancying other nurses' boyfriends. I asked them what they thought they were doing. She sloped off and I had a blazing row with Colin. I was supposed to be staying at his mum and dad's house for the weekend. I couldn't get back to Wakefield that night so I still went to the house. Phyl's boyfriend, Colin's older brother, took me back to Wakefield on the Sunday morning on the pillion of his BSA. I saw Colin occasionally after that. Once, when I visited his mother, I spotted him with that nurse sitting on his knee in a car.

I don't know if Colin knew how much he had hurt me. I was left heartbroken by the way he had behaved. From the moment I had seen him at the Town Hall dance in Wetherby, I knew he was the one. I stayed weekends with his family and slept on the sofa in the front room. After he made it clear he didn't want me I didn't know what to do. I couldn't go home and talk to my mother about how I felt. Mum was of the school of thought that said, 'You make your bed, you must lie on it.' The only person I could talk to was Phyl. She was good at looking after people with problems. She thought that I ought to find myself a date. We discussed a bloke who was a patient on my ward. He was called Don and was a coalminer at North Gawber pit. His father had not long since been killed at the same pit, leaving his poor mother with ten children. Don was the oldest, he was twenty-three, and the youngest was just six months.

When Don was discharged I went on a date with him. We started seeing one another. His mother took the younger kids off somewhere and while they were away I stayed with him at his house. I was completely naive and probably became pregnant the first time I had sex. At that time if you were a pregnant 18-year-old girl you must marry choose what. I tried to ignore my condition at first. Then I started to get morning sickness. I was working night shifts, I was sick both in the evening when I woke up from my sleep and in the middle of the night when I was working. I'd be putting thermometers into patient's mouths to take temperatures, then running off to the toilet to be sick. It didn't go unnoticed. I was really poorly one shift and the night sister put me in the sick bay. They had heard the gossip that one of the nurses was pregnant and it was on that night that the penny dropped. At that point I realised that my nursing career was over. I was just a month away from my final exams. I daren't tell my parents, I was hoping that the earth would open up and swallow me whole.

Don decided that he would go to South Elmsall and tell my mother and father. He'd only been there once before. On that occasion there was just my dad in and he had given him the third degree. Where did he work? What were his prospects and plans? What about ambitions? I don't think my dad was impressed because when I asked him if I might get engaged to Don he said 'Definitely no!' My mother was the same, in fact she got down on her knees and begged me to be careful because she thought Don was unsuitable. If you were under 21 then your dad had to agree to you being married and sign to say so. When Don told Mum and Dad that I was pregnant they reluctantly gave way and agreed to our marriage.

I was in denial about everything. I didn't know if I wanted to be married, whether I was coming or going, I just didn't care what happened to me. I had stayed in touch with Colin's mother and carried on paying visits. I had to tell her that I had become pregnant; I sat on her sofa holding back tears. I planned to leave before Colin got home but he came back early from work. When he found out the news that I was carrying another man's child, he looked straight at me and said, 'What the hell did you think you were doing you silly fool.' I was already feeling down. His comment made the upset worse and I felt completely humiliated by his reaction. I didn't know what to say and I couldn't face him so I walked out of his mother's house.

My mother had a word with the pit bobby. The pit bobby was someone highly respected in the community and this one was a member of the Gospel Hall. She explained that I was expecting and asked him to take pity and allow us to be married there. He wouldn't allow it. Mum then went to the Spiritualist Church. They agreed and I married Don there in November 1956. I stood in that church, a very naive, immature young girl about to marry a coalminer who I'd known for a few months. My dad gave me away but he hardly looked at me all day and didn't speak a single word. Mum spent the day organising the catering and reception. All the food had been homemade by her and the Armstrong family.

We arranged to live with Don's Aunt Elsie and Uncle Major at Mapplewell until we could get a pit house. On the Monday morning after the wedding, Don took me into the village and showed me where the shops were. Then he turned round, said 'I'll see you at dinner time' and went off to sup ale in The King's Head.

Sudden And Unexpected
Anne

I was out with Arthur one day near the Yorkshire miners' union headquarters on Huddersfield Road in Barnsley. I happened to mention that I'd helped my dad to sweep the chimneys on the big houses there. Arthur told me to look up at the union building. He pointed out the turrets and said that they were there to disguise the chimney pots because the posh residents whose chimneys I'd helped to sweep had complained that too many chimney pots would spoil their view.

Arthur loved to tell stories. His favourite happened late one afternoon when he and Goff Sunderland were in the pit yard and a youngster came running up to them saying that they had to come quickly to the top row because there was an emergency. Both of them thought that someone had been run over by a lorry on the narrow lanes leading up to the pit. They followed the youngster to one of the pit houses where they found a union colleague lying on his back on a fireside rug, stark naked. A much younger woman who was not his wife was in great distress kneeling beside him. The house belonged to the young woman and her husband was down the pit on the afternoon shift. The pit doctor was summoned and pronounced the man dead but could not certify the cause beyond 'sudden and unexpected'. The police and the police surgeon had to be summoned.

The police surgeon examined the body and noticed some bruising on the heels. He mentioned that he thought because of the pattern of the bruising, this had happened after death. The young woman confessed that she had panicked when the union man had fallen ill. At first she had left him, but then decided that before her husband came home from the pit she would have to move him. She had dragged his body downstairs from the bedroom and bumped his heels on every step.

An inquest was held and it was decided that death was due to cardiac arrest. The union officials asked the coroner if he could save any further distress to the young woman by keeping the more lurid details out of it. The story was that the union man had taken poorly as he walked along the top row and had staggered into the woman's house for help. To be fair, everybody in the village knew what had really gone on. At the next union meeting, the men paid a mischievous tribute.

'Our comrade was a man who had made mistakes in his life, as we all do from time to time. His final mistake came near the end, just when he thought he was coming, he was actually going.'

Sex was never discussed at home and I certainly didn't get any advice about men from my mother, but I did know about the results of unwanted pregnancy and children born out of wedlock. During the war some Canadian troops were stationed at Cawthorne, two or three miles up the road. We kids used to follow them about and shout after them, 'Have you got any gum chum?' Near Christmastime the Canadians brought McIntosh apples to our school, they are the last of the season to ripen and are bright red. They were the sweetest I ever tasted. When the Canadians went home they left behind some women who were carrying their children. I remember well some of these kids being talked about and the awful names they got called.

I was nineteen and I'd known Arthur less than a year when I realised I was pregnant. The thought of how I would cope frightened me. I didn't know who to tell first. I told Arthur because I was frightened to tell my mam and dad. I sat down one night with Arthur and said. 'Look! You will have to tell them.' Arthur agreed that he would.

'Well we haven't any money,' he said, 'but we will get married and I'll tell your father.'

My dad was upset. I think my mam was more angry than upset; she wasn't too carried away by Arthur. Still, they all agreed that there was no alternative but for us to be married. Arthur and me were wed at Gawber Church on 16th September 1961. We then went away for four days to a caravan at Chapel St Leonards that was owned by a friend of the family.

Arthur's mother had died when he was eighteen. It was something he never got over. To this day he still makes a pilgrimage every year to Sheffield Crematorium where her ashes were scattered. He couldn't stop himself talking about her all the time. He was still doing it long after we were married. Harold, his dad, took up with another woman called Gladys. Arthur couldn't bear it and went to live with his grandmother, Harold's mother. Arthur made up with his dad when he went to tell him we were to be married. Harold lived in a council house on Wellington Crescent at Worsbrough. He said that we could live at his house after the wedding. We moved there at the back end of September 1961.

Our Margaret was born in April 1962. Arthur was working nights at Woolley pit at the time. We decided we needed more money if we were to have our own house, so when Margaret was six months old I made my mind up to go back to work. Brook Motors had started using home workers, mainly women like me who had started families, so I decided I would have work brought to me. They had a van going round that would deliver half a dozen motors at a time for me to wind with copper wire. Mrs Netherwood next door heard me tapping all day with a little hammer. She asked what I was doing and when I told her, she said that I was causing her lights to fuse. I told her I wasn't touching any electricity. She reported me to the council for interfering with her supply. After that I set myself up in a wooden shed in the back garden.

I listened to the BBC Light Programme. 'Calling All Workers' would come on and I knew it was time for *Music While You Work*. It was a programme the BBC did for lasses in factories to make them work happier. In the afternoon I listened to Mrs Netherwood's daughter Clara playing her piano. Clara had what we would describe these days as learning difficulties. She picked up what she'd heard on the radio that morning and played it beautifully on the piano.

Harold had a lot of books in his house. He was an avid reader. He took the *Daily Worker* and read it every morning A to Z. He looked after Margaret while I worked in the shed, spending hours on end reading to her. By the time she started school she could already read and write. Margaret still likes to say that when all the other kids were reading Enid Blyton, she was listening to her grandad reading from Jack London and Somerset Maugham. Harold hadn't a clue when it came to cleaning up but he was a very good teacher and he schooled our Margaret well.

I decided to go back to Brook's factory when Margaret was about three. I didn't stay there long, there was a lot of gossip amongst the women and I didn't enjoy the sort of things they talked about. It dawned on me that they might be gossiping about me behind my back, so I decided that I would try for a job in an office. The one subject I had been good at in school was maths. I thought I might be able to get a job in accounts somewhere. In the middle of the 1960s, calculations were still done on comptometers. Every firm had women comptometer operators. You could pay for private tuition on a course in Sheffield that ran for three or four months. I joined and drove to Sheffield every day to a place over the top of the Castle Hill market. I got my diploma and Arthur said he might be able to get me a job at the coal board. I said no straightaway, I wanted to find my own job. I went for an interview at the Co-op offices on Wellington Street and got a job in the cash office on a comptometer. It was my responsibility to check incoming invoices against what the Co-op had actually ordered. I started work there in 1967.

Anne with Arthur and Margaret at Wellington Crescent, Bank End, Barnsley, 1962.

Two-up Two-down
Betty

Michael, my first baby, was born at Don's Aunt Elsie's house. It wasn't too long before I was pregnant again. As good as Aunt Elsie had been, we desperately needed to move to our own house. By then Don had found work at Woolley Colliery. Another of his uncles, Joe, was well in with Elijah Benn who was in charge of dishing out the pit houses. He kept pestering Elijah until he gave in and handed us the keys to an old two-up two-down. It was in a bad state with no hot water and an outside toilet we had to share with the neighbours.

On my first night in our new home, I sat on a high-backed kitchen chair in my small living room. My back ached, my bottom ached, but most of all my heart ached. I looked round my domain, a tiny two-up two-down on Brick Row in Woolley Edge. It was draughty, cold and in desperate need of repair. The floors were covered in lino and mats. My mother had bought the lino otherwise we would have walked on the bare stone floor. There was no money for carpets, chairs, a suite, certainly not a telly, not even money for a book and I'd been an avid reader before I was married. I sat on that high-backed chair because there was nothing else. I wanted to go to bed, at least the warmth there would ease my aches, but Don would be coming home from the pub expecting a cooked supper. I winced at the thought of that. In the kitchen I had a sink but only cold water, a copper boiler and a paraffin stove in place of a cooker. I didn't know how I would manage to feed my family on that stove. Upstairs my baby was asleep and I had another one sleeping peacefully in my womb. That my husband had left me on my own on our first night in our house was beyond me. It upset me enough that tears slid down my cheeks. As a child, I'd been cosseted, loved and led a very protected and sheltered life. I'd had a good education and after school became a nurse. I was determined that I would pass on my own memories of happiness in childhood to my own children. I wanted to make sure they wouldn't go short and that they would feel love and protection from a cold and hostile world outside. I didn't realise then how hard that was going to be.

When my first big washday came round, I lit the fire under the copper time and again but it refused to catch light. After an hour my hands and face were black with soot and streaked with more tears. In the end I despaired of not having hot water. I washed my hands and face and dried them on my apron. I picked up my baby and walked round to the house next door. I nervously knocked on the door unsure of what sort of reception I would get. I had moved to this pit village from another one, but that didn't qualify me as a local girl. I'd already found the people here hard to understand. My neighbour had six kids and though her husband worked long hours at the pit they still struggled. They had a television and a washer, but it was all on hire purchase. I'd always been taught that if you didn't have the money to buy something, you had to wait until you had saved up for it. My neighbour Nancy opened the door. She told me to come in.

'I'll make you a cup of tea, love. I've no milk, we have Nestlé in ours,' she said.

The tea was extremely sweet but I savoured every drop. I think in my frustration and loneliness I was glad of the chatter and friendliness.

'Them old coppers are a bugger to light and get going,' she said. 'I'll just have a cigarette and I'll come round and give you a hand. I've got the knack.'

I asked her what we should do with the children.

'Don't worry about that, my mother-in-law is upstairs, she'll sit with them while we've done.'

Within a few minutes Nancy had a blazing fire under the copper. I felt like an idiot. Nancy laughed.

'We call them set pots love. They're handy for getting hot water for a bath.'

I shuddered. At home I'd had a bathroom. At this house the tin bath hung on a nail on a wall in the yard. I hadn't tried it yet, I was frightened of sitting in the kitchen in a bath in the draught.

'If you need me anytime, love,' Nancy said, 'don't bring your baby out in the cold, just knock on the wall. And if me and my mother-in-law are having a cup of tea, I'll give you a knock.' I thanked her but I was still unsure what to make of her. She was a very direct, harsh speaking woman.

I set about the washing. I had all day to get it done. Don was on afternoons. He would go straight to the pub after work and roll home after 11 o'clock expecting a dinner put in front of him as soon as he walked in. I stoked up the set pot and filled the washer to start on the whites. The washer was a peculiar contraption. It stood on four legs, had a handle in the middle of the lid and a hand wringer on top. I wound the handle round and round until I thought the clothes were clean. After that I wound them through the wringer and into a dolly tub where I possed them with a posser and then back through the wringer. After that they went into the set pot to be boiled and then put into dolly blue or starch or both. Finally they were swilled and put back through the wringer. Once the first lot were done, the whole procedure started again with the next load.

I didn't have any clothes posts to hang the washing outside, so I hung it inside on two lines strung across the ceiling. It was hard work emptying the washer. I did it first with a jug and then lifted the washer up to the sink to tip out the remaining mucky water. I then refilled the washer to start on the coloureds. In between I talked to my little lad and fed him. I took him to bed when he was ready and carried on washing until about eight o'clock, then I started cleaning the house. By ten o'clock the house was spick and span but a bit humid from all the drying clothes.

I was ready for bed but I had to get Don's supper ready. I put a pan of potatoes on my paraffin stove and balanced a pan of carrots and a kettle on the coal fire. Don always demanded a pot of tea as soon as he was home from the pub, to drink while I put his supper out. I had to keep stoking the fire to keep the meat cooking in the coal oven. My mother had bought me an electric kettle for boiling water for tea but I didn't know how to put a plug on and Don wouldn't do anything in the house. I made a mental note to ask Nancy if she knew anyone who could put a plug on and how much it would cost.

Don came in and moaned straightaway about wet washing drying in the house. He started to eat his dinner and read the paper at the same time. It had been a tiring and lonely day for me, I wanted to talk to Don or for him to at least acknowledge me, but he just carried on eating and looking at his paper.

'Don, why don't you come home for your supper before you go to the pub? I'm busy and up with that baby all day, I'd like to be in bed before midnight.'

He just lowered his paper and glared at me.

'Are you bloody stupid? A man can't drink beer on top of a belly full of food. And if you can't cope, that's your own fault. My mother did it and there was eleven of us.'

I cleared the table, boiled some water on the fire and washed up.

'And another thing, I don't like coming home to wet washing all over. Peg it outside like my mother does.'

I had to talk quietly. I asked if I could have some washing line posts.

'I'm not buggering about putting posts up when I work at that pit all day. The neighbours have clothes lines, wash on a different day and use theirs.'

I told him that I didn't like to ask the neighbours for things.

'Well I'll tell you this Miss High and Mighty, if this is going to happen every washday, I'll go round to my mother's out of the way and you can stay up until I decide to come home for my supper.'

Then he stomped up to bed.

Harold
Anne

There was more than just me and Arthur in our marriage. Arthur's dad Harold always lived at the same house as us. From the time we moved into his council house there was never a time when he wasn't with us. We lived with him at Wellington Crescent until 1967. We saw a house on Ardsley Road that we liked and agreed a price before being outbid by a higher offer. We couldn't afford to match it, so we lost out. Arthur was fed up and took himself off into Barnsley to buy a new car. As he went past the bottom of Yews Lane he saw a for sale sign in the window of a bungalow. The woman's husband had just died and she wanted a quick sale. We bought the house for £3,000; it was a lot of money for us, but it was our first home and I was happy. Harold came with us.

We'd only just nicely moved into the bungalow when cracks started appearing. There was some mining subsidence which caused a problem with the roof. Harold had carried on paying his rent at Wellington Crescent, which was a good job because we had to move back there while the coal board worked to mend the bungalow. When we flitted back again, our Joan and her husband Geoff moved into Harold's old council house.

Arthur's dad was shy, but at the same time very witty and quick. He always said that in order to argue a case you must know more about your subject than the person you are arguing with. He had spent lots of time in the reading room in the miners' welfare where he developed a passion for current events and literature. He read a page of the dictionary each day and said that reading was something you should do two or three times a day as a command of words stands you in good stead. He was a staunch atheist, but read the bible. When the Jehovah's Witnesses came knocking, most people shut the door in their face but not Harold, he engaged them in conversation and wore them down until they wanted to be away.

Harold believed that people in power didn't take working-class people seriously when they spoke in a strong local accent, so you had to tone it down. Harold could have been a great political speaker but one big thing held him back: his father Joe McQuillan wasn't married to Harold's mam when she had him so Harold had to take his mother's surname, Scargill. Joe and Clara did get married later, which meant that Harold's brothers and sisters were called McQuillan. Harold was deeply affected for most of his life by the social stigma of being illegitimate. I think Harold wanted Arthur to achieve things that he had held himself back from. It was only when Arthur became well known that Harold became proud enough to take back his own name. The irony is that the trade union leader who became world famous as Arthur Scargill would not have been called that had his grandfather had the decency to call his own son after him. He would have been Arthur McQuillan.

Arthur likes to tell a story about his dad having a conversation with some other miners one snap time. They were talking about what they wanted for their own sons instead of the pit. One bloke said he'd like his lad to be a schoolteacher, another one said his son was trying to get into law school, and a third one said he hoped for his boy to become an engineer. Harold was sitting quietly eating his snap. One of the blokes said, 'What about your Arthur, Harold, what do you want him to do?' Harold didn't hesitate, saying quietly, 'I know what Arthur will do, he will become the president of the Yorkshire union.' Years later when Arthur did become president he declared that the victory was Harold's.

On Thursdays, Harold would go out with his brother John, get well oiled, and come home saying 'Margaret my brakes have gone' and he'd bounce off the walls up the hallway. At Christmastime in our house we had a tradition of opening our presents at midnight on Christmas Eve. Harold came home one evening the week before Christmas having won a prize in the Swaithe Club raffle. His ticket was the first to be drawn out so he had first choice of all the prizes; everyone expected him to pick the bottle of whisky but instead he picked a big teddy bear. He weaved his way home with the teddy under his arm and gave it to Margaret as soon as he got in. Arthur took it back off her and said he was going to send it to Father Christmas for it to be delivered on Christmas Eve. That teddy became a globetrotter, she took it on trips all over the world. She still has it now.

Harold was a fan of Laurel and Hardy. He used to have Margaret sat watching them with him; they must have seen every one of their films. He would sing that song 'The Trail of the Lonesome Pine' from *Way Out West*, and he would imitate the dance steps they did outside of the saloon. He was a lovely singer and very light on his feet. He loved watching comedies on television like *Dad's Army*. When *Fawlty Towers* came out, him and Margaret would be rolling about laughing with tears in their eyes. I didn't get it and Arthur used to tut and say, 'This is just bloody daft.'

He liked to tease Arthur and often said, 'Our Arthur's no sense of humour.' Then he would torment him. Many is the time he's sat on his chair in a string vest and his tubeteika hat that Arthur had brought him as a gift from Russia, refusing to move until minutes before Arthur had important guests coming for a meeting. Other times he pretended to be drunk in front of visitors to wind Arthur up. The visitors would be in on it, but Arthur never knew that. An American union leader rang for Arthur one day and Harold answered, as he often did. Harold put the phone down and went looking for Arthur shouting, 'It's a bloody Yank on the phone.' Arthur was mortified knowing full well that the American would have heard. As luck would have it, he had a sense of humour and whenever he phoned after that he'd start his calls with, 'Hi Harold it's that bloody Yank again, can I speak to Arthur please?'

Harold loved watching and listening to people and then he'd make stories about what he had observed to tell Margaret. He was a master of words and he liked to play with them. He loved overhearing people using malapropisms; when pedestrian crossings came out he told Margaret that he'd heard people calling them 'Presbyterian crossings'. He read the *Reader's Digest* and I'd often come home to find him telling Margaret about an article he'd read. He always did the word definition at the front and had the dictionary at hand's reach if he came across a word that he wasn't familiar with.

Harold could be serious when he wanted; he had a lot of compassion and could explain important world events. He and Margaret watched the moon landing together. He explained it to her in a way that a seven-year-old girl could understand. Our Margaret still says that she was shaped far more by her grandad than she was by either me or Arthur. He ought to have been a teacher really. That might be why he came to dislike going to the pit. Even though he came from a mining family he was never cut out to be a collier.

Harold liked to dress in good quality, fashionable clothes. He bought what he thought was a lovely brown suit but he was colour blind and the suit was green; for ages he couldn't weigh up why his pals called him 'the green man'. His immaculate dressing meant that he became the target for women of a certain age and, being a bit of a ladies' man, he had quite a few girlfriends. At one time he had three on the go at the same time. There was Annie, Gladys and Emily. Annie was a down-to-earth Barnsley lass with jet-black dyed hair and a lovely nature.

One day he was getting ready to go to Emily's when by pure chance Annie called round followed ten minutes later by Gladys. There was an atmosphere in the room you could have cut with a knife. Both of the women sat on opposite ends of the sofa with pursed lips and their handbags clasped on their knees. Harold sat next to the window with his head buried in a big newspaper. He never looked up once while Margaret tried to be polite with the two women. She kept glancing at Harold, looking for him to say something, but he never made a muff. I don't know how it happened, but somehow his shenanigans with his three girlfriends got leaked to the press. He even made it into the William Hickey gossip column in the *Daily Express* and was pursued by reporters over it.

Harold used to smoke Player's Navy Cut, but he stopped when he burned a hole in the rug. He had a terrible habit of shuffling his feet when he sat in his chair by the window, so there was always a threadbare bit in front of where he sat. We had a beautiful thick-pile carpet which was lovely in every area apart from where he'd been shuffling. He would sit there looking out of the window or reading and when he wasn't doing that he told his stories. He liked to recall the war. Even though he was a coalminer and that was a reserved occupation, he was called up into the RAF; he said he went because of his political beliefs. He was based in Yundum in Gambia. Through an administrative error he ended up with an American unit. When the British moved on, Harold and five of his mates were left behind so the Americans put them to work. Harold used to laugh when he told the tale of how for two years he had two wages sent home; one from the British and another from the Americans. He was a cook and often served the officers. One day an important guest visited the camp so everything had to be tiptop – it was General Marshall, the US army chief of staff.

Harold sailed home at the end of the war on the Queen Mary to Glasgow. He was met with little ceremony and some disdain except from the Salvation Army who gave him tea and food and a friendly word. He told me many times that he never forgot what they did to lift his spirits when he was low and he always donated to their cause. He went home by train, then bus, then walked and greeted his wife Alice who had no idea he was coming. Arthur had not seen him for three years and ran away from 'the stranger' when he hugged his mother. Arthur used to tell this tale a lot about his dad and he'd well up as he told it. I think it had a big impact on him.

The more I think about Harold, the more I realise that he was a lot more than a collier. His love of teaching, his thirst for knowledge and his talent for storytelling were never put to good use. He wasted his life in a way. He knew it himself and came to hate the pit. When he was forced to retire early through ill health, he was finally able to spend more time with his books. He could really have been somebody, but he – like a lot of intelligent working-class people then – didn't get the opportunity.

Brick Row
Betty

When we moved into the house at Woolley Edge, I was already four-and-a-half months pregnant with Donny, my second boy. He was born at home in the September. It was a thirty-minute labour. The midwife just had enough time to throw off her coat and wash her hands.

I didn't understand the ways of the people at Brick Row. They were always shouting, especially at the kids. I was quiet, shy and reserved, and was completely intimidated by them. When my lads started to play out there was one neighbour who wouldn't leave them alone. She shouted at them every time they walked past her lavatory. I used to bring them in and sit crying.

Because Woolley Edge was an isolated community without a bus service or a shop, we relied on mobile shops and a travelling butcher. One time our Michael was staying with my mum and dad at South Elmsall. I was in the butcher's van when this woman who didn't like my lads came and started shouting at me in front of the other customers and the butcher.

'It's a disgrace what your Michael's been doing, tormenting them poor kids at the bottom house.'

I looked at her and said, 'Are you sure it was Michael?'

She screamed at me, 'I know the difference between your bloody children.'

'Well it must be a miracle,' I said, 'because he's been at South Elmsall for the last few days.'

The woman didn't blink, she just said, 'It was your Donny then.'

I knew it wasn't and at that moment a lot of pent-up emotion came steaming out of me. I screamed in her face, 'Get out of this van before I start, because if I do you will be sorry!' The butcher's jaw dropped. He couldn't believe that this little mouse had suddenly turned and was threatening someone. After that I let the kids play out when they wanted. The woman still had a go at them, but we ignored her.

A rough family lived in the back-to-back houses at the bottom of Brick Row. The father worked at the pit when he could be bothered to get out of bed. There were two boys and a girl. One of the boys and the girl had learning difficulties and the lad was violent. One day the girl was scraping potatoes at the kitchen table when somebody lifted the table leaf and trapped her finger. Everybody knew that I'd been a nurse, so they sent for me. When I got there the girl was flapping her hand about with her finger almost severed. I held her arm and raised it to stop the bleeding while the doctor was sent for. The doctor decided he could stitch the finger back on. There was no access to hot water in their house so I went home to boil the instruments. Between us, with me holding the hand steady and the doctor stitching, we managed to save her finger. I then had to improvise a bandage that wouldn't come off because I knew the hygiene in that family was poor. A few hours later I saw the girl playing outside, she had a lid off a grate and was playing in the mucky water. Her parents didn't even notice. I took her to the surgery a week later to have her stitches out. Somehow the bandage had stayed on and, though her hands were filthy, the part under the bandage had kept clean.

At that time, whenever my neighbour lit her copper boiler our house would fill with smoke. It was so bad that I had to take the kids out for a walk. On these occasions I often took them to one of my husband's aunts and uncles who were very good to me and often fed us. One morning the lads came into our bedroom dancing on the floorboards. They were shouting, 'Mam, Mam, the floor's red hot.' It was, the house was on fire. A spark from the chimney over the neighbour's copper boiler had set fire to the beams under our bedroom floor. Don ran to a farm up the road to telephone for the fire brigade. After the fire was out, the chief fire officer said he was disgusted by the state of the houses on the row and blamed the pit. He marched up to the colliery and demanded that the coal board repair our house and look at the others on the row to check the state of the copper boiler chimneys. The NCB did the minimum of work that they could get away with.

Round about this time the colliery decided to build a new washing plant. I don't suppose a lot of people outside of the coalfields know that coal is washed when it comes out of the ground before it goes for sale. The pit was allowed to build the new washer on condition it only ran at night. They completely disregarded the condition and ran it in the daytime and this deprived the families in Brick Row of water. It happened too often. I was forced some days to put my children in the pram and walk the mile to my mother-in-law's house to fill old pop bottles with water. In the end I got on the bus to Wakefield with one toddling and the other in the pushchair and went straight to the Social Services. I put them both on the desk.

'You best look after them. I can't keep them clean or prepare their meals hygienically without clean water.'

They came rushing out of the office then. We had a discussion and they promised me that if I took the children back home they would have someone talk to the pit manager. By the time I got back home there was a man stomping up and down the row shouting and balling.

'Where's this bloody woman who can't make a bottle of milk for her baby?'

Things improved a bit after that until they started using up all the water again. A woman from down the row came with her baby. She said, 'I don't know what to do Betty.' I told her that she would have to do what I had done, that was help yourself. I was becoming a right hard cow. Circumstances forced me. I was changed by things I couldn't control. In the space of a few years, I had gone from a timid mouse to someone prepared to stick up for myself with the tough people in the neighbourhood and I wasn't afraid of anybody in authority either.

Just before election day one year, a van came round with a speaker on top of the roof. The people inside had a microphone and were telling everybody who they ought to vote for, but they made the mistake of leaving the microphone on when they stopped proclaiming. Everybody in Brick Row heard them say, 'Who the bloody hell can live here?' It was disheartening, especially as we struggled to keep a nice house.

I saved up for ages when I wanted to wallpaper the front room.

The day came when I had enough and I went into Barnsley to buy some paper. In those days wallpaper had an edge on it. You unrolled it to cut off the edge then rolled it back up again. I sat up in the evening doing this and put the paper to one side, telling myself I'd make a start the next morning. I got up to find the kids giggling and laughing. They had unrolled all the paper and put their hands and feet through it. I couldn't afford any more so I put plenty of paste on and pieced it together on the wall. Michael and Donny were mischievous kids but I loved them too much to be angry and, when they weren't there, I had a good laugh to myself about it.

I learned to stand up for myself on Brick Row. The shyness started to wear away, but it was replaced by loneliness and a lack of money to do anything. Don often stayed away from work and sometimes I didn't know where the next meal was coming from.

My friend Phyl got married to Colin's brother and carried on living in the Thorp Arch area. I often went to stay with her. Once my visit coincided with Open Day at the hospital. I went back to have a look and had my two sons with me. Matron Downs was still there. She was pleased to see me.

'I'd very much like to have you back here working with me,' she said.

I told her that I lived too far away now and it would be impossible. Although we didn't discuss it, I knew that she could see I was in an unhappy marriage.

'Come and live here,' she said, 'We'll find somewhere for you, the boys will be fine, they can play with the boys in the hospital during the holidays.'

I didn't know what to say, so I just said I was sorry and walked away. I was tempted, but I knew deep down that it would have been impossible. I couldn't have coped with all the fall out of leaving my husband and how my mother might have reacted. This was in the 1960s, in the decade when anything seemed possible. The reality for a working-class woman trapped in an unhappy marriage with two young children was that it wasn't possible.

Yews Lane
Anne

The bungalow at Yews Lane had an inside toilet and separate bathroom, a good-sized kitchen, a long lounge and dining room separated by glass sliding doors which were all the go at the time. Outside we had a big garden for Arthur's Airedale terrier, Lady.

The main feature of the bungalow was the enormous picture window at the front of the house which gave us a fantastic view over the Worsbrough valley. The only drawback was the poplar trees in Wilson's garden that spoiled the view. Arthur managed to persuade them to let him cut the poplars down and he asked his boyhood friend and best man, Derek Stubbings, to help him. Derek shinned up the trees and cut from the top section working his way down each one. He dropped his axe by accident one day and just missed our neighbour Olive Porter. The axe would have killed her if she'd been another foot nearer. Olive's brother was Reginald Porter-Brown who was an organist with the BBC at St George's Hall in London with his signature tune 'Oh, Mr Porter!'.

There was a pub across the road called The Cutting Edge. It was a popular place and always noisy and rowdy at turning out time, especially over the weekend. Because we lived opposite the pub, as soon as some of them had ale down them it gave them ideas. Folk were often knocking on the door asking for Arthur. It was usually something that had happened at work or something to do with pensions. Arthur never turned them away. We had got to the stage where we didn't go out much because folk wanted to ask him things all the time. Stopping in meant they knew where to find us. One night it was after midnight when there was a knock at the door. This bloke had come from The Cutting Edge. I was ready for bed but Arthur answered the door. I heard the bloke say, 'They've sacked me!' Arthur invited him in and sat him down. He fetched a pen and paper and asked the man which pit he worked at.

'I don't work at the pit, I work on the buses for Yorkshire Traction.' Arthur dropped his pen and said, 'I'm sorry lad, I can't do 'owt for you then.'

That sort of thing was happening all the time. I don't think I ever had my husband to myself, all he seemed to want to do was work and argue.

The fallout from the pub got worse during the strikes. When they'd had enough ale, those that didn't like us would shout and swear across the road. Then they started throwing eggs and grass sods; it's a wonder our window didn't get put through. The Cutting Edge employed an organ player and his regular piece on a Sunday night was Bach's 'Toccata and Fugue in D minor' played top note. If anybody had walked down our lane during the strike they would have wondered where in the hell they'd come to with drunken blokes effing and blinding and Bach blasting out. We managed to ignore it most of the time and it was rare we had to call the police.

We did have some good neighbours. One family we got on well with were Edward and Evelyn and their children Robert and Debra who were Margaret's age. They lived in a big white house perched on the top of the hill half way up Yews Lane. They were an eccentric family whose lives seemed to be dominated by animals. They owned and raced greyhounds but they also kept exotic animals. Evelyn and Robert took in any waifs, strays and orphans of the storm; bald parrots, poorly owls, they loved them all back to health. Everybody knew this and they brought all sorts of animals to them. They had a huge bird of prey which they kept in a caravan in the yard, I think it was a buzzard. Once, it escaped and flew into the graveyard. Evelyn called for Arthur to help her and they went searching through the trees for it. They found it high up in one of the tallest trees and Evelyn eventually enticed it down with some meat on her arm and chastised it all the way home.

Evelyn adopted and raised a magpie chick which became such a menace it made the pages of the *Barnsley Chronicle*. She named it Sherrie and it strutted about in her backyard. Visitors had to run past it because it pecked their heels. It was like Alfred Hitchcock's film *The Birds*. Margaret used to wear her wellingtons when she went round. Then it started dive bombing on people walking past or stood at the bus stop. It would peck them on the head and fly back onto Evelyn's shoulder cackling. One day it didn't come home. It was thought that someone had got fed up of it and wrung its neck.

On one occasion Margaret went to the house and was told to mind her step because the snakes had escaped. It was a laugh a minute at Evelyn's. She had a little monkey that had the run of the house. It loved her and she loved him, but he caused havoc at times. He took a liking to a man who came to see Edward. He perched on his shoulder and stroked the man's hair. Everybody was admiring the way the monkey had taken to the guest. Then the monkey started to get aroused and ejaculated in the man's ear. Evelyn as usual just howled with laughter. They had one creature from South America that looked like a giant badger with tusks that they walked in a harness and a lovely owl in the back bedroom. It was like a Doctor Dolittle house.

Harold with Margaret in the garden of Yews Lane, 1970.

New Shoes
Betty

My third son Glyn was born at Brick Row on 25th May 1965. Glyn was a pleasant baby and no trouble at all to look after. Michael and Donny were at school by then so I could spend plenty of time with him. Michael happily accepted his new brother. Donny was unsure. When I told him that we were going to get a new baby, he said 'Why can't we have a new sideboard or a doggy?' When Glyn arrived, Donny looked at him and said, 'He'll do.' His father had a different attitude. He had wanted a girl this time and when he saw it was another boy he blamed me for only being able to have boys.

By the time Glyn was three weeks old I couldn't fill him with milk. He was continuously hungry. I started to break Farley's Rusks into his milk and it wasn't long before he was taking it off a spoon. By the time he was a few months old he was eating what I put through my 'Mouli' – an old-fashioned milling machine that fit on the top of a pan or bowl and minced up food. Glyn had a good appetite, which he has never lost.

When Glyn was still in his pram, the council finally condemned all of the houses on the row and we moved into a council house. Don refused to pay for a removal van so we moved all of our stuff on the pram. I felt ashamed pushing that pram down the road, but the new house was warm, we had hot and cold running water and a bathroom with an inside toilet. I felt like I had gone on my holidays. I had been going up to my mother's every other weekend with the children for a bath in her bathroom. I hated the tin bath at home and the draughts all around me. The new house had a big pot kitchen sink. I bathed Glyn in that until he was big enough for the bath.

My life started to improve when I got to the new house. I made some friends and that helped to shed some of the loneliness. One was called Pat, she had moved to the estate from Woolley Colliery. Then there was Kitty who hadn't been well. Pat and I used to take

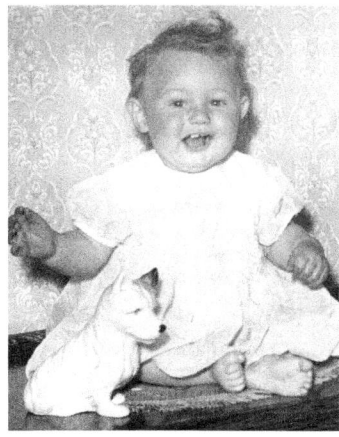

Michael's first birthday photograph, 1957.

Donny's grumpy day, 1961.

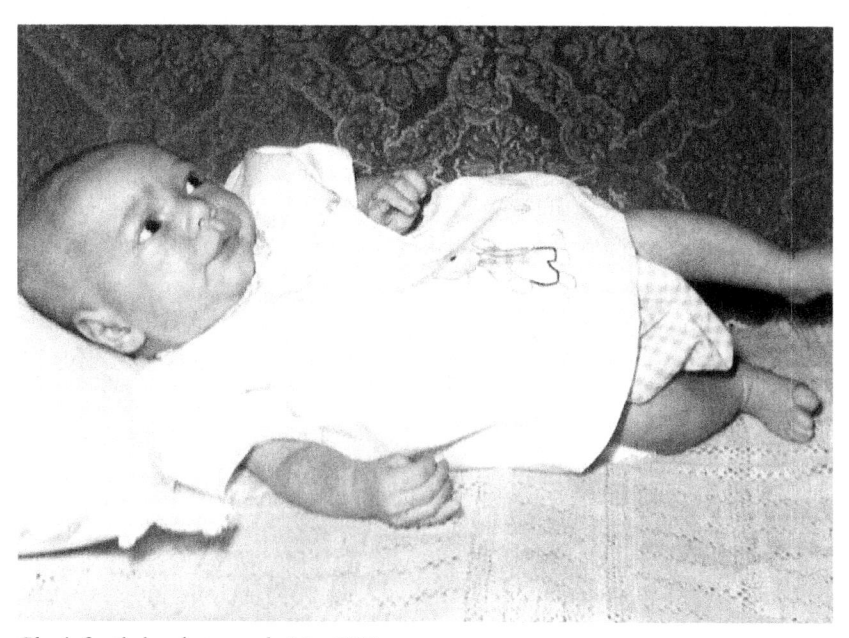

Glyn's first baby photograph, May 1965.

it in turns to do her washing. When Pat's washer broke down, her mother bought her a new one with an electric wringer on the top – we had never used one like that before. Pat had gone upstairs and I started to put a sheet through the wringer. The wringer started to swing round, I held onto the sheet and went round with it. There was water all over the lino and I slid round like an ice skater, all the time shouting for Pat to come round and turn it off. We had a laugh about it after and I did manage to keep the sheet off the floor and clean. We had a lot of laughs together Pat and I.

I had another mate called Tilly who told me that she had seen an advert in the paper for temporary workers at a mail order company in Wakefield called Empire Stores. The job was until Christmas. Tilly said if I applied and got in, she would look after Glyn for me. I loved the relationship I had with my new little boy, and the few friends I'd made on the council estate, yet I was still lonely and craved adult friendship. My mother agreed to take turns looking after Glyn so there was nothing in the way apart from Don, who I knew wouldn't allow me to work outside of the house.

I was very tempted by the job so had to think of a way of asking Don that would make him think it was a good idea and to his advantage. The key was the rent money. At the time he paid the rent – well he had to because he didn't give me enough to pay it. He was always saying he was skint. When I approached him to ask if I might go out to work he said 'No way!' I said, 'What if I use my wage to pay the rent?' He studied for a bit and then decided that it would be alright for me to have a little job. The feeling of loneliness was then replaced by one of guilt. I didn't like myself for leaving my lad to be looked after by somebody else, but the extra money would make life so much easier for me and my boys.

Don showed no interest in his own children. He lacked any sense of responsibility. He was only happy when he was in the pub. When I managed to ask him why he was like he was, his answer was, 'I've brought up ten children already.' By that he meant his younger brothers and sisters.

'I don't see why I have to bring up any more, let somebody else have a go.'

I don't know who he thought that 'someone else' was apart from me.

It wasn't just this belligerence, he could also be cruel. I asked him to take Glyn into Barnsley for some new shoes. Glyn tried some on which he liked that had plenty of space for his growing feet. Don said to the shop assistant, 'How much are they?' When she told him, he just said 'pap pap!' walked out of the shop and left Glyn sitting there. Another time he said, 'If you all get yourselves ready I'll take us to the pictures in town.' We all got washed and changed, the kids were excited. We waited for the bus on Coniston Avenue, but before the bus came Don said, 'I've changed my mind, I'm off to the pub.' He left us standing there. I had no money, and nowhere else to go, so I had to take the kids back home.

I worked in the warehouse picking orders at Empire Stores. I was nervous at first and I seemed to be continually saying sorry. It was all worth it though for the financial independence it gave me. When the supervisor asked me if I wanted to start a full-time job after Christmas, I thought about why I needed to work and about something that Donny once said to me. I always had to buy second-hand shoes for the children. One day Donny said, 'Please may I have some shoes that nobody else has worn before me?' Now, if the boys wanted a new pair of shoes, they didn't have to wait until I saved up, I could go out and get them a pair there and then.

Open House
Anne

Because Harold had been a cook in the RAF, he did a lot of the cooking at home. When we started entertaining people to dinner as Arthur got more well known, I decided to join a cookery and presentation class at a night school locally. They showed us how to do vol-au-vents and fish pies, the food that was popular in the 1960s and 70s. I wasn't used to doing that sort of food and I got tormented when I took my dishes home for 'critical tastings'. I didn't do it for long and went back to cooking the food that I'd been shown how to do at home. I preferred to cook traditional Sunday roasts and meat and tatey pies with crusts on that stuck to your ribs, as my mother used to say. I don't think I was cut out to be a hostess for dinner parties.

We always had a New Year's Eve party at our house. Vic Allen used to come. He was a professor at Leeds University and for a long time the official historian for the miners' union. He was a big ally and Arthur took him on as a trusted advisor, although it would be fair to say that Vic had a colourful past. He'd left school at fifteen in the 1930s without any certificates and worked as a brickie and a boxer but he read a lot of books. After the war he went to university and ended up with a PhD. He got arrested in Nigeria in the 1960s for giving out Marxist leaflets telling people to prepare for the revolution. He tried to escape dressed as an Arab, but they caught him and put him in jail. When he was an old man he got into a lot of bother when they started to publish papers from the old East Germany. It turned out that he'd been doing a bit of spying for the Stasi, the East German secret police. He had been on the committee of CND for years and admitted passing on information about them. He said he'd never been paid and did it for reasons of world peace. Our Margaret called him Mr Spock because she said he looked just like Leonard Nimoy. I remember him best supping fine wine. His wife Sheila liked a drop as well, I have seen her drunk a time or two. They had some right debates at our house. It made me laugh because I don't drink alcohol and never have. I have a condition that means I can't tolerate it, our Margaret is the same and she can't drink either.

Vic introduced us to Maurice Jones. Maurice was a journalist who ended up being editor of *The Yorkshire Miner*. Maurice looked like something out of *Citizen Smith*, a typical leftie of the 1970s. He had long hair, a beard and always looked scruffy. One day he came to our house wanting to talk to Arthur. I told him that Arthur was out but he shouldn't be too long. I asked him to sit down and wait, but he seemed agitated, up and down all the time looking through the window. He was like a cat on hot bricks.

'Do you want some hash?' I asked him.

He looked at me.

'Do you like a bit of hash?'

He looked flummoxed.

'Why have you got some?'

'Aye lad,' I said, 'I've got loads of it.'

He looked at me again, puzzled.

'Do you grow your own?'

'Nay lad, I don't grow it, I make it.'

I went in the kitchen and fetched him a plateful.

'Here lad, it's just some leftovers. Tateys, turnip, onions and a bit of chopped-up meat we had left from the Sunday dinner.'

I don't think he'd ever heard of tatey hash.

The bungalow was like an open house at times with a procession of visitors. Doug Stables lived across the road and would often come over. Dougie was an insurance man, a part-time painter and decorator, and secretary at the Swaithe Working Men's Club. In his spare time he went round churches and youth clubs showing Old Mother Riley films. He rarely came to our house before midnight. After the club shut at 11 o'clock he'd clear up and then come knocking on our door wanting to sit up into the early hours talking to Harold and Arthur before he went home because he lived on his own. I went to bed, but I could hear him, Arthur and Harold kallin' at 2 o'clock in the morning.

Another one who came round a lot was Percy Riley. Percy was a communist organiser and door-to-door brush seller. Going door to door like that meant he could spread his politics to ordinary people living in working-class towns all over South Yorkshire. He met Harold one day when it was freezing cold out and Harold invited him in to get warm in front of the fire. They became friends after that and eventually Percy became a good friend and helper to Arthur; he once offered to get him a job selling brushes but Arthur politely declined saying that he'd rather stay at the pit.

Percy had been born at the bottom of York Road in Leeds and remembered running about in his bare feet during the general strike. He was sent to approved school when he was six because one of his uncles accused his mam of neglect and said she couldn't afford to keep him. He was 16 when he went back to live with his mam and by then she had moved to a pit village called Goldthorpe, which is where he first came to know coalminers. He was an activist for the Communist Party in the 1930s depression and during the war he organised a strike. The miners were sent to harvest camps in Bedfordshire to help get crops in. Hundreds of them used to go down on the train from Cudworth station. The lads from Rossington didn't like it when they found out the rate for pulling peas down there was less than they could get in Yorkshire so they went on strike. After the war, Percy put up for the council in Hickleton and became the first communist councillor in South Yorkshire. He was a great help to Arthur during the 1972 strike and he was at his side at Saltley Gate and Grunwick later on. He had a tape recorder which he used to record what was going off. Arthur always thought it would be good evidence if ever there was a court case after.

Goff Sunderland was a good ally and friend to Arthur when he first got elected on the union. His actual name was Godfrey but we always called him Goff. He was a tall thin man, always on the go; I don't think he knew how to keep still. He was softly-spoken and never had a wrong word to say about anybody, but you couldn't argue with him. He never got nasty, but he was good at putting a case. He was also a stickler for rules, so he was perfect for his job as a union man but also for his other job as a football referee.

In the early 1950s he was invited to coach referees in South

America. He took time off from the pit to go. He sailed to Argentina and he'd only just got off the boat when some football officials told him they wanted him to travel to Chile to ref a match between Brazil and Uruguay in the Pan-American Cup. In his mild-mannered way, Goff tried to explain that he had come to coach and not to take charge of matches, but the officials were insistent and kept offering him more and more money. Eventually Goff gave in when he realised he could earn more from one match than he could earn in a month at Woolley pit.

It was a game full of high drama, a lot of goals and Goff had to send two off, one from either side. With only a few minutes to go Goff awarded Uruguay a penalty. There was uproar in the crowd, gunshots were fired and the linesmen ran away. There were rumours that some people had collapsed in the crowd with anxiety. Some high-up officials came running on and advised Goff to abandon the game. Goff, being the stickler he was, said, 'No, we have to complete the game.' You couldn't argue with him once he had his referee outfit on. They brought troops on to guard the penalty area. The Brazilian goalie saved the penalty and became a national hero. And Goff lived to tell the tale.

Goff never married. He lodged with a family in Higham and used to come to my mam's for Sunday dinner - he was a lifelong friend of my dad. After dinner me and our Joan would pester him to tell us his football tales and he always obliged us. He liked to tell us a tale about how he once refereed a match in Argentina in front of President Perón and his wife Evita. One player in particular kept fouling the other team. In the end Goff pulled him up and pointed to the VIP box and said, 'Hey up lad, if you carry on you're going to disgrace yourself in front of your own president.' The player in question was Alfredo di Stefano, the most famous Argentinean footballer of his time who went on to be the star of Real Madrid when they won all their European cups. Di Stefano was known for his robust play and great strength. Goff said after he warned him he played the rest of the game like a little fairy.

Another time Goff was in charge of a match in Brazil between Santos and Corinthians. He said that Santos had a very young skinny kid of about 15 playing for them. Goff was worried about him because every time he got the ball the opposition seemed to be trying to hammer him. A Corinthian player came flying in with a cruncher of a tackle but this young kid spun out of it like an acrobat and made a fool of the big defender. At the end of the game Goff went to shake hands with the kid and congratulated him on his skill. He said, 'What's your name lad?' The young man replied, 'My name is Pelé, sir.' Goff told us that every time Pelé came to England he got in touch with him and took him to a match. He never bragged about it, he just told it straight. Goff was full of great stories like that.

In Mexico he was on his way to the stadium when he saw some little boys selling rotten tomatoes. He asked them what they were selling rotten ones for. The boys said, 'They are for people to throw at the referee.' Goff told them that he was the referee and out of pity for the poor kids, he bought a couple of bagfuls. The story went round that the crazy English ref had bought rotten tomatoes to throw at himself. Then a buzz went through the crowd saying that out of respect fans were not to throw their tomatoes at a man who was obviously loco to start with. We right liked Goff. When he retired he got a little bungalow in Barnsley and our Joan used to go and clean for him.

Michael
Betty

My eldest son Michael started with convulsions soon after he started school. The first time it happened I'd just hung the washing up on the drying rack. The children were having their breakfast and Michael started looking up at the washing, rocking backwards and forwards in his chair. Then he started frothing at his mouth and fell onto the floor, his limbs flailing. I saw to him until he came round. I went to the phone box to call the doctor, who then came to our house on his round. He told me that I should try to keep Michael calm and that children often had convulsions when they were running a temperature. Michael had more convulsions over time, but I saw a pattern, so prepared as best as I could. My instinct told me that he had epilepsy.

By the time he was at junior school, Michael was referred to a consultant. The first question he asked was 'What is he like at school?' I told the consultant that Michael was extremely bright and that the headmaster had been boasting to other people that Michael was extraordinarily gifted and would go on to bring honour to Woolley Colliery School. The consultant shook his head and said, 'This is most unfortunate because he will regress.' Michael was put on medication and this seemed to work.

When he was about ten we had the chance of a family break in Amsterdam. I had a friend in Immingham who told me that a ferry went from the docks there. We took the train to Immingham, changing at Doncaster station. Michael was running up and down the platform pretending to be a locomotive. He loved trains and had a passion for trainspotting. Suddenly he fell down onto the lines convulsing. I jumped down and another passenger helped me while someone went to tell the station staff. Michael came round quite quickly and seemed alright. I put it down to over excitement with all the travelling, but in retrospect I realised that it was the start of a life to be lived with epilepsy and all that that entailed.

Instinctively I prepared and seemed to know when an attack would come on, but this pattern didn't always conform and over time Michael's condition grew worse. By now he was on a lot of serious medication, but none of it controlled his attacks. His learning and education were completely ruined. He still managed to go to school but he was no longer the quick, bright academic boy he had been. This was made worse by a headmaster who had once bragged about his star pupil, but now lacked both the compassion and the imagination to help Michael. This wasn't a surprise to me. That headmaster was next to useless when it came to empathy for anything but his own glory. When the school celebrated its centenary, the parents, Labour Party and ex-pupils really mucked in to make a special celebration day and the headmaster didn't even bother to turn up.

I had a lot of run-ins with that headmaster. He was a downright bully and was known to be violent towards the children. On one occasion in assembly he told the children to stand up. The whole class stood up, at which point Michael had a petit mal seizure. When he told them to sit down, Michael didn't hear him and remained standing, while all around started laughing. The head didn't think it was funny at all, he just saw disobedience. My boy came home that day with bruised and swollen legs where he had been beaten. If I could have got to the school before the head left I'm sure I would have swung for him. I contacted the local authority and they sent a health visitor to see me. She said, 'I believe there has been a little bit of trouble and perhaps a misunderstanding with Michael.' Then she started to laugh. I went mad. I told her to leave my house immediately before I threw her through the door and into the garden. She ran out of the house and I chased after her. The quicker she ran, the more I chased, round and round the estate. She took out her car keys but couldn't get them into the lock and I caught up with her. I looked her straight in the eye as she stood there.

'Now you can get off this estate and don't dare come back or you will have me to deal with and next time I won't let you off so easy.'

After that the other women neighbours would tell me if they were due a visit from this woman and I would wait for her. As soon as she saw me, she turned round.

When Michael got to Darton Secondary Modern things were no better. The teachers made next to no attempt to understand him and his condition. I had a letter from the head who said he wanted to see me fifteen minutes before parents' evening began. I went to sit in a corridor outside of the head's study, not in the best of moods. At one time I might not have had the confidence to even address a headmaster, but I was becoming increasingly confident. A well-dressed, middle-class couple arrived and the woman looked down at me as she sat next to the study door. Her husband said, 'I think this lady is in front of us.' She looked at me again, turned her head and said, 'Oh! I think he will see me first.'

The head opened his door, 'Mrs Cook, please come in.' I stood up, looked across at the woman over my shoulder and smiled. Some boys had been caught smoking in the bike shed. Michael was one of them. He had also been out to the corner shop without permission and bought a big bottle of lemonade, which now stood on the desk. Before he could say any more, I told the headmaster that he ought to understand that due to his condition Michael sometimes needed a sharp drink. The head said he had confiscated the bottle of pop.

'Well I am going to confiscate it back!' I said. 'Do you understand that Michael is on a lot of medication and you are suggesting he is a difficult child?'

The head didn't seem to know how to respond. I carried on.

'Where are the parents of the other boys who were smoking?'

The head said he hadn't invited them.

'Well until such time as you do, I consider this matter closed.'

At that I turned on my heel and walked out of the office. I offered my best smile to the woman who was waiting.

Some of Michael's schoolmates teased him. One afternoon I happened to have walked my mother back to the bus stop after a visit and waited for the school bus to drop off. As Michael got off, a big lad pushed him and said, 'Thy's done a good trick today, show us again.' Michael must have had one of his fits at school. I took hold of this lad and chucked him straight over a low wall.

'Don't you ever behave like that toward my son again.'

'I'll fetch my father to you.'

'Fetch him! He'll get some of what you have just had.'

Michael was referred to Dr Orme, a psychiatrist attached to Barnsley Education Department. One time he gave Michael a pencil and paper and encouraged him to draw something. Michael drew a children's playground with no children in it, just a man with a pipe in his mouth. Dr Orme showed me the drawing. He asked me what I made of it. I told him that Michael was missing a father figure. After that Dr Orme did a session with Michael and then one with me. He asked me why my husband never came with me. I decided to unburden myself and I told him just what things were like at home. I mentioned Don's constant drinking, his neglect of me and the children and just how unhappy I was. Dr Orme asked if I had thought of trying to make a new life for myself and the children away from Don. He even offered to support me if I could bring myself to get away. At the time I was so low that I couldn't even face the help he was offering.

'I believe that one day you will meet someone else and leave your husband,' Dr Orme told me.

I shook my head.

'I can't do that because it might mean leaving my children and I will never do that.'

'One day I believe you will.'

Don could drink any amount of beer, but never seemed drunk. If he was that way out at chucking out time he'd want to carry on with his mates. I've known times when I have been ready for bed and he's invited a gang of blokes back for some supper. I heard him outside, 'Come on lads, our lass will make us something.' Then he would have me put the frying pan on at midnight so he and his mates could stuff their faces with chip butties.

On week nights he drank his beer at the Liberal Club in Darton. He liked to go to a working men's club at Barugh Green at the weekend. I always stopped in to look after the children. One Saturday when the boys were staying at my mother's for the night, I watched Don as he got washed and changed ready to go to the club. Something came over me and I got washed and changed myself and announced that I was going to go out with him. He wasn't best pleased and told me not to follow him. He strode off down the road with me behind him. He stopped off at his mother's house. When he got up to leave I stood up as well, so he sat back down again. He did this two or three times. I was determined that he would not go out without me. His mother said, 'Why don't you come to the bingo with us instead?' I told her no, I wanted to go out with my husband as a couple. Don stood up again and sat down as soon as he saw me move. He liked playing childish games like that. I was always on my guard when he was stirring his tea because when I wasn't looking he would press the hot spoon on my hand. In the end, I got fed up and gave in and went to the bingo with his mother but I think I had put a warning shot across his bow. The next time Don was carrying on I plucked up the courage to say to him. 'These boys won't always be small you know.' He just looked at me and shrugged, but I knew that I had got to him.

My phone rang one evening. It was the lad who used to pedal on his bike to visit me in nurse training at Thorp Arch, the one who dropped a worm down my back. I hadn't seen him since he sailed off to Australia. We chatted for a good while and then he asked if I might meet him for a drink. I told him I was married and I knew he was married, but I agreed to meet him at a pub in Featherstone. We chatted all night about old times. We met again that Christmas for another drink. I got the feeling that he wanted more than just a friendship between old friends. This time I told him, 'This is as far as it goes, it's not fair.' He went off heartbroken for a second time.

Lofthouse Disaster
Anne

At the end of 1969 there was a strike in the Yorkshire coalfield which soon spread. It was Arthur who pushed for action. Arthur was one of a good number who thought that the union had lost its teeth and needed to make itself known again. There was a lot of senior officials who were happy to sit back and not get involved. Sam Bullough, the president of the Yorkshire miners, ruled that Arthur was out of order. The area delegates voted Bullough out of the chair and then voted by a big majority for a strike. It was during this strike that flying pickets were first organised. They managed to persuade Derbyshire to come out, but Nottinghamshire were slow on the uptake. This was the first time Arthur started to get noticed.

At the beginning of 1972, the miners came out on strike over wages. Coalminers' wages had fallen behind over the years and they had a very good case. Arthur organised the flying pickets at Saltley in Birmingham. This led to Ted Heath's government giving in and the miners won a famous victory after about seven weeks on strike.

Shortly after, Arthur became the compensation agent for the Yorkshire miners and took responsibility for the miners who were injured or killed at work. One night he'd been to a reunion of people who he had been on a day release course with at Leeds University and didn't get home until the early hours, I was already in bed. We were both woken up by the phone ringing. We had a so-called hotline for special calls. On the hotline was a mining engineer who said he had been asked by Norman Siddall, the chief mining engineer, to let Arthur know that there had been an inrush of water at Lofthouse Colliery and some of the men were trapped underground. Arthur got dressed straightaway and set off. He met up with Siddall and together they went down the pit with the rescue brigades. I didn't see him for three days except on the television news. When he did come home on the fourth day he was so agitated he couldn't sleep so he went back again. He ended up stopping with the rescue men and the families of the trapped lads for ten days.

A shaft from an old workings from bygone days had burst into some new workings and millions of gallons of water rushed in. It pushed muck and sludge down a roadway and blocked it off. The engineers thought that men might have survived beyond the sludge. Arthur went down the pit each day and was involved at every stage of the attempt to rescue the lads who were trapped. They tried to dig a tunnel above the rings over the roadway. Time passed and they said that it was impossible that anybody could survive, so they decided to look at recovery of bodies. There was a free vote amongst the union, families and those involved in the rescue attempt to create a tunnel into the workings to potentially recover bodies and find out more information as to why the accident had happened. Arthur wanted to go ahead with the tunnel but lost the vote, mainly due to fears for the safety of the operatives. It was a terribly sad event. Seven miners died, but only one body, that of Charles Cotton, was recovered.

The Prime Minister Ted Heath came to observe the rescue attempt. Arthur told me that he was impressed by how Heath showed genuine concern and said he was supportive. He asked for updates and said he would do anything he could to help. The Labour Party didn't send anybody and this sloughened Arthur. The following year Arthur went to see Heath in London over a dispute where outside contractors were getting paid more than regular workers for doing the same job. He said that Heath listened at first and seemed to be siding with what the NUM were telling him. Then he listened to what some of his advisors were telling him and came back and said he couldn't settle. Arthur always says that if Heath had gone on his instinct instead of listening to bad advice there would have been no need for a strike and Heath wouldn't have had to call the election that he lost to Wilson. If you follow that through, there might not have been Thatcher.

Arthur got on well with Heath. They once had lunch together, beef stroganoff with rice, and Arthur teased Heath about Russian influences on the menu. After their lunch, Heath showed Arthur and Owen Briscoe, general secretary of the Yorkshire miners, round his office. He wanted them to see the cups he had won for sailing on his yacht Morning Cloud. He even invited them to come sailing with him. Arthur gave a polite no, not mentioning that he suffered badly from seasickness.

There was a public enquiry into the disaster at Wakefield Town Hall. Arthur was the advocate for the NUM on behalf of the bereaved families. He went well prepared; he had spent a lot of time beforehand making a plan. He talked to folk in the village about the local history and looked at the lie of the land round and about with people who knew it well. Some of the miners told him that water in the old shaft had been bleeding through the coal for days before it burst through. Then he went to the geological institute at Leeds to look at old drawings of mines in the Lofthouse area.

At the enquiry Arthur showed that all of the drawings of old workings going back to the nineteenth century were there to be seen if the surveyors had looked for them when they were planning new workings. He then questioned the pit manager about attitudes to safety. He asked him what action he would have taken if a smell similar to rotten eggs had been reported. The manager shocked Arthur when he said 'that was normal'. Evidence from engineers said that in that situation, work should stop immediately.

I went on the final day when Arthur was doing his summing up. I think it was the first time he'd been at an enquiry in that way and he was as good as any lawyer. He argued that the coal board had failed in its duty and that they could have prevented the disaster if they had acted upon information that was readily available to them. Arthur kept his calm all the way through, but I knew he was upset by it all. He was angry and distressed when he came home and he told me that if the people who made decisions at the pit had done their job properly, those poor men would not have lost their lives in such a terrible way. Compensation for the families was awarded without fight, but Lofthouse had a massive emotional impact on Arthur that never went away.

Empire Stores
Betty

It was hard work picking at Empire Stores. The stock was on either side of an aisle in cardboard boxes piled onto high metal shelves. To reach the higher levels you had to monkey climb. There were no ladders or steps to help you reach and no notion of health and safety at work. After a few weeks I was put on stock control, which was less stressful, but still involved a lot of climbing up and down. The work was tiring, but I wasn't done when I came home. I still had all the housework to do and Don insisted that I still prepare the meals. He changed shifts so that he finished at 4pm and put the meal I had prepared the night before into the oven.

I applied for a clerical job that came up and I was successful. Don agreed to it of course because by now he was happy for me to be earning money; it meant he could keep more of what he earned for himself. The childminder agreed to carry on looking after Glyn for me and my mother said she would come one day a week to help with the housework. One of the supervisors there was unkind and did all she could to make my life difficult, to the extent that she questioned me every time I requested an afternoon off to take Michael to his consultant. Another supervisor was more understanding and encouraging. She persuaded me to join the Labour Party. I quickly started to learn about local politics and how you could strive to get things done.

When the flying pickets started in the strikes in the 1970s I got shut of Don for a bit. In the 1972 strike a lot of the miners were bussed to the East Coast to stop the boats bringing coal in. Don was sent to King's Lynn. While he was away we ran out of coal. I went into the woods between the pit and the Windhill Estate with a little handsaw, a chopper and a length of rope. I'll never know to this day how I managed it, but I cut down a tree and dragged it home with the rope. Don was one of the flying pickets who went to Birmingham to try and get them to shut the gates at the coke plant at Saltley. It was the biggest fuel store in the country and the lorries going in and out were keeping the fuel supply going to industry. The government declared that the plant would be kept open at all costs and that the gate must not be closed. After Arthur Scargill led a massive picket to blockade the place, the chief constable, Sir Derrick Capper, said the gates would have to close for reasons of public safety. It was seen as a great victory for the miners and Arthur made a big name for himself.

I was at work at Empire Stores when one of the girls fetched a message to say I was wanted on the phone. It was Don. He phoned me to tell me that they had managed to close the gates at Saltley and that he was coming home. It was like somebody saying they were coming home from a battle. I put my hand over the phone and told the news to the other women. One of the supervisors was sitting nearby and when I came off the phone she went mad. She said I ought to be ashamed of myself for being happy that men were being prevented from working. I found out later that her boyfriend owned a coal lorry and had been one of the drivers contracted to bring coal out of the depot. He was being paid a lot of money for running his lorry in and out. I could never understand how you could work in the same place as someone, who, as soon as you give them more money and a bit of responsibility, start sympathising with the Tories.

Don started drinking with some men who took their wives out on a Saturday night. Don was easily influenced and he decided that I ought to start coming out with him. I looked forward to the Saturday night because it was one way of getting him to spend a bit of money on me. Every time he went to the bar for a pint, I had a half. At the end of the night he sent me to the bar for the last one. He used to tell me to have a short. I'd treat myself to a double Pernod and lemonade and put some of my own money to it because I knew he would count the change.

The Barugh Green Club was a typical working men's place with a bar, a concert room and a drummer and piano player for the turns at the weekend. It was mostly men who went in during the week but at the weekend the women got dressed up and went there. Even then the men didn't talk to the women much apart from to ask if they were ready for another drink. The men congregated together and so did the women. It was a routine week in week out; same table, same seat, turns and bingo and ten minutes to drink up when it got to 11 o'clock.

It was a hard life being married to Don but I learned how to survive it. There was very little I wouldn't have a go at. I learned self-sufficiency and independence. In many respects this contributed to changing a lot of my previous attitudes and ways. My mother was a working-class snob who easily judged and looked down on people she thought weren't up to her standards. She wanted everything to be 'just so' and that rubbed off on me. Don was forever saying that I was the biggest snob he had ever met. Living with him knocked a lot of that out of me.

Russia
Anne

A letter came from Russia to invite officials from all areas of the NUM plus their wives and children on an all-expenses paid trip to the Soviet Union for a five-week holiday. Arthur had only recently become the compensation agent, so he wasn't on the original list. Sid Schofield, who was the general secretary of the Yorkshire miners at the time, dropped out because he was poorly. Sid said that Arthur, me and our Margaret could have his place. About a fortnight before the trip, they told us that we could go if we could get visas. In those days it was almost impossible to get a visa for the Soviet Union in such a short space of time, it normally took about eight weeks. Arthur got in touch with Bert Ramelson who was high up in the Communist Party. He told us that he could get us some visas sorted out. We wrote a letter to the embassy in London and told them that Arthur had been to Moscow when he was nineteen to attend the World Youth Conference. Arthur went to the Co-op to ask for five weeks off for me. The trip was organised and paid for by Soviet coalminers who offered their generosity to people who had been prominent in the strike. They were impressed with the success of Arthur's flying pickets. When we travelled down to Tilbury docks to board a ship called *The Baltika*, we still hadn't got the papers to travel. Just as the rest of them started boarding, a Soviet official stepped out of nowhere and handed over an envelope marked 'Special Privilege Guest'.

Arthur had told me many stories about his first trip to Russia when we were courting. In 1957 he went to the World Festival of Youth and Students in Moscow. Nikita Khrushchev was trying to open up the country more at the time and sent out invitations to young people all over the world. Arthur was invited as a representative of the Young Communist League in Great Britain, but nobody had any money to send him. Frank Watters said they ought to do fundraising and ask for donations. They called it 'Send a Young Miner to Moscow'. Tommy

Degnan, who was an important mentor to Arthur, advised him to go and see Alwyn Machin who was the president of the Yorkshire miners' union at the time. Tommy had an interesting past, he was wounded in the Spanish Civil War and thought to be dead – a funeral was held with an oration by Sir Stafford Cripps – but was later spotted by Will Paynter in a hospital bed very much alive. He worked with Stalin, Lenin and Trotsky, and was subsequently blacklisted by many employers. He ended up as checkweighman as this was a job appointed by the men themselves. Acting on Tommy's advice, Arthur went to see Alwyn Machin who gave him £5 and this encouraged more people to make donations and they ended up with £35 in the kitty.

Arthur went on the train across Europe. He told me that the Russians had a different size of track so when they got to the border they had to wait for a train that ran on their rails. Arthur said that when the train turned up is was like something out of *Doctor Zhivago*, a huge steam train with a massive red star on the front with steam and smoke blowing all over. The young delegates got on and well-wishers passed food to them. Arthur said it was the first time he tried salami.

All the delegates stayed in the same hotel in Moscow, but sixteen of them were invited to a special dinner in the Kremlin hosted by Khrushchev and Nikolai Bulganin, the Chairman of the Council of Ministers in the Soviet government; Bulganin had been the armed forces minister at the time of Stalin. Arthur said that the whole of the Politburo was at the dinner and that he sat near the top table next to Kirichenko, who had something to do with the Young Communist League in the USSR. Sitting at the other side was an African man who had been badly beaten by government forces. Arthur said he was spellbound by the personality of Khrushchev, he thought he was magnetic. He wasn't sure what to make of it when Khrushchev leapt over the dining table to hug the African man. Arthur was never one for men putting their arms round one another. He wasn't comfortable with all that hugging business. When we went to the international gatherings together I can remember seeing the delegates sniggering. When Arthur used to put his hand out to shake hands they used to embrace him and kiss him on the cheeks on purpose. The French ones like Alain Simone and Augustin Dufresne were the worst for it, they were always trying to kiss him. Arthur was still a pit lad at heart and he didn't like it.

When we went on our five-week trip, Arthur didn't get off to the best of starts. It turned out that the Russians had a practical solution to spare cabin space and they put a young man in to share ours. Arthur complained and the poor lad was evicted. Arthur was seasick every day and spent most of the cruise somewhere down the bottom of the ship. We stopped off in Copenhagen. I can remember looking at the Tivoli Gardens and on the way back we must have strayed into the red light district. Arthur had to grab our Margaret's arm and pull her away before she could look in the windows. There were lasses of all shapes and sizes displaying their assets. Before we got back on the Russian ship our Margaret went for a walk up the dockside and started taking photos with a little instamatic camera I'd bought her. She was fascinated with a massive aircraft carrier that was loading aeroplanes onto its decks and she started snapping away. Some men came running up and told her to stop. It turned out that the ship was *USS Nimitz*, the famous US aircraft carrier that was still undergoing tests at the time before it went into service.

Ron Rigby, a delegate from the Shafton workshops, was with us on the trip. He was a lovely dancer; he used to do the jitterbug with his wife and throw her over his shoulder. Clive Jenkins came as well. Clive was high up in the TUC at the time. His daughter Bronwyn was about the same age as our Margaret so they palled about together. They explored that ship top to bottom. They got in bother when they went down to the engine room but most of the time the crew were brilliant with all the kids.

When we docked in Leningrad there was a bus waiting for each area of the union – a Yorkshire bus, a Welsh bus, a Nottinghamshire bus and so on – each with its own interpreter assigned. Our interpreter was called Valery and he wasn't too keen on Arthur. They fell out a lot on that trip. Arthur kept asking him for fresh milk for the kids and Valery said he couldn't get any.

We were waltzed off to the hotel and everything went like clockwork. We were taken to see inside the Winter Palace where the Russian emperors had lived before the revolution. We were told not to touch anything, but Arthur couldn't resist it when he saw a door knob made from gemstones. He put his hand on it. A babushka came running up, slapped his hand and swore at him. They showed us Catherine the Great's peacock clock with its mechanical birds and then they took us to see a battleship that had been preserved since the war with Japan. Everything was exciting. The one thing we struggled a bit with was the food. Our Margaret is a faddy eater at the best of times. The only thing she would eat was smoked sturgeon so she had smoked sturgeon and a beaker of water for every meal.

We travelled down to Moscow on the overnight train. This time they put a young woman in our sleeping cabin. In Moscow we were taken to the theatre to see a medley by the touring Kirov Ballet and then to the Moscow State Circus. It was a busy schedule but even when we were in the hotel Arthur couldn't sit still. A lot of the delegates were happy to lounge about drinking and smoking. Arthur always wanted to explore. He took me and our Margaret on the underground railway. It's beautiful. We must have got off at every station to stand and look at the walls. We even went exploring down the back streets by ourselves. A policeman stopped us one day for running across a busy road. He couldn't speak English but he was waving his arms about and pointing at us. Arthur pulled out his special visa and showed him it. That calmed him down but he was still gesticulating that we must be crazy as we walked off. He seemed angry because we had crossed a busy road.

At the space museum we saw Yuri Gagarin's capsule. Yuri Gagarin was a massive hero. I can see Margaret now playing on a model of his *Soyuz*. She got upset though when they told her about the dog Laika that had died in space. I think to appease her, the guides said Laika was put down humanely by an injection that was timed to go off once the spacecraft started orbiting.

We went to see Lenin in his glass case. It's a very cold, eerie place and the Russians insist on keeping it solemn. If men put their hands in their pockets while they are looking they get told off. I saw a man stopped from going in because he was wearing shorts. I was asked to cover my shoulders as we filed passed. The casket is bathed in yellow light. Margaret had never seen a dead body before and she was scared, but said she was glad she'd been in when we came out. Arthur asked a woman tour guide where Stalin was. She wasn't best pleased. Of course Arthur wanted to debate with her. We were told that Stalin had been moved to a place behind a wall. He said that they shouldn't be airbrushing history like that. Arthur's hero, Arthur MacManus, an early activist for the Socialist Labour Party, is buried in the wall as well. He died when he was visiting Moscow so they gave him that honour. Arthur was happier later when we were shown Stalin's summer house at Lake Ritsa in the Caucasus Mountains. The water trickles down the mountain side there, they say it is a monument to weeping mothers.

Arthur was constantly debating with the tour guides, the officials and the delegates on the trip. In the end the delegates on our bus got fed up with him and an argument started. Frank Warboys, an official for the Nottinghamshire miners, said that our family could travel on the Nottinghamshire bus for the rest of the trip. It suited our Margaret because she had made friends with Frank's daughter Pamela.

We went to the coal-mining district at Donetsk in the Donbass. The men went down the pit, but they didn't invite the women. Arthur asked if we could see how some ordinary people lived. The next day the bus turned up at a housing estate. They herded us through a woman's house. I don't know what she must have thought of all these strangers traipsing through her front room and looking at her furniture and kitchen. While we were in the Donbass we were invited to a reception. The governor came with gifts for all the miners and their families. We got a beautiful samovar, Margaret still has it. The governor was Alexei Kirichenko and he recognised Arthur from the dinner in Moscow in 1957. He laughed about teaching him to sup vodka. Of all the things Arthur could have asked about, the first was fresh milk for our Margaret. He'd been going on about fresh milk since we'd landed. Kirichenko laughed, clapped his hands and in a flash some people came running in with fresh milk for the kids. The next morning we saw the tomb of the unknown soldier. It was built over a pit shaft where they told us a lot of women and children had been thrown down alive. It was a sad and very moving place with just a simple flame burning on top of the capped-off shaft.

The last place we went to was Pitsunda, near to Sochi. It's the seaside town where Khrushchev used to go for his holidays. Arthur can't swim at all, but he likes to paddle. He was wading out to sea when the shelf he was on suddenly dropped away. I saw him flailing about and thought he was going to drown. I had to fish him out and swim back to the shore with him. The resort was lovely and safe enough to let Margaret and Pamela wander about unsupervised. They made friends with a young lass called Natasha who'd have been about twenty. She was on her holidays there and was keen to learn English. She invited Margaret and Pamela back to her hotel room once or twice and in return for a few English lessons she bought them ice creams. They came back giggling one day and told me that she had got undressed to get changed in front of them. I think the Eastern European women are a bit less inhibited than we are.

We flew back to Moscow on a big Russian aeroplane with propellers and a glass nose. The pilot let our Margaret and some of the other kids sit in the cockpit. Our hotel in Moscow had faulty plumbing. The water wouldn't stop dripping so we asked for room service to send a plumber. By the time he came it was after midnight and we were all in bed. He ignored us and started to fix the taps. Halfway through doing it he must have realised it was snap time. He put down his tools, unwrapped his sandwiches and poured a hot drink out of his flask. After he'd supped his tea and eaten his bread he got his paper out and had a squint at that for ten minutes. He was completely oblivious to us peering over our blankets. Then he folded his paper up, shoved it back into his jacket pocket and carried on until he'd finished the job. He then shut the door behind him and went whistling down the corridor.

We did a bit of shopping before we came home in a state shop called GUM. Margaret bought a guitar with seven strings on it and some nesting Russian dolls. I bought a Russian hat. I still wear it now when it's cold. Margaret wrote about her trip for her English O-level. She told me that thirty years later she got talking to a schoolteacher at a dinner party. The teacher said that she had marked Margaret's paper and was fascinated that a pupil at a Yorkshire school could write so vividly about a trip to the Soviet Union in the middle of the cold war. Then she saw the surname.

We had already been to Russia together a few years earlier, but only for a day-trip on a short excursion from a family holiday to Bulgaria. A bloke called John Bloom had set up a holiday company in the 1960s offering cheap holidays to the Black Sea coast. Bloom was the man who had made a fortune selling cheap washing machines; firstly door to door and then on hire purchase by mail order. He liked to sell himself as the housewives' friend and a helper to the working class. He started offering holidays to Bulgaria for £59 for a fortnight. This was at the time when only a few people had been to Spain. Bloom ended up bankrupt but a tourist industry was up and running in Bulgaria with some nice hotels. Arthur was fascinated by the idea that you could go to a communist country with sunny beaches so he booked for us to have a family holiday. We flew there with a Freddie Laker package tour.

It was unusual for working people to go abroad for their holidays then, mostly people still went to Blackpool or Bridlington. Arthur liked to be the first to do something new. He loved to know about advances in science and technology, he was the first on our street to get a video when they came out and a cine camera. When travelling abroad came within the pockets of workers, Arthur obviously wanted to be the first to do it. We flew to Varna Airport and travelled to the Golden Sands resort on the Black Sea where we stayed at the Morsko Oko Hotel. Our Margaret took Big Ted with her, the teddy bear that her grandad had given her that she insisted on taking everywhere. Golden Sands was overrun with brussen East Germans, but the Bulgarian people were lovely, very generous and giving. We met some English people as well. They were John and Volantina, or Vol as we called her. He was a lecturer and she worked for a law firm in Hertfordshire. When they found out that Arthur was a coalminer they were delighted. They told us that Vol's dad was Arthur Horner, the general secretary of the NUM in the 1940s and 50s. Not only that, Vol had once been the girlfriend of Mick McGahey, the Scottish union leader.

Arthur wasn't satisfied to be sitting on the beach all day, he liked exploring. There was a big forest at the back of the beach, so we went for walks in there amongst the gypsies with dancing bears on big thick chains. Our Margaret made friends with one of the lads at the gypsy camp, she went about holding hands with him. We ate at a restaurant at the edge of the forest, they served fresh spit-roasted chicken and warm bread. The locals looked after us well when they saw us red raw from sun bathing. They lathered us with natural yoghurt and it worked.

When we found out that a cruise ship sailed across the Black Sea to the shores of Russia, Arthur was very nervous due to his fear of water and seasickness. Vol came to his rescue. She had some pills that she said were superb for preventing seasickness. Arthur took one. The trip went smoothly and Arthur said he felt champion and hadn't felt sick at all. He asked Vol what the medication was for future reference. She admitted they were pills that she took when she had period pains.

In the evenings we walked up and down the sea front. We called into a posh hotel called the Astoria for a coffee and a slice of Black Forest Gateau which was all the go then. Back at our hotel I went to sit in bed with my Mills and Boon books. Arthur and Margaret went onto the balcony where it was cool. I used to listen to Arthur reading to her. He was a great storyteller and put a lot of emotion into his reading.

We went back to Bulgaria again a few years after, but the whole place seemed to have changed. It had become totally commercialised. You didn't spend money, instead they had started a system of vouchers. Only the tourists could spend vouchers but the locals were keen to get hold of them by any means necessary. They were ripping the tourists off left, right and centre. They never gave you the right change and they were trying to pull a fast one at every turn. Arthur went mad one day when he got short changed for the umpteenth time. He grabbed a pouch off a woman who had ripped him off and said, 'I want my change.' She complained that everybody who worked in the holiday villages were on low wages. Arthur told them to get organised and form a union instead of pinching off people. When we got back from that trip Arthur said, 'If that's communism they can keep it.'

Margaret
Anne

Margaret had a Chopper bike that she loved riding about on but what she really wanted was a pony. There was a woman called Janet at Staincross who bought New Forest ponies at auctions, then trained them up before selling them on. We bought one off her called Salty. It was salty by name and nature. There is a word that horse people use for a horse with a bad trait and that's 'vice'. Salty had a lot of vices. If they were going through a gate, Salty would get as close to the fence as possible in order to knock Margaret off, at other times it would buckle its knees on purpose and try to roll on her. Arthur went to see Janet and told her he wasn't happy. Janet agreed to have a go at retraining Salty and said that in the meantime Margaret could borrow her daughter's horse. This horse was called Coco and he was in a bit of a sorry state when he came to us. He was bald in places and generally unkempt. Apart from that he seemed gentle and Margaret liked him. Arthur talked to 'Knocker' Cole, the horse keeper at Woolley pit, about him. Knocker prescribed feeding with molasses treacle and some skin rub. He said that Coco was a sound horse and would get right. Knocker knew what he was talking about and Coco turned into a fine handsome horse with a lovely shiny coat and not a bad bone in his body. If Margaret fell off, he stopped straightaway. We loved Coco, he wasn't an ounce of bother. The only thing he didn't seem to like was brass bands.

Margaret went to local gymkhanas and won a fair few rosettes and trophies. She was thrilled to bits when she won an RAOB award at Higham. We knew a local artist, Ashley Jackson, who had become quite famous in the 1970s for his landscape paintings of the Yorkshire Moors. Our Margaret pestered him to death to paint her horse. In the end he gave in and did one for her.

We kept the horse at an ancient farm owned by the Elmhirst family. Arthur was up there one day and was bragging about his prowess with horses. There was a big troublesome one and Arthur decided to have a go at riding it. The horse shot off as soon as he mounted and was heading for a wall until it swerved at the last minute. Arthur managed somehow to stay on and came back at a gentler pace grinning. Everybody clapped him. One Saturday, Margaret's close friend Penny was kicked by her own horse there. Penny died. It was a terrible tragedy. It was never the same after that and Margaret decided to let Coco go. We got an Airedale terrier that we called Ginger. She was a lovely dog. Our Margaret loved Airedales.

I have fond memories of my own childhood days at the miners' gala when I sat on the rail beneath the banner swinging my legs. When I married Arthur and we had Margaret we had some lovely days out at the gala. Arthur always marched at the front with the delegates, Margaret and me marched with the Woolley pit banner. When Arthur became president of the Yorkshire miners they started inviting famous people as well as politicians to take part. I sat down with Arthur and Margaret and had many a laugh about who we should invite. Margaret always wanted John Noakes from *Blue Peter*. We never did get him to come but we got Lesley Judd, another *Blue Peter* presenter, instead. Joan Bakewell came one year and so did Michael Parkinson. Michael didn't charge a fee, I think mainly out of respect because his dad had been a miner.

Most of the celebrities were lovely but one or two were stand-offish. When Julie Goodyear came, she was massively popular on *Coronation Street*. We thought she was going to be down to earth but she turned up with an entourage and minders. When our Margaret ran up to get an autograph, the minders wouldn't let her anywhere near. Arthur was a big fan of the Welsh singer and comedian Max Boyce. He really wanted him to come. When Max Boyce's people sent us a price, it was eye-watering. Arthur exhaled and said, 'Nay! We don't want a full concert, we just want him to come and say hello to the children.' Different again was Tom Baker. He was fabulous. He turned up in his full Dr Who outfit; wide-brimmed hat, long knitted-scarf and overcoat in the middle of July. He spent ages with all the kids. He was like the Pied Piper with them. I'll never forget the announcement over the tannoy.

'Will your kids all get off Dr Who now. We want him to judge the Miss Miners' Lamp contest.'

Out of the politicians Michael Foot came, he was a grand fellow, so was Tony Benn. Harold Wilson came and Dennis Skinner was a good supporter. Jimmy Reid came and stayed with his wife at our house. In fact Jimmy Reid stayed with us a few times, he and Arthur had been friends since their days together in the Young Communist League. Jimmy became famous for organising the work-in at the Clyde shipyards. He was a great speaker and a persuasive man. He was the one who inspired John Lennon to support the shipbuilders. He was also a popular local councillor and represented the Communist Party in Clydebank. He always seemed drunk to me. He liked the top shelf. He'd have one or two pints then he'd be on the shorts. You'd have to watch yourself then because when he'd had too much he used to get loud and boorish.

In 1974 Arthur was asked to do a television programme with the well-known broadcaster Jonathan Dimbleby for Thames Television. Afterwards he got friendly with Jonathan and his wife, the writer Bel Mooney. Jonathan ended up doing a lot of work for Yorkshire Television and presented the famous documentary series *First Tuesday*. When Arthur got arrested during the strike Jonathan offered to stand bail for him.

Jonathan and Bel came to visit us and they both wanted to have a look down a pit. Arthur arranged for them to see Emley pit, an old-fashioned mine with very low seams. In 1842 when they passed the Mines and Collieries Act that banned children under the age of ten and any females from working underground after the Huskar Pit disaster, Emley was one of the handful of mines that was allowed to continue sending kids down due to its low seams. We took Jim Parker, Arthur's right-hand man, and his wife Elaine went with us as well as Bert Beaumont, a teacher who had helped our Margaret with her science O-levels. We crawled on all fours to get to the coalface and I got left behind with the under-manager. He said to me, 'I expect the mice will be out to play in a bit.' He couldn't have said a worse thing, I'm terrified of mice and I froze. He had to crawl round the gob to coax me out.

Jonathan and Bel enjoyed the visit. They were lovely people and very supportive towards Arthur. I was sad when they parted. They were always good to our Margaret. When they lived at Clapham Common they invited Margaret and one of her mates to stay with them for a week. Bel took the girls to see *Annie* in the West End and after the show they were invited backstage to meet the cast. Margaret was thrilled when Sheila Hancock made a fuss of her.

Jonathan's older brother David Dimbleby decided he wanted to make a programme with Arthur. It was an hour-long programme but it took ages to make. We had big lorries parked outside our house for above a week, with make-up artists, hair stylists and all sorts. Again it was our Margaret who enjoyed it all, she was having her hair and make-up done while everybody was standing about waiting.

The more famous Arthur became, the less I knew him. He was out a lot. I started feeling lonely very early on in our marriage. Not only did Arthur go to meeting after meeting, he also went to night school classes run by the Workers' Educational Association and he studied at Leeds University. He missed all of Margaret's birthday parties and school concerts when she was growing up. It ended up where I had to go with Arthur to see him and I'd take our Margaret with me. One time we went to a conference in Blackpool; our Margaret must have been only little because Lady Mason and Nellie Gormley, Joe Gormley's wife, were babysitters for her. There was also a Co-op conference on the Isle of Man. My sister Joan came on that trip. It was only a small aeroplane and it was so overcrowded the air hostesses gave up their seats. We hit a thunderstorm over the sea. I thought we were going to die, but Margaret was shrieking with laughter, she thought it was great fun. I think she thought she was on the roller coaster at Blackpool Pleasure Beach.

I liked the Isle of Man. We had great fun in the evenings. Freddie 'Parrot Face' Davies was one of the big turns at the time and the delegates' kids loved him. On the last night they got some of the officials up to perform a party piece. I remember Peter Lazenby the reporter getting up and reciting the poem 'The Lion and Albert'. They tried to make Arthur sing a song but he can't sing so he performed a piece about a cigarette in a speak-singing style like Rex

Harrison did in *My Fair Lady*. As usual though, Arthur got involved in some controversy. He found out that the hotel staff were all low paid, non-unionised, mainly immigrant workers. He convened a meeting and encouraged them to go on strike for better money and conditions. Within a day or two he won a deal and by the time we left they had formed a union branch.

On the notice board at the secondary school in Worsbrough I saw that they were doing a night class called 'Judo for Ladies'. Arthur already went to a judo club to keep fit. I studied that notice for a bit and thought, 'That's something for me, I'm going to give it a try,' so I signed up. The class was run by a woman from Kendray called Marie. I really enjoyed practising judo and I never missed a Tuesday night. Marie taught us a lot of moves. I can't say that I used any of it for fighting anybody apart from on the mat at the class. Though there was one occasion. We had a soft spot for Leeds United because Uncle Bernard had once played for them and we used to go to matches at Elland Road. There would be me, our Joan, Arthur and George Duncan, who was the manager of Woolley pit. George's brother was a staunch communist who was tragically killed in the Spanish Civil War and was buried in Spain – Franco wouldn't allow access to the grave. We stood at the back of a rail on the terraces. At one match we had been stood a good half hour in our places when a woman came up, tapped our Joan on the shoulder and cheekily took her place as she turned round. I challenged her and she put her arm up as though to hit me. I don't know what came over me, I just grabbed her arm and chucked her straight under the barrier. She didn't come back. It was a shame when they cancelled the judo class. Like a lot of night classes the numbers dwindled. It went down to half a dozen of us at first, and then when there was just three of us they closed it down.

Part Of The Union
Betty

When I started work at Empire Stores it was a non-union place. When the rules changed to allow unions, the office controller addressed the staff.

'When you go down to the canteen for your break, there might be some union men who want to talk to you. You don't have to talk to them if you don't want and you don't have to join the union, you will be alright here, we will look after you well enough.'

I didn't believe that. I made a beeline for the union reps, filled in a form there and then and said, 'Right! When do I get my whistle?' *The Rag Trade* was popular on the telly at the time. Miriam Karlin played a shop steward who was always blowing her whistle and shouting 'Everybody out!' I was elected rep for the clerical staff at the first meeting. One of the girls in the office asked me 'What went off at the meeting?' I put her straight.

'You are not a member of the union. If you want to know about what goes off at union meetings, join!'

I was also appointed health and safety rep, something that was certainly needed. They had run out of space for storing folders in the office. This meant they stored them in the warehouse down two flights of stone stairs. Every time the girls in the office wanted a file they had to carry it up from the warehouse. One girl had already fallen on the steps and had time off work badly shaken. We managed to persuade them to use a forklift truck after that to raise them up.

I did well in the union and became branch secretary. This meant I had to attend high-level meetings at the head office in Bradford. I went there to negotiate everything from wages to sickness benefits to working conditions. One day I went with Pat, the branch chair, to a meeting with the personnel director and his sidekick. They were acting the old trick, 'Iron Fist and Velvet Glove'. The sidekick was the first and he quickly lost his temper. I can't even remember what it was over now, perhaps something to do with money. He jumped off his chair and snapped.

'Look you! If you are so unhappy here, why don't you piss off down the road and work for Grattan's.'

Grattan's was another mail order catalogue firm. He picked up his chair and threw it at us. The director called an adjournment. We sat outside the office and waited until they cooled down. Pat fetched out of her handbag a packet of what I thought were mints.

'When we go back in,' she said, 'I'm going to offer these round, don't take one, they're laxatives, they'll be shitting through the eye of a needle in no time.'

The same supervisor who had earlier encouraged me to join the Labour Party also persuaded me to go on the governing body of Woolley Colliery School. I saw it as an opportunity to exercise some control over those who assumed they could scoff at complaints from people like me, but mainly to ensure that no other child would suffer in the way my lad Michael did. At my very first meeting I was voted chair of governors. I didn't even know at the time what that entailed, but the rest of the people seemed supportive. There was one in the meeting whose face spoke a thousand words. The headmaster twitched at first, then trembled when I asked if I might see his punishment book. There was a pause.

'It's in my office but my office is locked at this time.'

There was a time when I might not have been confident enough to pursue him, but something came over me.

'Well I imagine you will have a key won't you?'

'Yes,' he said sheepishly.

I looked straight at him.

'I suggest in that case, that you take your key, open your office and bring your punishment book to this meeting directly so that we can have a look at it.'

He did as he was bid. I opened the book, it was empty. I had heard many stories from neighbours about how their children had been hit by this man for doing nothing. There had also been times when I knew for a fact that children were being punished because if you stood near enough to the school you could hear them crying out.

I stood up and addressed the meeting.

'In future this book will be produced at every meeting and I expect to see a detailed written account of who was punished, what they were punished for and what exactly the punishment meted out entailed.'

The headmaster went grey in the face. At another meeting I noticed a broken windowpane in a classroom door with shards of glass still hanging. The headmaster admitted that he had done it during a fit of temper. I asked him why he hadn't had it repaired. He said, 'I want to remind the children that I can lose my temper.' I told him that I wanted it boarded up immediately and re-glazed by the morning. I still get angry about that man and the children he was supposed to look after. One of the happiest days of my life was the day when we got a new headmaster who truly cared for the children.

Bombs, Bullets And Bare-naked Ladies
Anne

When Arthur's profile grew, so did the extent of the shenanigans. We were used to people coming to the door with local disputes and coal enquiries, we even had someone call during Christmas dinner with a query, but things started to take a bit of turn. Our Margaret tells a story about one weekend when I'd gone to bed for an early night. She stopped up to watch *Appointment with Fear*. There was a knock at the door. Arthur answered it to a woman in a raincoat holding a tulip in her hand, complete with the bulb attached. She offered him the tulip and said, 'I admire your mind and your body.' Arthur panicked. He thought straightaway that it might be one of the newspapers trying to set him up. He shouted for Margaret to come to the door. The woman in the mac unfastened it and she was stark naked underneath. She said, 'I adore you.' Arthur asked her to leave. She offered her address and phone number. He declined that as well. We never saw her again but Harold picked the bulb up and planted it. The tulip came back year after year.

We once helped an old chap who had fallen outside our house and was in bad shape with a busted face. Arthur helped him inside, called an ambulance and sat with him chatting while holding a tea cloth to his bleeding nose and split forehead. The man looked at him and said, 'Do you know Scargill, I bloody hate you.'

We received a gift pack in the post from an ex-pit manager who had suffered a nervous breakdown. It consisted of a letter outlining the demise of Arthur and enclosed a pack of supplies that Arthur could enjoy and reflect on in his final few days on Earth. This included records to listen to, books to read and chocolates to eat as a last swansong. The police checked it all out and said they felt they were not poisoned or contaminated but advised us to discard the food items just in case. We kept the books and records as he had quite good taste.

Other people filled in the forms for book clubs with our address and we received numerous books that were offered on approval as we had 'signed up' for their book clubs. Obviously the forms were forged. The companies were informed but the cost of collection of the books was not deemed worthwhile so our library increased daily. For some reason most of the books were military and sex manuals. Harold was well taken up with Alex Comfort's *The Joy of Sex*, the one with the bearded hippy on the front. I remember him reading it studiously.

A file of 'fan mail' was created at the NUM. People sent shit in the post for some reason, often on toilet paper mixed with glass or smeared on writing paper. Another favourite was a razor blade attached under the seal of the envelope so if you opened it as normal you would slice through your thumb and finger. We started to use letter openers. The content was vile, often involving threat of torture, kidnap and rape. This became a daily occurrence. We got to the point where we were wary about answering the phone due to the barrage of verbal abuse and murder and rape threats so we decided to change the number to become ex-directory. This was a shame as in the early days Arthur liked to be accessible to members but the abuse and impact on the family could not be tolerated.

An incendiary bomb was sent to the Barnsley NUM. Arthur's secretary had found a package that felt odd so the local police were called. They snipped open the end and found wires inside. They sent for the bomb squad, evacuated the NUM building and the device was taken to London in an armoured vehicle to be exploded remotely. This was followed by an odd incident when Arthur returned home from a meeting and heard a weird ping in his ear from a car that had stopped outside the house. The police were called and they noticed a mark on the side of the house near the door. They decided that the ping Arthur had heard was the ricochet of a bullet. On further investigation the police found a bullet stuck in the jamb of a door on a house further up the hill. This caused the police some concerns. Then they had a tip-off that they said was a significant threat and decided to post two police officers at our house and two Special Branch bodyguards would accompany Arthur. During the hot summer and with the cricket on the television, Harold felt sorry for the two policemen on the door. He asked them in and they sat drinking lemonade watching the test match. The chief constable turned up that day with a stone face.

'If they throw a bomb in are you going to bend down, pick it up and chuck it back out? Get back outside now!'

The police gave us tutorials in how to check for car bombs. We always had to check under the back wheel because they told us that bombs were often placed there to detonate as a car reversed out of a yard. The death threats carried on and the police advised us to have a panic button fitted. We had three in different parts of the house. One was in Margaret's bedroom as she spent a lot of time on her own in the house when we were away at functions. One weekend we had guests to stay; Michael Mansfield, his wife Yvette and Jean McCrindle. Jean slept in Margaret's bed and decided to do some late-night reading. She pressed what she thought was the light switch but when it didn't work she turned in for the night. Everyone else had gone to bed except Arthur who was still up reading when all of a sudden there was flashing lights and sirens and the house was surrounded by armed CID officers. They confronted Jean barefoot in her nightie. After that we had to warn everybody who stayed.

When the women at Grunwick came out on strike in 1976, Jack Dromey, who later married Harriet Harman, and an Indian lady called Mrs Jayaben Desai asked Arthur if he could help them. It was a disgrace what the management there were doing. They were paying mainly Asian workers far less than a normal wage and sacking them for working too slow. Arthur went down to their picket line and he'd only been there two minutes when he got arrested. Arthur went again with pickets from Wales, Kent, as well as our lads from Yorkshire, and they managed to block the place off. The strike at Grunwick lasted two years. Maurice Jones got arrested and they fingerprinted him. He was terrified because he had been fingerprinted before outside a National Front office in Manchester. Maurice alleged the police had said, 'You have a delightful daughter and the roads are very busy round here.' Poor old Maurice, he didn't know if he was coming or going. He packed his bags up and fled to East Germany with his wife and daughter to claim asylum. The trouble was the East Germans didn't appear to want him.

The first thing we knew about it was when the East German embassy phoned up and asked Arthur if he could intervene. Then Arthur got a letter from Maurice. Arthur went to East Germany with Owen Briscoe, the union secretary. They reassured Maurice that he would be safe to come back home and that he would probably just get fined. Maurice decided to come back with Arthur. When they got to Heathrow airport the police pounced on Maurice and dragged him to the cells, but then let him out on bail. Arthur went to see a left-wing lawyer called Michael Seifert. Michael seemed to be the one everybody went to over union causes. Michael did a good job helping Maurice, who was soon back editing *The Yorkshire Miner*. Arthur's relationship with Maurice eventually went sour. I don't know for certain what happened, but I know that Maurice said that Arthur was interfering too much with what went in *The Yorkshire Miner* and Arthur said that Maurice was being a bit too gung-ho about what he wrote, putting stories in without much evidence to back them up. They were getting in bother and having to retract and apologise for articles too often.

Michael Seifert became a good friend to our family. He was a grand fellow, a born storyteller. We loved listening to him telling the tale. His mam and dad had both been communists. Michael always dressed casual and used to talk between puffs on his cigarettes. He came to our house one day with a colleague. I thought I'd prepare a good lunch and put on a buffet. When Arthur looked at the spread he went mad because amongst it were ham sandwiches, sausage rolls and pork pies.

'You can't offer them that,' he said.

'What's up with you, they're Albert Hirst's from Barnsley market and everybody knows they're the finest pork pies in the land.'

Arthur said, 'You silly bugger, they're Jewish!'

Poorly
Betty

In the middle of the 1970s I became poorly. The specialists thought that I might have renal tuberculosis. It turned out not to be the case but my consultant Mr Smith told me that I had a serious kidney complaint. I was in a lot of pain but managed to keep going to work. I'd been told not to take painkillers because in the long term they would do more harm than good. I started to self-medicate and always took a bottle of whisky about with me in my handbag. The whisky seemed to kill the pain. My office manager must have got wind of what I was doing. One day he said to one of the supervisors, 'If Betty has got that bottle of whisky of hers in her handbag, tell her to take a sip, I've never seen such agony on a woman's face.'

Mr Smith always greeted me at my appointments with a warm welcome. I'd go to Pinderfields Hospital straight from work, wearing my shop steward's badge. He would remark that his favourite union organiser had arrived. He always called me Ma'am. My condition was not improving. One day, Mr Smith said to me, 'Ma'am, you are dying.' Just like that. He must have seen the shock on my face. He told me that a streptococcal infection in my throat had led to damage in my immune system and this in turn had caused problems for my kidneys. I was having regular attacks of nephritis and pyelitis.

'I have been thinking about a certain surgery that I would like to perform. I have great faith in you and if you will have faith in me, I think it will work.'

I told him I had every faith in him. He found me a bed at Pinderfields. The surgery worked but I was in recovery for a long time. The manager who told me to take a sip of my whisky visited me twice, even helping me back into bed on one occasion. Sometimes the ward sister would not let my visitors in, saying that I was too ill, and would only allow close family members to visit. I was in hospital quite a long time, in a lot of pain and dosed quite heavily on pethidine to relieve the discomfort.

One day when I was feeling a little better, the tea trolley came round after lunch but three of us were not given any. When I asked for a cup of tea for us I was told by the nurse, 'Sorry we haven't enough cups, you'll have to wait until the others have finished with theirs.'

At that time I was co-opted on to Wakefield Metropolitan Council and had my council diary in my locker. I asked the nurse if she would get it for me.

'What are you going to do?' she asked.

'Please bring me the phone,' I said, 'I am going to ring the leader of the council and request that he contact the relevant department and request more cups.'

'Please wait a minute,' she replied. After about ten minutes she appeared with some new cups filled with tea. Although I was ill, the fighting spirit re-appeared.

I was discharged after about six weeks but was still very fragile. The weather was good and although I was still in nightclothes and dressing gown I aimed to take six steps outside and then add an extra step each day.

The office controller from work who had visited me in hospital several times started ringing me at home. In October she started harassing me to go back to work. Eventually I caved in, not just because of her but I was desperately short of money. My GP was horrified, her opinion was that I should have not gone back to work until twelve months after my surgery.

My dear friend Phyl was golden at this time. She took my youngest, Glyn, to her house and put him into a school at Bramham and did a lot of running about for me. I could never repay all the things she and her husband Derek did for me and my boys. Another childhood friend who had also supported me throughout was Marjorie and her husband Bill.

I finally recovered from the unique surgery that my brilliant surgeon Phillip Smith from St James Hospital in Leeds had decided to try for me. In his words he had made me a 'new woman'. It worked.

Personal Guests Of Fidel Castro
Anne

Me and Arthur were invited as personal guests of Fidel Castro to the 11th World Festival of Youth and Students in Cuba in 1978. Arthur was appointed a member of the festival committee. I sat down with Arthur when the invitation came and said, 'I wish our Margaret could come as well.' She was 16 at the time. I wanted her to see something different and perhaps get a political education. We arranged for her to be a youth delegate and we paid for her airfare and board. I'm not sure what the political education did for her, because she is stubborn. She never did get involved in politics like Arthur and me, though it's fair to say that she is a great believer in social justice. I've heard her say sometimes that she is 'soft left'.

The list of delegates at that festival included Barry Gardiner, who went on to have a high profile in the Labour Party; Paul Boateng, who sits in the House of Lords now; and Peter Mandelson who was nothing but a nuisance on that trip. He spent most of his time trying to organise a protest about human rights issues in the Soviet Union and wanted to demonstrate in Havana. A good half of the delegation was troubled by what he was doing; they found it embarrassing to the hosts and the Russian delegates. A meeting was convened, a vote was taken, and Mandelson's idea was turned down. Mandelson put a lot of people's backs up on that trip. He was very unpopular with guests and hosts alike. It was rumoured that at the end of the festival he was given a good hiding in the gents' lavatories by a group from the delegation.

I loved Cuba. The people there are grand and the beaches are spotless clean with lovely white sand. We travelled down to Santiago de Cuba for a few days with some friends we'd made; a brother and sister called Sean and Noreen Jose. Sean had been in jail in South Africa for giving out anti-apartheid leaflets. We stayed in a complex of bungalows round a big swimming pool. I liked to get up early every morning to go swimming. There was a big athletic man with a body like a Greek god and a handsome face in the pool every morning. I got talking to him as we did lengths of the pool. He was softly-spoken and ever so polite. I kept thinking, 'I'm sure I know you, where do I know you from?' Later on someone told me that the handsome man was Harry Belafonte. We ended up palling about together and struck up a friendship.

We all went back to Havana for the closing ceremony, it was like the Olympics. I was with Arthur in the VIP area and then he was invited to take his place on the stage with the dignitaries. Fidel was there, so was Yasser Arafat with his silver revolver and Joshua Nkomo from Rhodesia. Arthur sat next to Harry Belafonte. Harry leaned over to Arthur and whispered, 'I hope if there is a sniper here today they are a good shot, because we are sitting very close to them.'

In Havana we stopped at the Hotel Capri. Arthur was delighted when he found out our room was the one that George Raft used to stay in. The bed was as big as a living room. While we were at that hotel I met Hortensia Bussi, the widow of Salvador Allende, the president of Chile who had died during Pinochet's military coup. She had recently lost her daughter. She was a beautiful and kind person with a gentle way about her. She seemed to have no bitterness about what had happened to her. At least she didn't show it if she did.

Harry Belafonte kept in touch with us after we came home from Cuba. He wrote to Arthur to say that he was coming to England and could he come and see us. Arthur said that he could stay at our house. Before he was due to arrive, Arthur went up to the Swaithe Working Men's Club at Monkspring to see the concert secretary Harry Carr. He told him that we would be welcoming Harry Belafonte as our guest soon and wondered if the club might like him to sing a few songs. Harry Carr thought for a bit.

'Ooh! I'm not sure about that Arthur,' he said. 'I've got plenty of top turns booked up well in advance. I can't just make exceptions at the drop of a hat. Harry who did you say?' Belafonte didn't come to the UK in the end.

In the same year we went to Cuba, the NUM delegation was due to fly to America. Arthur got into difficulties trying to obtain a visa.

I seem to recall that the Americans declined him on the grounds that he was an undesirable. Joe Gormley got going behind the scenes. I don't know what he said but in the end Arthur got a limited visa. Sid Vincent, the Lancashire miners' leader, was with us on that trip. He hated flying and took plenty of drink to calm his nerves. By the time we got to Washington he was in a stupor. We were all tired but Joe Gormley insisted that everybody should stop up and have some dinner. Gormley's wife Nellie was trying to look after Sid who was still drunk and wobbling about all over the place. She asked him what was up with him. He said his feet were killing him. It turned out that while he was three sheets to the wind on the plane he had managed to jam his shoes over the top of his complimentary flight socks. Sid was a comical bugger with unnaturally black hair for a man of his age. We were at a conference in Jersey once and I watched him dive into the hotel swimming pool, leaving a black trail like an oil slick behind him. He never lived that one down. I've still no idea what he had been dying his hair with. Sid only knew one song, 'I Left My Heart in San Francisco'. He thought he was Tony Bennett when he sang it.

In Washington we stayed at The Watergate Hotel, which is part of the Watergate complex that was made famous by Nixon. The mineworkers' pension fund had investments in that place. I loved it and I was fascinated when they started to tell us about the history. I pinched one of their ashtrays as a souvenir. We went to some remote region on that trip as well. One of the parts was where Buffalo Bill once roamed. I don't think the folk there liked us at first and there was a bit of friction but as soon as they realised our mining heritage was similar to theirs they were alright with us. On the plane home I showed Arthur the ashtray I'd taken from the Watergate. He went mad.

When Arthur became the national president we went to Australia for discussions about joining the international miners' organisation. There was a scheduled stopover at Hong Kong on the way so we took the opportunity to visit China. We went to Beijing and explored the Forbidden City and Tiananmen Square. We got a certificate for climbing to the highest part of The Great Wall of China. We were

Anne, Elliot, Harold and Harriet with Margaret on holiday in Exmoor.

Noreen Jose, Harry Belafonte, Julie Belafonte and Anne in Cuba.

Anne, Arthur, Margaret, Mary Stubbings, Derek Stubbings and Volantina in Bulgaria.

hosted by some diplomats who put a banquet on for us. It was a magnificent spread of traditional Chinese food and solid silver cutlery with a crest on every piece. Arthur made an after-dinner speech. He made a joke that when we went for our dinner to the Golden Dragon in Sheffield, it was a tradition that the guests took home the chopsticks that they had used to eat their meal with.

'I have enjoyed this dinner and I hope that the tradition will extend to this banquet as I am looking forward to taking home a set of this fine cutlery.'

The Chinese didn't get the joke and it caused a bit of a stir until the diplomats smoothed it over by explaining that Arthur had a Barnsley sense of humour that was difficult to translate.

They took Arthur down the pit. He was shocked by the conditions. In the pit bottom, some of the Chinese miners were cooking their food. Arthur said he'd never seen anything like it and asked to be brought out immediately.

Frying Bacon At Greenham Common
Anne & Betty

Anne
I went with Arthur to a debate he was having about coal and nuclear power. A professor had brought a rod of uranium in a plastic case as a prop. Halfway through the debate he put some white gloves on and picked up his rod to show it to the audience. He told them how clean and safe it was and mentioned that the security record at nuclear power stations meant it could not be stolen or go missing due to very stringent checks. He had also brought a lump of coal and he picked that up and passed it from one hand to the other. He got muck all over his gloves and smirked.

'What would you prefer?' he announced, 'The nice, safe, clean technology of nuclear energy or Mr Scargill's dirty, polluting, nasty piece of coal?'

While he was on with his bit of theatre, Arthur put the professor's rod under my coat. When he'd done Arthur stood up and picked the piece of coal up.

'When I was a young man working down the pit,' he said, 'I occasionally suffered from dyspepsia and heartburn. I relieved the symptoms by sucking on a piece of coal, as it is a good antacid.'

Arthur turned to the professor.

'I will eat this dirty lump of coal if this gentleman will eat his uranium rod.'

The audience was in uproar by now and the professor obviously said no. Then he started to panic because he realised his rod had disappeared from the table. I passed it back to Arthur and he made a big play about looking after it in case of theft. The professor was as red as a beetroot.

I enjoyed myself that night. I'd never really got involved with Arthur's debating. I supported him in any way I thought might be a help and I used to drive him to meetings, but I didn't always go in. I don't think I was confident enough to start speaking up but as time went past I decided to join the Labour Party. I had always voted for them and I thought it was about time that I started knowing a bit more about what I was voting for.

When the protests at Greenham Common started against the American cruise missiles, I went with some local women who wanted to join in. I was there one Sunday just before Christmas and not long after some of the missiles came. It was a bitter cold day and a lot of the women were wearing woolies they had knitted themselves. Everybody was singing and dancing. We all held hands and made a circle by the fence.

At Greenham Common I made friends with women who I wouldn't normally have met. There was one called Ann who lived in the camp. She'd managed to get through the wire and spent three days inside the base hiding from the soldiers. They found her and she was arrested and sent to court. She expected to be fined and had already decided that she wouldn't pay even if they sent the bailiffs to her house. Her husband worked abroad and she wasn't bothered if they took her things. The court took a dim view of her and sent her to prison. As she was being taken to the cells she was wiping dust off the window sills with her finger. She told them that the place could do with a feather duster. They reminded her that she was a prisoner and not a prison inspector. In the cell she decided that the layout was all wrong and she tried to move her bed and table. It was then it dawned on her that everything was bolted down. She sat on her bed and studied her predicament. That night one of the guards lifted the flap on the cell door and asked her if she would like anything to help her sleep. They meant sleeping tablets.

'A glass of warm milk or a cup of cocoa might be nice.'

I liked the ways and manners of these middle-class women. They had a self-confidence about them that seemed to rise them above the situation they were in.

We used to take our own bacon, lard and a frying pan to Greenham. A lot of the women had decided to be vegetarian so they turned their nose up at us at first. Then there would be this smell of bacon frying and we'd see women coming out of the woods like fugitives creeping about.

'Will you make me a bacon sandwich Anne, but don't tell the others please.'

They were all at it. We ended up like the Salvation Army, frying bacon and handing it out.

We used to go on a Saturday for the day. One Friday night I thought I'd make a big pan of corned beef hash to take down. I used my biggest stew pan and warmed it up when we got there. When we were ready to come home there was plenty left. I told the women that I didn't want to leave my pan, but if they brought me one of theirs I'd empty mine into it. The pan they fetched me was a disgrace, they'd been boiling gooseberries and blackberries in it or something and not washed it out properly. I said, 'I can't put my hash in there!' They didn't seem bothered. I think they had got used to not being able to wash their utensils properly.

I saw things at Greenham that were different to what I was used to and I felt engaged in politics and protesting in a way that I'd never felt in all the time with Arthur. I travelled all over the world with Arthur, but I was the one who was expected to smile and be nice to the other officials' wives and laugh at the jokes that the men made. I was never asked my opinion on anything, not that it would have been listened to if I'd offered it. At Greenham I found something. It was myself. I can't say that I had a lot in common with most of the women there and I wasn't a big fan of their ways at times, but I admired their togetherness. I suppose it was at Greenham when I first came across the word 'feminist'. I shied away from it at first, I didn't consider myself to be one. I have always enjoyed being a woman, a daughter of a coal-mining family and the wife of the man who became the president of the most powerful trade union in the country. I like it when a man opens a door for me and I like it when men pay me a compliment.

I haven't always had the best of experiences with educated women and academics. This comes from sitting in meetings with intelligent women and feeling hopelessly lost when they said things that I couldn't understand. When I spoke to Arthur about this he said, 'You have to realise Anne that the academics rarely call a spade a spade.' I always thought there was a gulf between the women who had been to college and those such as me, a simple working-class lass who struggled at school. This gulf was never properly addressed and I was left thinking that the educated women were secretly laughing at my ignorance and naivety. I have come to realise that a lot of it was down to my own insecurity. These women were really trying to help and they did a lot of good. I felt that when those women joined hands they meant it. For the first time I was able to join in.

Betty
I travelled down to Greenham Common on a bus with some women activists from Wakefield. It was a freezing cold day. We had taken some candles so that we could have a candle-lit vigil. We spent half the time shivering, cuddled up to one another with our hands cupped round the flame on our candles. The helicopters were flying round low and blowing up all the autumn leaves and muck onto us. One woman near me slipped in the mud and put her hand out to stop herself falling. As soon as she touched the fencing, one of the security men hit her on the arm with his baton. It was horrible, I really didn't like it. I didn't go again for a long time after that because even though I was a shop steward and a member of the Labour Party, I wouldn't say I was a political campaigner. Then, on 6th March 1984, the NCB announced that they were going to shut Cortonwood pit. Within a few days, half of the miners in Yorkshire were out on strike and on 12th March the NUM executive committee sanctioned the strike as official. That changed everything forever.

Strike
Anne & Betty

Anne

When Cortonwood came out, the union official there, Mick Carter, had a brazier out straightaway at the top of the lane and in no time at all the lads had built themselves a hut out of scrap wood and painted 'The Alamo' on it. I started baking buns and cakes and taking them down for the pickets. A lot of people pipped their horns as they drove past. When the delegate from Cortonwood went to the Yorkshire Area meeting and asked for support, every hand went up. I could feel that this strike was going to be a long one.

It took less than a fortnight for women to get involved. I saw Marsha Marshall on the television news being asked about the strike and how long it would last before the men had to go back to work.

'We'll eat grass first,' she said.

It was the sort of thing my dad would have said, rather than give in to Tories and bosses. Shortly afterwards I was getting out of my car in Worsbrough when I bumped into Lorraine Bowler. Lorraine lived in our village and was a mature student at Northern College in Stainborough.

'I'm glad I've seen you Anne,' she said. 'We're having a meeting and we'd like you to come.'

The meeting was at a big house near Locke Park where Joan Davis lived. Joan ran the reception at Northern College. I think about twelve women turned up, some were connected to the college and some were miners' wives. They were there to try to find a way to help the striking miners.

Betty

I was determined that I wasn't going to stay at home like I had during the strikes in 1972 and 1974. I'd cried a lot then. I was cold and hungry all the time. I got sick and tired of seeing baked beans; beans and egg, beans and chips, beans on toast. I told myself I wasn't going to cry this time and I wasn't going to go hungry. I was behind the strike from the start and I wasn't going to give in or change my mind.

My boys were men now. Michael was still poorly, so he was at home. Glyn was at home as well and he was on strike. Donny had got married by then and had moved out, but he worked at the pit and was on strike. Don was on strike as well of course, he decided that he wasn't going to go picketing this time, instead he mooched about at home and did a bit of cooking.

At an USDAW conference in Eastbourne, I met some miners from Kent who were collecting in buckets. They gave me loads of leaflets. When I got home I wanted to do something with the leaflets. I had heard about a group of women who were getting together a campaign to stop pit closures. I asked round some of the lads at Woolley and they told me to get in touch with Jean Miller who was in the Communist Party in Barnsley. Her son gave me her number.

Jean Miller told me that there was a meeting at Joan Davis's house on the Sunday. I went there and sat in a massive front room next to a woman who introduced herself as Elicia Billingham; she said she was a miner's wife from Barnsley. Nearly all the women had cigarettes in their mouths and you could barely see for the smoke. Jean McCrindle came in with Anne Scargill and introduced me to her. Anne was wearing a beautiful white blouse.

Jean chaired the meeting. She was a lecturer at Northern College and seemed very confident and sure. She went round the room and asked us to say what was happening where we lived. When it came to my turn, I mentioned that I'd being going round with some other women asking for donations and food. Jean McCrindle said that if we set up a soup kitchen, she'd be able to help out financially with money from donations.

I decided to change my work pattern and went part-time. This meant starting at 4.30pm and finishing at 8.30pm. I could then go home and catch up with my housework, leaving me free in the mornings to help out where I could. There was a community centre for Windhill and Woolley Colliery run by the Social Services. I applied to ask if I could use it for a soup kitchen. They let me have it for three days a week, so we started doing hot food there for miners and their families. Then I was summoned to a meeting with the local union branch officials. They had their own kitchen at a sports pavilion down the road from the pit, but it was only for pickets. It was run by the wives of the union men. They asked me what I thought I was up to. When I explained that I was helping to run a soup kitchen for all, they weren't best pleased. They told me that I didn't have the right plates and cutlery to be doing something like that and that theirs was the official soup kitchen. They didn't like it when I pointed out that their kitchen wasn't open for all miners and families, but just for the lads that went picketing. They said that there was one for families at the Civic Centre in Barnsley. I wouldn't give in and told them.

'Look, I know a young man who is a single parent, he can't go picketing because he can't afford to pay somebody to look after his children. Do you expect him to pay bus fares to Barnsley and back to feed his family when we can do it here?'

In the end the union men said, 'Well you will have to have a word with our wives, they're in charge.' It was laughable.

Anne
The women at Northern College were some of the first to talk about what ought to be done. They started to discuss how the press was reporting the strike. A lot of publicity had been given to some women from Nottinghamshire who were backing their husbands for carrying on working and there was some suggestion that women elsewhere were against their husbands striking and wanted them back at work. At a meeting we came up with an idea to have a rally for women in Barnsley town centre. Jean McCrindle suggested that I ought to ask Arthur if he would speak at the rally.

Jean organised a social evening and the women talked about how they might get behind the miners. The same women had a meeting the following day and called themselves 'Women in Support of Miners'. They sent a letter to the *Barnsley Chronicle* asking for other women to get involved. That letter touched a lot of women all over the district.

The decision of the Yorkshire miners to strike in the defence of their jobs and their industry has raised strong feelings in the Barnsley area. We women would like to express our support for the strike action.

The first official meeting took place at Joan Davis's house. It was at that meeting that they decided to call themselves Barnsley Women Against Pit Closures. They also talked about going picketing. There was some resistance at first from the men who claimed that it was hard enough to organise groups of men without women being involved. When the women pointed out that they didn't need organising by men and could organise themselves, the blokes had to step out of their way. The first women's picket happened at Newstead Colliery in Nottinghamshire at the end of March. By the middle of April a public meeting was held at the Trades and Labour Club. Seventy women came in support.

March Through Barnsley
Anne & Betty

Anne

On Saturday 12th May 1984, the biggest gathering of women ever to march through Barnsley took place. It was a beautiful warm day. I'd organised for five hundred tea cakes to be delivered from White's bakery. At that time we thought that about five hundred women might turn up and if we had any leftover food we would give it to the striking miners' kitchens. When Sheila Capstick arrived she told us that she'd mugged the milkman. She'd realised that he hadn't given anything for the food collection so she took a tray of eggs, a crate of orange juice and a crate of milk off him.

I had to tell off one or two of our lasses. I think they'd got carried away with it all and forgot to muck in. Only five turned up to cut sandwiches. We were at it all morning. When we realised that there was going to be far more people than we could cater for, the NUM gave money to go round local shops to buy more food. Talk about the feeding of the five thousand.

We stood near Churchfield car park and watched them coming in. We kept saying 'Look there's another bus! There's another bus!' as they rolled in from Kent, Staffordshire, Scotland, Lancashire, Durham, from everywhere. They got off the buses displaying their homemade placards and banners. Some girl majorettes came from Royston and Worsbrough, there were jazz bands and folk musicians. A group of Welsh women turned up in traditional costumes singing Welsh songs. We tried to join in with the ones we knew. Then we were off.

'Chocker' Reeves, one of the NUM officials, tried to get himself on the front line. The women there shouted at him, 'Get to the back.' He just lifted his shoulders and moved back. It was the day for women to be at the front. Even Arthur and Jack Taylor, the Yorkshire NUM president, realised that they should make way and came off the front line to walk with the children and the women pushing prams and pushchairs. The crowds clapped us all the way down Regent Street and Shambles Street; there was a lot of abuse shouted at the Yorkshire Electricity Board offices as we passed, venting anger for the way they'd harassed people to pay their bills. When we got down to the Civic Hall, the police asked us, 'How many women will come?' We laughed and said, 'Thousands love, thousands!' They told us to leave our placards outside. We told them where to get off and just carried on marching and singing all the way into the hall.

All the seats had been taken out of the hall, both downstairs and on the balcony, but they still couldn't fit everyone in. Some speakers were put up on a bit of spare land to relay the speeches outside. I think around three thousand women came in the end and they had only fetched about a dozen bobbies, not that there was any bother. It was a day full of emotion. I looked round and saw women crying, not because they were upset, but because they realised that they weren't on their own and that there were women just like them who had made it out into the sunshine and were doing things that meant something.

Betty

I had been on one or two demonstrations but I have never been to one like that before or since. I got the feeling that day that working-class women like me were finally getting their chance. I could see on their faces that there was a determination to fight and try to win this strike, but there was something else as well; I got a sense that it was more than just a strike we were going to win. I think it was the women who first realised that the fight to keep pits open was about the future for our family life, for our children and their children to come.

I made my own placard from some cardboard and a stick. I wasn't used to making placards then so I put too many words on it. It said, 'Barnsley wives and others support the miners in their struggle against pit closures, we coped in 72 and 74 we will cope even more in 84.' It wasn't perhaps the most dynamic of messages but it was heartfelt. Some people were carrying placards that said 'Coal Not Dole', a phrase that became famous during the strike. I saw it for the first time that day. My mate had one that said 'Yank Go Home' which was directed at the American Ian MacGregor, the coal board chairman who started the pit closure programme. The best one I saw said 'Close a Pit, Kill a Community'. It was painted on an old bed sheet and was being carried by some women and children who lived near me. I came to know that this wasn't just about keeping men in work and fighting against a government that didn't seem to care, it was about where we lived and how we needed to look after it.

Before the speeches in the Civic Hall, the groups from the different areas were mentioned and cheers went up from their section. The best cheer went up for the Nottinghamshire lasses whose husbands and boyfriends had done the right thing and come out on strike when most of their workmates had scabbed. Annette Holroyd was about to speak on their behalf when somebody said, 'It's her birthday.' So, like women do in a group, we all sang happy birthday to her. It's not the sort of thing you normally see at a rally, but this wasn't a normal rally. Annette was moved to tears. Ann Hunter was the chairperson. I don't think she was used to public speaking with a PA system, they had to tell her to stop shouting down the microphone.

The first speaker was Lorraine Bowler. I think it was the first time she'd spoken in public, certainly to a crowd of that size. She spoke well and even started making jokes. She said that there had been arguments in her house over the past few weeks about whose turn it was to go picketing and who was to babysit. She told us that her husband would rather do a month on nights than mind the children. She then made a point that was in many minds when she said, 'Things will never be the same after this.' She also had a message for the government.

'If this government thinks its fight is only with miners, they are sadly mistaken. They are now fighting men, women and families.'

Arthur was obviously touched by what he had seen and spoke well even though he kept being interrupted by singing every ten minutes. But this was a day for the women. When Annette Holroyd from Nottinghamshire and Maureen Douglass from Doncaster spoke, they did so from the heart and with a lot of confidence.

Anne
The only upset that came from that day was that in all the haste to get it organised and publicised, we forgot to let Betty Heathfield know. Betty was the wife of Peter Heathfield, the general secretary at the NUM, and was a fantastic activist and speaker for women. She went to see Tony Benn who was MP for Chesterfield where she lived. They decided amongst themselves that it would be a good idea to have a national organisation that the different local groups could send a delegate to. That's how the national movement 'Women Against Pit Closures' got started. I was the delegate from round our way.

Soup Kitchens
Anne & Betty

Anne

By the beginning of July, Women Against Pit Closures had an office at the NUM in Sheffield. It was staffed every day by volunteers and we had regular meetings. The first conference took place at the end of July at Northern College. Miners' wives and women supporters from every coalfield across Britain came to that. The main idea of the conference was to organise a big demonstration in London. While we were in London we planned to present the DHSS with a bill for all the money that they had withheld from striking miners' families for all the weeks that the strike had been going on.

At the start, a lot of the union men were against women being involved. There was a bombastic bugger called Dave McDevitt who was a union official at Barrow pit. I knew there was a kitchen at Worsbrough Miners Welfare so I went to see Maureen and Jim Exley who were the caretakers to ask if we could set up a soup kitchen there. They were a lovely couple but they told me that they couldn't give me permission so I would have to apply to the union. I approached McDevitt.

'We're not having women coming here and organising,' he told me. 'This is where the pickets set off from and we have our meetings here.'

I argued with him but he held firm and told me that it was a matter for the area union. In the end I told him a little white lie.

'Look here Dave,' I said. 'I've already asked Arthur and he says we can. And as you know very well if Arthur says we can, we can.'

McDevitt got out of my way after that and we got set up. We made dinners and puddings for everybody that wanted one. I used to make custard for 120 people in an old boiler, the sort that you use for boiling whites on wash days. When Jean McCrindle brought Peter Hain the MP to see us, I gave him some apple pie and custard.

He wanted to know how I could make enough custard to serve that many people. I showed him my boiler. I'm not sure whether he ate his custard after that.

We had some good lasses at that kitchen: old grandmas came who could make a dinner out of a dishclout, sisters, daughters, our Joan was another, and two retired blokes used to wash up. We had that many pots and pans to do they washed them in a shower. The caretakers Jim and Maureen joined in and they were brilliant. Gladys was in charge of chips. Once she got going she insisted that only she was allowed to cook chips. I don't know why because they were only frozen ones.

Betty

A lot of those who helped out in the kitchens weren't political at all, just ordinary working-class women who wanted to help. They used to say, 'We don't want to be activists, we just want to help out in a way that we know. You keep raising funds and we'll do the cooking.' They were doers rather than talkers, and hard workers at that. Some lads used to come to our kitchen at Woolley with meat to sell it to us cheap. The women weren't sure where the meat came from and didn't like the look of the lads who were selling it.

'I think that meat might be pinched,' one whispered to me.

'It doesn't matter where it comes from,' I said to her, 'I won't say anything if you don't, just get it cooked.'

Another time I came round to the kitchen and saw a policeman stood near the door with a mug of tea.

'Who's give him that tea?' I asked them.

The lasses in the kitchen looked at me and admitted they had. I went mad and told them not to give tea to policemen. The lasses couldn't weigh up what I was saying.

'Nay he's t'local bobby, we know him.'

I put my foot down that day. I told them that while the strike was on, he wasn't on our side, even if he did live round the corner.

One of our best supporters was a bloke who had a meat warehouse in West Melton. He gave us meat at very good prices and always put a bit extra on. My grandparents had lived at West Melton and the

Souper Women soup kitchen volunteers, Betty on right.

building where the butcher had his business was where we queued up for food handouts during the Second World War. The first time I went there to buy meat for our strike kitchen, the irony dawned on me; it was the same spot where I had gone with my basin when I was a little girl.

We were becoming very excited about all the organising, demonstrating and petitioning we were doing, but there was still the everyday to see to. My mum was helping me at home. She didn't agree with a lot of what I was involving myself in but she still came round to my house to hold it together. Don was doing a bit of washing up, but when the house needed a good bottoming it was my mother who did the cleaning and ironing while I went to the soup kitchen.

As the strike went on we were getting a lot of food sent from abroad, including some big tins of eastern European goulash soup. It didn't look too appetising, it was full of gristle and fat, but it smelled alright. We strained all of the fat and gristle out and used the liquid as a base for our own soup by adding vegetables to it. The lads ate without complaint so we carried on sieving and serving it. The women at North Gawber had taken delivery of the same stuff. They were going to throw theirs away because they didn't like the look of it. We told them to give it to us. When we finally ran out and had to go back to making our own the lads wanted to know why we couldn't get any more of that other tasty soup.

We will never be able to thank people enough for the donations they gave to keep our kitchens going, most of whose names we will never know. There is nothing better than sharing food to bring folk together. I saw people who hadn't been acknowledging each other for years, sat talking. I was thinking about this one day and I was inspired to write my first ever poem.

> They tried to starve us out
> You were there
>
> We needed food and donations
> You were there
>
> We needed strength on demonstrations
> You were there

When we needed help to picket
You were there

Whatever help or task, we only had to ask
We need not have worried
You were there

The papers tried to tell us
You weren't there

Maggie tried to tell us
You weren't there

Oh! Where could they be looking
What did they think they were cooking
You certainly showed them
You were there

Words can't express our thanks
You were there

We will always remember
You were there

And if you ever need us
You only have to call us
And we can guarantee that
We'll be there

Not everybody was kind. We got one letter from a 'working' miner, anonymous of course. This scab said that he would like to spit in our soup, called us scroungers, beggars and bastards and said the troops ought to be turned out to shoot us. He bragged that by blacklegging he had earned £136.06p that week and he sent us the odd penny for our kitchen.

Picketing
Anne & Betty

Betty
At one of the meetings it was decided that we would go on the picket lines. I went along with it at the meeting, but on the way home I realised that I'd need to pluck up the courage to tell Don. I had to pick my time because I thought he would go mad. He surprised me, he didn't bat an eyelid, just shrugged his shoulders and went back behind his paper.

We hired a minibus and set off in the middle of the night. Anne drove us. We were supposed to be picketing at a pit in Nottinghamshire called Shireoaks. We got lost on the way and ended up in a supermarket car park with the police following us. There was a car full of women there, one of them introduced herself as Liz Hollis. She told us that she and her friends were going to picket at Silverhill Colliery and that if we followed them they would show us the way. Liz Hollis became a friend to Anne and me. She was a cousin of Hilary Wainwright whose dad was the Liberal MP for the Calder Valley. She had a great sense of social justice and this had led her to move to Nottinghamshire once the strike had started to help out where she could.

It was still early in the morning and the sun was just coming up as we followed the car down some country lanes. When we got to the pit there wasn't many about apart from half a dozen policemen from Avon and Somerset Constabulary. They were smiling. We had a bit of light-hearted banter with them and told them to get off home. We stood on a gravelled area opposite the pit gates. Then the scabs came. There was a bit of pushing and shoving and two of the scabs chucked their sandwiches at us. After they went in we just stood there wondering what to do next. We decided to set off back because some of our lasses had to go to work themselves. As we were coming away I saw the bobbies putting their chin straps on.

'Watch your backs girls,' I shouted, 'there's going to be some trouble here.'

A scuffle started when the police started shoving us for no reason. Liz Hollis and one of her mates got arrested and then Lynne, one of our lasses who'd just had a baby, got dragged off. I couldn't see any reason apart from her just being there. I went up to the inspector.

'Will you take me instead, she's got a new baby at home.'

The inspector was unmoved.

'She wasn't bloody bothered about her baby when she came here shouting and bawling.'

Anne
I went up to the inspector.

'What are you arresting Lynne for? She's done nothing wrong.'

'Let's have this one as well,' he said.

I chucked the van keys to Jean McCrindle as they arrested me. They put us into the police minibus at first and asked us our names.

'You tell me what I've supposed to have done and I'll tell you my name.'

They kept asking and I kept telling them the same answer. The Black Maria came and they put us in cages inside. I was frightened. They drove us to a police station. I was desperate to go to the toilet. When we got to the station it was chucking it down with rain, so I started to run. A bobby grabbed hold of me.

'Nay lad,' I said. 'I'm only running so I don't get wet through.'

They put us into a dog pound full of dog shit. Some of the women were a bit squeamish about it. It didn't bother me. I'd been brought up with dogs and pigs.

I was still desperate for the toilet and started shouting. A woman police officer came. She showed me to a bathroom. There was a toilet at one end, a bath tub down one side and a wooden bench down the other. After I had been for a wee, the policewoman came in.

'Right! Get undressed,' she said.

I must have been a bit naive.

'I don't need a bath,' I told her, 'I had one before I came out this morning.'

'I said, get undressed!'

I started to get undressed. I asked her what it was all about. She told me that I might have dangerous weapons or drugs concealed. I told her not to talk so daft. She made me take everything off and turn round. When she was satisfied she told me to put my clothes back on. She then took me to a cell. The other bobbies kept walking past trying to torment me.

'What's your name?'

'I've told you already, you tell me what I'm here for and I'll tell you my name.'

They brought the other lasses in. They had been stripped as well. After about half an hour a senior policeman came and took me to an office. He told me to sit down and asked me my name. I told him what I had told the others.

'Look here,' he said. 'I've got a pack of people from the press outside. They're telling me I've got Arthur Scargill's wife in my station, so I want to know your name.'

I didn't tell him. He said I could make a phone call. I suppose he thought I might be daft enough to phone Arthur. I phoned Brian my office manager at the Co-op.

'Tell Keith Batty I can't come today, I've been arrested in Nottinghamshire and they won't let me go to work.'

I could hear Brian laughing at the other end of the line.

'We know, it's all over the news, we've got it on the telly now.'

They put me in a cell on my own after that. They kept walking past and looking in. They asked me if I wanted something to eat. I remembered what a lad had told me who worked at the Co-op before he joined the police. He said, 'Never eat food in a police station because they spit in it if they don't like you.' I didn't have anything to eat. I had to go to court at seven o'clock that night. The magistrate adjourned the case until September.

Betty

After Anne and the others were arrested we decided to follow them down to the police station in our van. Jean McCrindle wasn't used to driving it and couldn't reverse it from where we had parked. We ended up jumping out and pushing it back. At the police station we couldn't get any sense out of them so all we could do was come home. As Jean drove us home, I looked down at my lovely, bright red stiletto boots. I'd just got them at an Empire Stores sale where staff can buy stuff at knock-down prices. All that pushing and shoving on the gravel had ripped the coating off them. They were ruined.

Ann Musgrave who worked in our soup kitchen was on that first picket with us. She was traumatised by the whole experience. On the way back home on the bus she said she would never go again. We were a mixed bunch who went that day: Anne, who was married to the miners' leader; me, married to a good-for-nothing lazy miner who hardly did a hand's stir at home; Lynne, who'd just had a baby; poor Ann who was frightened to death by it all; and Jean McCrindle, a middle-class academic whose dad was a famous actor. Alex McCrindle had been in *Star Wars* and the Alfred Hitchcock film *The 39 Steps*. We remembered him for playing Jock in *Dick Barton* on the wireless.

Jean was quite posh, if she made you a sandwich it was cucumber. She was a no-nonsense sort as well and didn't suffer fools. Once, we were pulled up by the police and asked if we were miners' wives.

'That's a bloody silly question Officer!' Jean told him, 'Do I look like a bloody miner's wife?'

Another time we were in London driving to a demonstration. Jean was pulled up for not wearing a seatbelt.

'If you had tits like these my dear, would you wear a seatbelt?'

Jean was a good friend of Sheila Rowbotham and Sally Alexander who had been married to John Thaw. Sally had been one of the organisers of the first women's liberation conferences. They were a circle of academic feminists. Our lives and theirs were far apart until the miners' strike.

Anne
When they strip-searched me in the police station I felt humiliated, but it didn't deter me. If anything, it made me worse. When my mother found out that I had been arrested she told me that she was ashamed of me. Her first words were, 'What's your Uncle Alfred

going to say? I don't know what your Uncle Charlie will think.' She was more bothered about what folk might think than she was about my feelings. I suppose she thought it showed her up. My dad didn't bother much. He just dropped his paper down a bit and said, 'What's it like doing porridge then?' Then he laughed.

I listened to women telling me that they wouldn't go picketing again and that motivated me even more. As soon as things settled in my mind I decided that I would get my own back. Before the strike I wouldn't have dared to say boo to a policeman, but I have never trusted one since. I decided that not only would I go picketing again, but I would go regularly.

Kettled At Kiveton
Anne & Betty

Anne
Arthur talked to me about how many pits the government really wanted to shut. It was a lot more than they were saying on the news. I used to think to myself, 'There will be nothing left.' Sometimes you just have to get off your arse and do something. You can do your crying, but there's times when you have to stand up to them.

I saw even less of Arthur in the strike than I had done before. We had a lot of threats made against us. I was frightened on my own, but just as frightened when Arthur did make it home. The police came round one night and told us that they were acting on reports that a gang were coming up from Birmingham to shoot us. They sat in the house. Dougie Stables came back from the club one night, knocked on the door and tried to get in. The police got hold of him and were about to wrestle him to the ground when Arthur told them that it was just Dougie Stables. Poor Dougie, he was only a little fellow, he wondered what the hell was going on.

Me and Betty started going picketing nearly every day. We had to organise ourselves because we were both working. I came home from work at five and had some tea. Then I'd do a bit of housework and go to bed. I was up at two in the morning to pick up the minibus from a garage at Darton. I'd pick the lasses up and Betty used to meet us at Worsbrough. We would be off for three o'clock so we could get into Nottinghamshire before five. We'd boo the scabs as they went in and then come straight back home so that we could get ready to go to work ourselves. On the rare occasions I bumped into Arthur, he'd ask me to let him know what's going on.

'Have a nosy round Anne. See if you can count how many are going in and how many bobbies they are using to take them through.'

We started going to Kiveton Park a lot. There was a mounted officer there on a big white horse. We had to watch our backs when he was about because he was nothing short of vicious. We used to sit on a wall in front of a row of houses and watched the lads who were picketing going by. One day one of the lads came up to me.

'You want to get down there and have a look at the photograph they've got taped up on the window of the police minibus.'

'Come on,' I said to Betty. 'We'll have a look at what the bastards are up to now.'

When we got there, they had a photograph of Arthur with a moustache drawn on him like Hitler. I went mad. Not long before I'd been to see Jimmy Rae the union man and he'd got me a pair of size seven pit boots. I started to kick hell out of the side of the van with my toe caps. The chief of the police that day came down carrying a long stick. I set about him before he could say anything.

'I've been looking for you! Look at that photograph of my husband. Would you like them to do that to a photo of your wife?'

He sighed and shone his torch on the damage I'd done to the side of the van. He sighed again and said, 'Take it down Clive.' Clive took the photo down straightaway. After that 'Take it down Clive' became a bit of a saying for us when we needed to lift our spirits a bit.

Betty
The police kettled us at Kiveton, it was very rough there. If you went down a certain lane you couldn't get back out, so the police used it to trap us. One morning they pushed Anne and me down there. We ended up hanging onto the side of a lorry and we wouldn't let them pull our fingers off. Another time when I was driving I told the lasses to stop in the van while I had a spy around. I walked down a country lane and a bobby jumped out of the hedge bottom.

'You take another step and I'll have you for unlawful assembly,' he said.

The police were terribly childish at times, they were quoting these ancient laws that nobody knew existed before the strike. 'Watching and Besetting' was another. Who would have thought that you could be arrested for looking at and talking to somebody?

Three actresses got in touch with us. They were doing a play about the women's movement in the strike. They travelled from London and we met them at the Welfare. We took them down to Kiveton with us. Things got incredibly rough that morning. The actresses got separated from Anne and me within minutes of us getting there. We looked all over for them. We found one wandering about in a terrible state, we found the second one cowering in a bus shelter and then it took us ages to find the third. She was laid down in a field in the rain, absolutely petrified. They couldn't believe how we could put ourselves through it day in, day out. They never came again. Some time after that I was in London to give a speech. The organisers took me to a pub afterwards. A man came up to me and told me that his wife was one of the actresses we had taken on the picket line. He said that she still had nightmares about it and he thought that she would never get over it.

Anne
We always pushed Marsha Marshall to the front when we smelled bother. She was the biggest among us. She used to say, 'What if he sets about me?' We told her, 'If he does 'owt to you, we'll all kill him.' We stopped a full coal lorry in a country lane and trapped him with our van. Some of the lasses went round the back and tried to unfasten the tailgate to let the coal out onto the road. We couldn't unfasten it but Marsha frightened the coal lorry driver to death when she threatened to fill his petrol tank full of stones and muck.

Betty
We sang songs on the pickets to keep our spirits up. We sang 'Don't underestimate the women, cos the women are here to stay' to the tune of 'John Brown's Body'. We sang 'We Shall Not Be Moved' and one we made up called 'Little Boys in Blue Don't Scare Us'. One clever bobby said as we were going past, 'The cows are singing well this morning.' Irene Battye was quick, she came straight back with, 'At least these cows don't smell like pigs.'

One day we were on a country lane going towards some pit gates and there was just one bobby guarding it. He stopped us.

'Where do you two think you are going?' he said.

We told him we were having a ride out.

'No you're not,' he said. 'Turn round and go back to where you came from.'

'Who says?'

'The Chief Constable of Nottinghamshire.'

All of a sudden, a media crew passed us on the other side and screeched to a stop. They shouted across wanting to know what was going on. We told them that the Chief Constable of Nottinghamshire says that nobody is allowed to drive down this road. Then a big black car pulled up and dragged the policeman in and drove off.

We had a full-page photograph in the *Daily Mirror* the following day. I was supposed to be on a trade union course at Wakefield College. I got there a bit late. Les Clark who was running the course said, 'What have you been up to now, Cooky?' I told him about getting stopped for no reason in Nottinghamshire. One of the other delegates on the course said, 'Bloody miners, I'm sick of hearing about them.' I rolled my sleeves and went to confront this ignorant man. Les jumped up and shouted, 'Cooky, sit down!' Then he turned to the delegate and said, 'You, get out and don't come back!' I was glad Les stepped in like that. We had enough on with the police abusing us without getting it from people who were supposed to be on our side.

Letter To The Queen
Anne & Betty

Anne

One of the women at our soup kitchen idolised the queen and couldn't understand why she hadn't stepped in to stop her policemen beating up ordinary working folk. I sat with her one day after half a dozen of our lads had come back from picketing badly knocked about with cuts and bruises all over their faces.

'I wonder if the queen knows what they are doing to our sons and husbands?' she asked. 'They might be keeping it from her. I think I'm going to write and tell her.'

She wrote a beautiful letter and came into Barnsley day after day asking people to sign it.

> From the women of the mining communities
> to HM Queen Elizabeth II.
>
> Your Majesty
>
> We, the women of the British mining communities, appeal for your support in our struggle to defend an industry which is crucial to the future well-being of all.
>
> Our husbands, our sons, our fathers – and indeed many of ourselves, have been on strike for nearly five months. Ours is a campaign to save the British coal industry, to preserve the jobs that should be passed on to our children and grandchildren, and to hold together the very lives of our communities.
>
> We are proud of the determination and courage of our men. We support them wholeheartedly. We have, over recent years, seen the horrors of mass unemployment cripple other industries; we have witnessed the slow death of communities dependent on them, and the tragedies that fall upon families and individuals.
>
> We also share with them the intimidation and intense hardship levied against us by those who oppose our fight for pits and jobs. As loyal and law-abiding citizens of this country, we never thought the violence, the denial of civil liberties, the day-and-night harassment employed by police forces from around the nation against us would enter our lives.

But we are determined people with a strong sense of justice.

On the picket lines, in the streets of our villages, and indeed in our own homes, the police have been used to terrify us and try to silence our opposition to pit closures.

Our children go without proper nourishment; indeed, they often go hungry. We care for them and comfort them, but their distress is a constant reminder that this dispute must be settled quickly.

We ask you, Your Majesty, to speak up on our behalf and help us to defend our families, our communities and a source of energy which can only grow in importance as oil and gas reserves diminish over the years to come.

We the undersigned support the above statement.

That letter and petition got over 100,000 signatures in less than a month. On the day of a big rally in London, me and Betty Heathfield marched up to the gates of Buckingham Palace to deliver it to the queen. They put us in a room that wanted a good clean and took it off us. I don't know whether the queen got to see it. If she did she never bothered to write back. It was a sad day for me in a lot of ways. When I got back home our Margaret told me that Ginger our lovely Airedale had died that afternoon.

Betty
When Anne and Betty Heathfield handed the petition in at Buckingham Palace, we wanted to march past there but the police wouldn't let us, saying that there were too many of us for that area. On that rally we remembered Joe Green and Davy Jones, the two lads who had lost their lives on the picket lines early in the strike. A lot of the women wore black armbands and Ann Musgrave made loads of black petals.

Some of the women had never been to London before. Everybody was singing and chanting. We got a few funny looks but most of the people on the route were cheering and clapping us. As we came past Downing Street we went silent. The women took their black armbands off and threw them down onto the road along with Ann Musgrave's black petals.

We had a forwarding address for Women Against Pit Closures at a little mews house in the middle of London. Jean McCrindle took us there to pick up some cheques. I have never seen as much mail, all in sacks from the GPO. We sat there for ages opening envelopes. Every one had a cheque in and some of the letters were heart rending. There were letters from old-age pensioners on tight budgets who apologised for only being able to send just a few coppers; letters from single-parent families who said things like, 'We can manage on beans on toast for a few days, use this to buy a chicken.' There were letters from people in Cambridgeshire, folk who had done well in life but remembered coming from mining families and, of course, ones from political people on the left. But most of all the letters were from ordinary working-class people who knew that we had a just cause; even though they might have been in a different industry, they were in the same boat as us.

The Best Christmas
Anne & Betty

Anne

Kathy Michaels was a coalminer and union activist from America who decided to come to see what was happening in the strike. She was a keen amateur photographer and took hundreds of pictures. When she went home she must have been telling her friends and fellow activists, because the next thing three more women coalminers came over and stopped at my house: Kipp Dawson, Margi Mayernik and Libby Lindsay. Kipp has a history as a civil rights activist starting when she dropped out of college and campaigned against the Vietnam War. She worked down the pit in Pittsburgh and became a great union activist. Libby Lindsay was one of the first female coalminers in modern times and worked at Eagle's Nest coal mine in Boone County, West Virginia as far back as the 1970s. They wanted to show their solidarity to the miners' strike and particularly to Women Against Pit Closures. They themselves were extremely well organised. They belonged to a woman's organisation which held a conference every year that moved around the American coalfields called Coal Employment Project. They came to see us to offer help and advice and to share their experiences. There had been some rough strikes in America and they knew how to handle themselves.

Fundraising was an important part of keeping things moving. Billy Connolly, the Glaswegian comedian, came to Leeds to do a benefit show for the striking miners. He was on stage for more than two hours and was brilliant. He came to meet Arthur, me and our Margaret after the show. We took him for a meal in a Chinese restaurant. He was a vegetarian at the time and nothing like that rough Glaswegian image he portrays on stage. He was gently spoken, had some lovely manners and never swore once.

Just before Christmas we had a day out shaking our tins and buckets at York. Percy Riley had done a collection at Sheffield and sent us some money to pay for the bus. A group of students came to meet us and offer their support; it was the first time that some of the lasses had had anything to do with students. Some of the women had never been anywhere without their husbands. We went with our buckets round the market and down The Shambles. We collected a lot of money that day and enjoyed the sightseeing while we were at it. On the way home, loads of the lasses came up to me and said, 'It's been grand today, can we come again?'

Betty

Christmas during the strike was exciting. We ended up working twenty-hour days to prepare for it. We were determined that the kids wouldn't go without. One of the lasses in our group showed us a letter that her daughter had written. It said:

> Dear Mum and Dad,
> I love you a lot. I know my dad is on strike so I don't mind if you can't get me a lot of things this year. All I want is a radio cassette player and a game.
> Love, Gillian.

We were determined to do roast turkey and all the trimmings. A young woman from Germany had come over and was volunteering to help us. She was brilliant and ran round Barnsley market like an athlete to get the best price on turkeys. In the end we got some from a shop outside town after we met a butcher who said he had plenty left. Our friend Sandra Hutchinson then had a great idea. She went to the weights and measures department at the council and asked them if they had any toys that had passed health and safety tests. She came back with toy lorries with just a scratch of paint off them and dolls that had been tested. They had a big party at North Gawber and the kids who came to our kitchen were invited over to join in with them.

Anne

I'd go as far as to say it was the best Christmas I can remember. We decided to have a big party at the Welfare. Arthur invited the folk singer and comedian Mike Harding to come. Mike was a loyal supporter and had played benefit concerts for the strikers at Hebden Bridge Trades Club. Jim Exley got dressed up as Father Christmas and Alain Simone, the French miners' leader, fetched sackfuls of toys over with him. We got the lasses organised, wrapped all the presents and put trimmings up. On the day we put the trestle tables out and had a lovely meal. The meat came from National Kitchens and the bakers' union gave us some apple pies. I put my boiler on to make the custard. The night before, somebody came knocking on our door. I answered it and there was a bloke wheeling a small bike. He told me that his lad had grown out of it and he wondered if I knew somebody who might want it. I knew just the kid. There was a little lad from a poor family and I wanted to make him feel special. His eyes lit up when he saw that bike.

The Bum Waggers
Anne & Betty

Betty
I came to know Frank Watters during the strike. It was the first time I had met a Communist Party activist. Frank had been a promoter of communism in the coalfields, going back a long way, and a big influence on Arthur. He was in Birmingham at the time and arranging support down there. Whenever Frank came up from Birmingham he needed somebody to drive him about because he didn't know how to drive. He was always asking for lifts. I didn't mind doing it because he was raising much-needed funds for the miners. I was appreciative of all that the Communist Party did for us. I was never tempted to join them though. I stuck to the Labour Party.

Near to the beginning of the strike, the Barnsley Women Against Pit Closures were invited by Ken Livingstone to speak at the GLC. It was the first meeting of that sort that a lot of us had been to. Valerie Wise chaired the meeting. She is the daughter of Audrey Wise, the socialist MP for Preston, and she worked for Ken Livingstone on the Council's Women's Committee. We hadn't got our confidence up at that point, so we often stumbled over what we wanted to say. I think Valerie was aware of this and was a sympathetic chair.

We talked about our experiences and time was left at the end for questions. One bloke stood up and rattled on for a good ten minutes without really coming to a point or asking a proper question. I think he just wanted to hear the sound of his own voice at the same time as trying to test us. I didn't understand many of the things he was saying. Jean McCrindle was in the audience with her head in her hands. I think she realised how uncomfortable he was making us, so she moved it on to the next question. The other questions were easier to understand and simpler to answer. At the end Anne leaned over to me.

'Let's not finish without saying something to that bugger with the long words, put him right Betty, don't let him get away with it.'

I leaned forward and spoke directly to the pompous man.

'As you can well see we are miners' wives. We haven't had the opportunity to get the same education that you have had. But when this strike is over, we will seek out education and I hope we will be asked to come back here and then I will answer your question.'

It took us a while, but we came to realise that not everybody who talked to us during the strike was doing it to befriend or support us. The reporters were the worst; they were always trying to trick and deceive. We got a letter from two women in Lancashire who told us that they worked for a company called 'Knobs and Knockers', a factory that purported to make doorknobs and knockers. They said that they had taken up a collection amongst their fellow workers and that they would like to deliver a cheque to us in person. It turned out that they were both journalists for the *Daily Mail*. They wheedled their way into the launch of a book we had done with Yorkshire Art Circus about our soup kitchen. They slipped up though because they featured a poem I had written without my permission. Brian Lewis of the Yorkshire Art Circus rang me to say that he had a friend who was socialist lawyer and he would pursue them for breach of copyright. They paid out £200 in compensation.

There was also tension and stress amongst ourselves, including a certain amount of jealousy. Barbara Jackson was speaking at Northern College one time and nobody told us, we only found out by accident. When we asked why we hadn't been invited we were told, 'Well nobody is stopping you, you can come if you want.'

We weren't always the one big happy family that we wanted to be. This came mainly from the different levels of development that the women had got to. The middle-class women in the movement already knew about feminism through their reading, campaigning, and the camaraderie that had developed from being together as women with ideas. They saw the miners' strike as a great opportunity to spread their message. The clash came when some of the miners' wives brought their own brand of working-class feminism to it. Some of the middle-class women got impatient about trying to spread their message and some of the younger ones simply didn't understand how the mining communities worked.

A young woman came up from Greenham Common to help us. When she saw that men were helping us as well, she got angry. She told us that we shouldn't allow men to help because women could do anything by themselves. A lot of the women couldn't make head nor tail of her arguments. They'd say to her, 'Well so and so is a good lad, he fetches wood for the fire every morning that he has scrounged and that other lad brings gallons of water.' The Greenham lass said that women were strong enough to do that and didn't seem to understand that our village relied on men as well as women to make it work. It all came to a head one day when the young Greenham woman rushed out to confront the men. She screamed at them, 'Why are you here? We don't need you and we don't want you.' The blokes just stood there, they couldn't weigh up what was going on. She carried on screaming and swearing at them. In the end one of the lads came to tell me that they were going home and that they wouldn't be coming back anymore. I went out and said, 'The shit has hit the fan now.' Then I turned on the Greenham lass and said, 'And you! If you don't like it, you go home!'

We were fortunate that the academics like Sheila Rowbotham, Sally Alexander and Jean McCrindle were happy to accept us for who we were.

The constant organising, picketing, cooking food for a lot of people with limited facilities, and worry about money was hard work. And lack of sleep did catch up with us. It became stressful in a lot of ways. After Christmas some cracks started to appear amongst ourselves. We were a lot of women thrown together all of a sudden, many of us from different backgrounds. At first we were all pulling together but as time went by we started to notice that there were differences.

We were on a picket at Woolley and some German political activists came to join us. They brought with them some lovely raincoats, very high-quality branded garments. When these coats were handed out, they all went to the students and political women, the miners' wives didn't get a look-in. As soon as these women saw the labels they were like lightning grabbing them. I didn't say anything at the time, but it didn't go unnoticed. Another time Anne was invited to speak and fundraise in Ireland and that caused a right set-to.

Anne

A letter came inviting me to go over to Ireland to explain what was happening in the strike. I invited Maureen Exley from the Miners' Welfare and Marsha Marshall to come with me. We were met off the ferry by Des Bonass, a prominent figure in the Irish trade union movement. He took us to a bed and breakfast place on the edge of Dublin where we stayed for four nights. Des showed us round various union meetings and let us take up collections. The people in Ireland were very generous and kind to us. In return, we helped out on a picket line. A young woman called Mary Manning who worked on the checkout at Dunnes supermarket had been suspended for refusing to handle a grapefruit that had come from South Africa. Her union was boycotting anything to do with the apartheid regime. Mary, her shop steward, and about a dozen more women who sympathised went on strike. The strike ended up lasting for three years until the Irish government banned fruit coming in from South Africa. Mary Manning and her sisters were recognised by Archbishop Tutu when he called in to see them on his way back from picking up his Nobel Prize. They even met Nelson Mandela years after when he visited Ireland. We spent the day with them outside Dunnes on Henry Street.

Before we came home Des took us to a pit. The manager came out, he didn't look best pleased.

'If I give you some money, will you go and collect somewhere else?'

He gave us a good donation, in fact we came back from Ireland with a lot of money for our soup kitchens. We took it straight to the meeting on the Sunday afternoon at the Park Road Club, and that's when the balloon went up. A certain group of women, mainly the ones from Northern College, complained that the invitation for the trip hadn't been brought to the meeting. They said that things like that should be discussed properly and that the whole group should decide who would go to such things. They were angry that me,

Marsha and Maureen had gone without their permission. 'Well look at all the money we've brought back,' I told them, but it didn't wash. It was a horrible afternoon. The meeting closed on a sour note. I was very upset by it.

The telephones were red hot that night. Jean McCrindle phoned me and said she thought it hadn't been a very nice meeting and that some of the women were thinking of forming their own group without the women from Northern College. I talked to Marsha Marshall as well. She was never one to wallpaper over the cracks.

'We've been all the way to bloody Ireland, raised all that money and instead of being bloody happy they're moaning, they're never satisfied! Meanwhile my husband's still on strike. We might as well just organise ourselves.'

Betty

We formed the Barnsley Miners Wives' Action Group and referred to ourselves as 'The Bum Waggers'; not the best of terms, but it fit the letters. Lynn Hathaway from Great Houghton joined us, as did the Woolley/Windhill group and the Hoyland lasses. We started having our meetings at Worsbrough Miners Welfare. The women from Northern College and some from Royston stayed with the other group. I think the top and bottom of it was plain to see. There was a bit of jealousy towards Anne because she was Arthur's wife and she attracted a lot of attention from the media. Beyond that there was the matter of working-class women, real miners' wives, finding their voices. It didn't sit well with some of the educated middle-class women and that's what was causing the tension. Marsha put it best.

'We're strong women and we've got something to say and choose what they think, we're going to bloody well say it, whether they like it or not!'

I was completely inspired by the way working-class women in our group came to the front. Elicia was a shining example of that. She was involved right from the start. Her husband Danny came home from picketing one day and told her what the police had been doing. When it came on the news it was a different story to what Danny had told her. She decided there and then that she would go picketing and see for herself. After that she threw herself into supporting the Women Against Pit Closures group with all of her heart. Elicia was the youngest of sixteen children and the only girl, her mother must have kept trying until she got one. All fifteen of her brothers worked at the pit and she left school at fifteen to work at S.R. Gent's clothing factory. Her mother was a right character, they called her the 'Old Rough Diamond'. When she went out she smoked and drank and stood with the men. She lived to be eighty-four and died the year before the strike. Elicia told us that her mother was mannish in her ways and that she stood up for herself and taught Elicia that she had to as well.

It wasn't long before Elicia was going to meetings and then speaking at them. She entertained supporters from around the country and abroad. Two Yugoslavian women came to her house in the New Year of the strike and it was her husband's birthday. They went to Marks & Spencer's and bought him a cake. They could only get a leftover Christmas cake, but it was a lovely thought. Elicia spoke abroad, in Holland and Italy. She became our treasurer when we decided to carry on with the group.

Marsha was our secretary and a fantastic inspiration. She decided that she would back her husband and son from the start and she never wavered. Marsha's passion before the strike had been sausage dogs. She lived at Wombwell and had a houseful of dachshunds yapping all day long. Marsha had plenty to say for herself at the best of times but when the strike was on she really found her voice and was always intent on making sure that it was heard. She was very bright and saw immediately that the strike wasn't just about now, it was about the future and that was the reason to fight. She was also witty. Her husband was arrested for obstruction on the M1 twenty miles before he got to the pit he was picketing. Marsha said, 'It's funny, loads of miners manage to get arrested on the way to somewhere, but there doesn't seem to be any who get arrested coming back the other way.' Marsha was the first miners' wife to get herself on the television right at the beginning. After that, whenever they wanted an angry miners' wife, they got in touch with Marsha.

The first time I was on TV myself was with Marsha. Jean

McCrindle said to me before we went on that we ought to ask for a donation for the soup kitchen. The producer said he couldn't possibly give us any money. Marsha waited until the programme was due to start and then said, 'It's alright love, we don't want to be on your show!' The producer panicked and agreed a fee as quick as a flash.

Anne
We still met on Sundays. We were also still part of National Women Against Pit Closures. Something positive came out of the bit of animosity. We discovered that there was a lot of smaller groups working on their own without much support and we brought them in. These were groups in outlying districts like Frickley, Cudworth and Hemsworth, and there was a tiny kitchen at Park Mill Colliery, an isolated pit out near Skelmanthorpe. It was run by just two women who were struggling.

We still did our picketing and started going into Lancashire. We got pulled up at every blockade. We had a whole list of excuses ready when the bobbies shone their torches and put their head in the window.

'We're strippers on a late-night engagement.'

'We're on our way back from a hen do at Blackpool and we've got lost.'

If that didn't work we used to make Betty start crying. She always sat in the back seat and she could turn the waterworks on like an actress.

'I've got to be at home in bed with my nightie on before my husband gets in from the club, else he'll beat me up.'

Blood Running Out Of All Of Us
Anne & Betty

Betty
Some scabs started going in at Woolley. They didn't go in through the main gate, but on a back route off Woolley Edge Road where the washing plant was. It's an exposed road, high up and the wind there means it's bitter cold in the winter. The farmers say the wind comes straight from Siberia. Woolley was a picket line with a lot going on at the best of times, but on this particular day there was a massive turn out to try and turn the scabs round. There were strikers there, the women's groups, the trades councils and the Socialist Workers Party people. We had a caravan doing hot food. The police brought their dogs slavering, snapping and snarling right up to the counter. You could see that the dogs were as agitated as the police were. I served an older miner with a cup of hot soup and I leant on the counter to watch him drink it. A motorbike policeman with long boots on just like a Nazi came up to him and beat him for no reason at all, then arrested him on some trumped up charge. I ran round to try and remonstrate. The policeman told me to move or I would be next. I looked him straight in the eye.

'I am not frightened,' I told him. 'Look around you, there are some very tough lads here. So I will tell you just once, if you hit me, I will be the last woman you ever do it to!'

There was blood all over the grass. The bobby dragged the miner away and I just stood there in the cold, trembling with anger. I watched the blood mixing with the rainwater and running down the lane. It was as if that blood was running out of all of us. I was determined to go to court when that miner was up. It was heard at Wakefield. We sat there all day, waiting, waiting, waiting for the police witnesses. The arresting officer was from somewhere away. They finally arrived in the late afternoon, claiming they had been unable to find Wood Street Police Station. The magistrate wasn't impressed and reminded them that Wood Street was the main headquarters of West Yorkshire Police. He dismissed the case.

A women's photography co-operative from London got in touch and asked me if I would take one of them on the picket line. There were four of them and each went to a different pit. The one who came to us was Rai Page, a well-known Canadian photographer who had been all over the world working with mainly indigenous people. We got to the picket line and went up to the front where it was heaving. The police were hitting out with their truncheons and, as usual by then, I was mouthing off at them. As I turned to look at Rai, one of them belted me across the knee with his truncheon. He laughed in my face.

'It serves you right you silly old cow.'

I stared at him.

'I'll be back in the morning though and you need to wash your mouth out with soap and water.'

When we came away I looked at my knee, it was bleeding badly. Rai wanted me to go to hospital straightaway. The thing was I had promised a woman in Nottinghamshire that I would go to court to support her. She was conducting her own defence after being arrested on another picket line. I decided to patch myself up. I put some butterfly stitches into my kneecap and wrapped it with a padded bandage. We set off for Nottingham and made it to the court there on time. Rai kept asking me if I was alright. I must have looked dreadful, I had lost a fair amount of blood. At lunchtime I finally gave in and said, 'I think I need to get home.' Rai then wanted to take me to a hospital in Nottingham. I told her 'No!' and half joking said, 'They're liable to bloody amputate down here.' We got to Barnsley A&E and they X-rayed my knee. They found it was broken in three places. They suggested I might need an operation, I told them to put it in a pot and let me out, I was too busy for staying in hospital. They plastered my knee and Rai drove me home.

Rai had never been to our house or met my husband. She knocked on the front door and told Don what had happened and that I would need assisting from the car. Don told her to get off home and that he would see to me. He came to the car, picked me up and carried me to the sofa. He sat with me for five minutes and then went off to the pub. I couldn't get upstairs and I badly needed the toilet. I'm ashamed to say it but I crawled over to the coal bucket on the hearth and I had a pee in that.

Anne
Betty still had her pot on when we set off to do a series of talks in Switzerland. A young woman whose dad was a doctor had been over to observe the strike and she invited us there to collect and tell our story. Betty made a joke of it.

'Most people come back from Switzerland on crutches, I'm the first one to go there on them.'

We landed in Geneva and they transferred us to a plane no bigger than a tube of Smarties to fly over the Alps in. We went somewhere down near Italy where our hosts ran a pizza place. They took us round to visit trade union and socialist groups. Betty made some speeches and talked about us being mother hens folding our chicks under our wing.

There was a big conference going on in Geneva regarding the food and pharmaceuticals industry and we were invited to make a speech about our experiences during the strike. Betty and me were both members of USDAW and at the time USDAW were having a really big push to bring women to the forefront. A lot of people came to see us, but we were disappointed when we found out that our national organiser, Geoff Martin, hadn't turned up. The official explanation was that he'd had to fly home early. One of the bakers tipped us the wink that he hadn't and he was swanning it in a local pub. We marched down to the pub, burst through the doors like in a cowboy film and confronted him. His face was a picture. We were fuming. We called him all the bastards under the sun. His union was trying to get more women to speak up and there he was with a big glass of beer in his hand when he ought to have been in the hall listening to what women from his own union had to say.

We still came home from Switzerland happy. We collected a lot of money for the kitchen. The only problem was it was in Swiss francs and you were limited to how many you could take out of the

Betty on crutches, Woolley Edge, February 1985.

country. You could only change so many at a time so it took us all day driving from one town to another to different banks to change the Swiss francs into sterling before we came home.

Marching Back
Anne & Betty

Betty
The strike seemed to end all of a sudden. It knocked me back when they made the announcement that there would be a return to work. We were still planning rotas and menus for the soup kitchen and organising for picket lines. I was left with an empty feeling inside me. All sorts of memories went through my mind. I thought about the time when we dropped a pan full of liver and onions out of the oven and onto the floor at the soup kitchen. We had loads of hungry bellies waiting. Everybody stood there not knowing what to do. In the end I scraped the liver up and ran it under the hot tap and put it back into the gravy. Then I thought about standing at the door after dinner was over. They always thanked us on the way out. One day the last group going out said, 'Don't think we don't appreciate it, but that custard was a bit salty today.' Somebody had put salt in it instead of sugar. I thought about a march I'd been on from Chesterfield to Liverpool called 'Mines Not Missiles'. We went via Stoke-on-Trent. It took us three days. I met some women from the North Staffordshire coalfield there who were brilliant. On that march I walked alongside a young woman from near Doncaster who worked at a pit canteen. Her husband worked down the same pit. She told me they had lost everything, including their house. Remembering made me want to weep. I felt betrayed as well.

Anne
On the day the strike ended the union decided that everybody would go back behind the bands and banners with their heads up. We set off from near the Red Lion pub and marched to Barrow pit. One of the lads came up beside me and almost whispered in my ear.

'Anne, I want my wife back now.'

I laughed.

'Well you have got your wife, she's marching alongside you.'
He studied for a bit.

'No! I mean I want my wife to be like she was before.'

I knew that wasn't going to happen. She had changed like a lot of us women had. I didn't say that to him though.

'Well, that lad, is something you are going to have to sort out amongst yourselves.'

I don't think that they did sort things out amongst themselves because I heard not long after that the couple had parted.

I was disappointed when they called the strike off. I hadn't had enough. Arthur was the same. Though he rarely spoke about it with me, I know from talking to him on the phone and the few times he did come home that in that whole year he never once wavered. He always thought that the strike was there for us to win. He once told me that in one meeting MacGregor was about ready to concede. They were close and MacGregor had to excuse himself from the meeting because he wanted to make a call to his 'sister'. When he came back he had changed his mind completely about what they had been talking about. Arthur thought that he had been on some sort of hotline to Thatcher and she had told him not to give in to anything.

I often think if they had asked the miners' wives to vote, we would have still been out. In a lot of ways the women despised what Thatcher and her government and police force did more than the lads did. I sat down on my own on that Sunday night and thought about where we were with it all. I couldn't get it out of my head that we had come all this way and now it was suddenly over. I was still proud that day we marched back. I was proud of the struggle we had been in, proud of the way my husband led the men, and proud of the lads who stuck behind him for twelve months. Most of all, I was proud of the women who joined in at the soup kitchens, the marches and the picket lines.

I am the daughter and granddaughter of coalminers. I married a coalminer who worked his way up through the union to be president and he too was the son of a miner. Like in a lot of mining family houses, the men always wanted their way. I had two men to deal with at our house, Arthur and Harold. I know about male chauvinism because I had seen it first hand. As soon as my mam saw the pit bus coming she used to have a warm plate and the knives and forks on the table. It's fair to say that some women did go back to that, but most women were changed forever by the strike. They realised that they no longer had to be just a mother or a wife, they had a political education and a wider view. When that happens the boundaries alter. The strike taught us all a lesson. We knew things were about to change and I saw that on the very day when we marched back at the end of the strike.

Back to work march behind Barrow Brass Band, March 1985.

The Struggle Continues
Anne & Betty

Betty
When you come from a coal-mining community, you know that digging for coal isn't just a way of making a living. Coal is in your heart and blood; it links you to where you are from unlike any other industry. My grandparents on my mother's side and my grandparents on my father's side came from Staffordshire looking for work. My paternal grandfather helped to sink Frickley pit to the Barnsley Bed seam in 1903. My husband's grandparents came from Staffordshire for the same reason, to make a life for their families by digging for coal. My husband was a collier, two of my three sons worked at the pit. They never knew their father's dad. He was killed in an underground accident at North Gawber Colliery before they were born. He left a widow with ten children. Three of her boys were working at the same pit as their dad on that day. The other kids were in school or toddling at home and one was a six-month-old baby. My own father died two years into his retirement after a lifetime down the pit.

I am very proud to say that I was involved in the struggle against pit closures during that bitter strike in 1984 and 1985. I, like many women in pit villages before the strike, was expected to conform to the traditional role; I was to look after my husband and family and make a comfortable and clean home. Very few women from mining families were involved in political or trade union activity. The only women remotely connected to the National Union of Mineworkers were the handful who worked in the pit canteens or as cleaners in the offices; none of them had roles of any influence. All of that changed. I was just one of thousands who stood up and got involved in that struggle. For women, the strike was just the beginning.

Perhaps the most important thing to come out of the strike was the women's movement that flourishes across former mining communities. Women like me have become involved in things far beyond the normal life we had before. I have become interested in issues around social justice, the peace movement, the health service, cuts in social provision, strikes for better wages and conditions. When the strike finished and the shock subsided I made a joke that at least now I would be able to catch up on my housework and decorating. That day is still to come.

We decided to carry on with our meetings and moved to Elicia Billingham's house on Western Street. Jean McCrindle stuck with us, Noreen Pendleton, Margaret Ince, Marlene Thompson, Bernadette France and Maureen Exley, all good women. Over a period of weeks we decided that because we were interested in social justice we should carry on with our political campaigning. For a start there was the matter of a lot of young miners who had lost their jobs through being arrested and something needed saying about that. We also wanted to ally ourselves to different political causes; Greenham Common and the wider peace movement was one and we were also determined to carry on picketing. If we saw a strike that interested us, we would offer our support. This led to us making great friendships with other working-class women in struggle.

Anne
We had a stall in aid of the sacked miners. These were the lads who had lost their jobs through being arrested. Not all of them had been on the picket lines; some had been caught foraging for coal, some had been nicking scrap, and there were even some who'd been caught poaching on the big estates. We sold badges, plates, books, pamphlets and little ornaments carved from coal. We toured that stall to union events, festivals, conferences and anywhere working people gathered. We went down to Coalville in Leicestershire to have our plates made; they featured pictures of collieries that were being shut and knocked down. Arthur had a load of copies of Vic Allen's book *The Militancy of British Miners*, there were piles of them at the NUM offices. He signed them and gave us them to sell.

I was spending most of my time with the women's groups. Betty and me got nicknamed 'Rent a gob, Rent a Mob, Rent a Picket Squad'. We travelled to wherever we thought we'd be useful.

My cousin Jack Harper, a union man, came to see me during the Wapping dispute when Rupert Murdoch was using scabs to break the printers' strike. Our Jack asked me if I would round up some of the lasses to go to a place near Rotherham that was a distribution centre for early morning newspapers. We had to be there in the middle of the night because that was when the papers were transferred into smaller vans for local delivery. It was bitter cold. Betty had fetched some hot milky coffee in a flask. There was a long line of policemen rubbing their gloves together and stamping their feet. Betty went up and down the line with the stopper off her flask asking them if they would like to smell her coffee. We didn't have much luck stopping the distribution that night so on the way home we pinched piles of *Sun* newspapers from outside the newsagent shops. It was ages before I got shut of them all.

When the Silentnight mattress factory went on strike we showed our support to them. That turned out to be a long job and another where we stood outside a wire fence for ages. It was about showing solidarity of course, but it was also our opportunity to point a finger at the policemen. We used to say, 'It was us in the miners' strike and it's these today, but don't forget, it might be you next.'

Betty
I fell out with the Labour Party shortly after the strike was over. Some members organised a social evening and didn't tell me about it. Then I found out why they hadn't. They had invited some scabs and, not only that, they had recruited them into the party as paid-up members. I resigned immediately.

Elicia Billingham and her husband Danny moved on and bought a guest house at Blackpool. It was called Chesterfield House. Danny had collected a lot of memorabilia from the strike and had lamps, plates and all sorts of souvenirs that he displayed in the bar. One evening Elicia overheard two guests talking quietly and realised that they had been scabs in the strike. She confronted them there and then.

'Hey! Have I heard it right, did you two go to work during the strike?'

They looked sheepish, but then admitted they had crossed the picket lines. Elicia made nothing more to do of it.

'Right! Get your bags packed now, you're not welcome here, you can find another bed and breakfast somewhere else.'

Not long after that, the Tories were having a conference in Blackpool. Every time the phone rang with someone asking for a room that week, Elicia asked them if they were coming for the conference. If they said yes, Elicia told them to find somewhere else as they were not welcome. One bloke chastised her.

'You're not going to make a very good living behaving like that.'

'Don't you worry about me flower,' Elicia said, 'I make enough and besides I'm particular about who I let into my house.'

Durham Miners' Gala, July 1985. First left is Maureen Exley, Betty, Anne, Jean McCrindle in the black jacket and trousers. To the right, Lynn Hathaway in the sunglasses next to Doreen Jones, mother of Davy Jones who was killed in the strike.

American Sisters
Anne & Betty

Anne

An invitation came from America to visit a conference with the women coalfield activists who had come to support us during the strike. Betty went with Gwen White and I went with Betty Heathfield. We stayed with Marat Moore. Marat had worked underground at a pit before going to university. She ended up being an advisor to the union and then a photographer and writer. She wrote a book about women working at the pit called *Women in the Mines: Stories of Life and Work*.

Betty

Gwen White and I stepped off the plane for the first time in America and sat down to wait for Kipp Dawson to come and meet us. I'd only met Kipp once before when she came to stay with Anne during the strike. She was a great campaigner who had been investigated as a young teenager by the House Un-American Activities Committee. Her grandfather had been murdered by the Ku Klux Klan. We were terribly excited to be meeting her again.

 The excitement started to wear off an hour later when there was no sign of anybody meeting us. Gwen was asking me what I thought we ought to do. We had some phone numbers and we tried to call from a phone box but it kept asking us to put more money in and we never got through. I think Gwen thought I was a far more seasoned traveller then I was and she seemed to think I knew what to do.

 'Well,' I told Gwen, 'we'll just have to jump on a Greyhound bus.'
 'Where to?'
 I hadn't thought it through. I had an address for where the conference was and I knew from watching films that everybody went everywhere on the Greyhound bus. I guessed that we could do the same. Just as we were beginning to panic the tiny figure of

Betty speaking at the National Conference of Women Miners, Paintsville, Kentucky, USA, June 1986. With Betty Heathfield, Anne and Gwen White.

In the USA again. Front row (L to R) Dot Kelly, Betty, Doris Meghan and Anne. Back row is Mary Smith with her arm around an American supporter.

Kipp Dawson came walking quickly towards us carrying above her head a poster saying 'Coal Not Dole' that she'd brought back as a souvenir from her trip to Barnsley.

After the conference, Anne went to stay with Libby Lindsay for a few days. Dot and I went to stay with Doris and Tony in Kentucky. Doris and Tony were both coalminers. Doris's family are close and they all live near one another. It was Doris's mother-in-law's birthday when we got there and they were having a family barbecue in the garden. Dot and I played down at the creek at the bottom of the garden with the kids and when we came back the children asked us if we would like to play croquet. When we told them that we didn't have the first clue how to play croquet they thought we were teasing them. They genuinely thought that all English people played croquet and they had asked us as a special treat. The kids set it up and told us the rules; they still thought we were kidding them about never having played.

In the evening we sat with the adults and talked about the strikes we had been through. In America, when the miners go on strike it's like a war and it's not unusual for both sides to get their rifles out. Tony took us into his workshop and opened a drawer to show us some metal spikes he had made to throw under the horses hooves to stop them charging.

One of my strongest memories of that trip is of being asked at the conference if we would like to visit one of the principal women organisers, someone they looked up to. She had taken ill and was in hospital. Gwen White and I went to see her. She was in a ward on her own surrounded by bleeping machinery. Her condition wasn't good and it was being made worse by a huge worry that her insurance money was running out. She was getting the best treatment money could buy but as soon as the money ran out the treatment would stop straightaway. When we asked about what would happen then, we were told that she would likely end up in a charity facility. I thought immediately about what a treasure we have with the NHS.

Anne
Betty Heathfield was a great woman and a lovely soul. Both her grandads worked in the pits in Derbyshire and they encouraged

her to get an education. She got a place at one of the best grammar schools and was a top class student. She should have gone on to university but the war was on so she left and got a job as a secretary in order to help out her family. She told me that she used to ride up and down on a motorbike delivering messages. She was with me and Betty on the picket lines now and again, but she wasn't like us. She was a lot gentler and didn't believe in direct action like we did. She never swore at the police. When we were down at Wapping supporting the printers' strike, me and Betty sat down in the middle of the road to stop the traffic. Betty H said, 'Oooh! Anne I'm not sure we ought to be doing this.'

Both her and her husband were health conscious and keep-fit fanatics; they each had a bike at the top of the stairs in their house. It was cruel that she should get Alzheimer's later in life. She went back to studying and was doing a politics degree but was too poorly to complete it. Betty and me went to see her in a nursing home at Chesterfield. They had left her a plateful of food but it was just sitting there going cold. Betty said, 'Would you like me to feed you?' She didn't say anything. She just looked at us both. Betty started to feed her off a spoon. She gave the most beautiful smile and then out of nowhere said, 'You can come and sit on my knee anytime,' then went back to being lost in her thoughts. We told her that we would definitely come to see her again. I think we both knew in our hearts that we wouldn't.

Further Education
Betty

Donny rang me to tell me that my dear friend Phyl had died. She had been to a tea dance and passed away suddenly: she died dancing. Phyl's funeral coincided with her son Carl's wife going into labour with their first child. He came to the funeral from the maternity ward and then rushed straight back to the hospital when it ended. I loved Phyl. We remained friends throughout all the ups and downs of life. I was flabbergasted when she told me that she had joined the Tory party, but she explained it by telling me that where she lived you had to be in the Tory party otherwise you would never get to know what was going on. After I left nursing to get married, Phyl moved to work in a hospital at Leeds. She came down with rheumatic fever. She was told she might not be able to have children. When she married Derek, a baby was all that she wanted. She badgered her GP at Thorp Arch and eventually he relented and said, 'Okay Mrs Barton, but only one.' Phyl had Carl and then Mandy. Her children were very close, they even had a double wedding. I still miss Phyl. I think about her most days. Those times when we were in nurse training together were some of my happiest days.

About six months into the strike, Northern College had organised a weekend course for Women Against Pit Closures. We were all suffering from a lot of stress and lack of sleep at the time. Northern College had started in the 1970s as a place of education for those who might for whatever reason have missed out when they were younger. It specialises in social and community education, and is supported by the trade union movement and other organisations. It's based at Wentworth Castle and set in beautiful parklands. We stayed over and had great fun that weekend. For the first time in ages we were able to let our hair down a bit. We sat in the bar every night telling stories and laughing. I can't recall much about what I learned that weekend, but I had a great time and it lifted the weight that was pressing on my shoulders. Shortly afterwards, I was at a function with Jean McCrindle and she introduced me to Professor Bob Fryer, who was the principal at Northern College. I don't know what came over me, but the first thing I said to him was, 'When this strike is over, I am going to come to your college.' He smiled and said, 'Okay Betty, you will be very welcome.'

After the strike, I stuck to my word. I signed up for two years to study part-time for a diploma in social and community studies with the idea that I might then work back in my own community and share what I had learned. John Goode, one of the education officers at my union USDAW, tried to persuade me to do an area organiser's job within the union and the college tried to make me do trade union studies, but I was adamant that it had to be community based. I'd always enjoyed volunteering and what I had seen during the strike made me realise that good things could happen in the heart of the community, outside of the workplace.

I decided not to go residential. There were too many jobs to do at home and I had to keep my eye on Michael. He had started drinking heavily and kept forgetting to take his medication.

I was outside cleaning my car one Sunday morning when one of Don's brothers came up to me. He stood there watching me with the sponge and bucket.

'What does my brother have to say about you going to college then?'

I was straight with him.

'Well, it's like this, he can have me and college or not me at all.'

He walked off muttering under his breath.

I was still unsure about my academic talents. My tutor was Ed Ellis. After my first essay I had a tutorial with him. He said to me, 'Betty, this is a first class A-level essay.' I believe he thought this was a compliment. I felt crestfallen. When he had gone I sat there and thought to myself, 'I've come to bloody college and he's putting me back to school.' It was a slow start. I was asking the other students question after question to get their opinions. After a couple of terms I felt alright. I still had a long way to go, but I started to feel equal to the others, or nearly equal. I always got my essays in on time.

One day in a lecture Ed Ellis asked a question, 'Is human behaviour instinctive?' One of the girls said yes immediately. Ed asked her to say in what respect. She just said, 'Sex.' I raised my hand.

'I think I can give an example, look at how birds look after their young and weave a nest without being shown.'

Ed seemed to like my response. He then asked another question, this time directly to me, about the human body. I remembered my nurse training and relied on that to give an answer relating to physiology and anatomy. Ed said, 'My word, you know your stuff.' I pulled him up sharp and told him that I didn't mind joining in with a group discussion, but he wasn't to put me on the spot like that ever again. My confidence was coming.

We were a mixed group, about ten of us in all. I became close to a young woman called Kate who had suffered sexual abuse as a girl from a man in her family. She told me that she couldn't trust men. And there was Kevin. He was so laid back he hardly bothered to say anything. When he did it was usually interesting, but most of the time he didn't seem to want to make the effort. We teased him. When he spoke we would immediately jump in and say, 'Kevin says and we all agree…' This ended up being like a saying for us, whenever we were stuck for words we'd say, 'Well Kevin says.' Then there was Frances. She was a single parent with a little lad. One of the big things about Northern College was that women with children could bring them. They either attended a nursery or, if they were older, they went to the local school.

I was progressing well and also enjoying the socialising that comes with college life. I was meeting male students who were a million miles away and a different species to Don. If you left your washing in the laundry room drying, you could go in a bit later to find that a man had actually taken it out and folded it up for you. Don didn't know how to turn a washing machine on or off. Because I was still living at home when I first went to college, Don still thought he had me under his thumb. He told me that I was too thick to pass any exams and that nothing would come of my studies.

My mother was so dyed-in-the-wool that I couldn't bring myself to leave Don. She constantly reminded me that I had married him for better or worse and that I must make do with what I had got. She wore me down. After my teenage years I don't think I even bothered to argue with her; I couldn't make her see my point of view. I wasn't frightened of her but I allowed her to control and rule me to keep the peace. I secretly told myself that when my mother died I would leave my husband.

After I'd been at college for about a year I had made a lot of new friends. I was getting invites to social evenings and was feeling more confident about myself. Occasionally I would phone Don and tell him that I'd decided to stay over at the college. I could almost see the shrug as he said, 'Well it isn't going to stop me going to the pub is it?' I don't think Don ever loved a woman apart from his mother, but as time went by any love that he might have had for me turned into a sour indifference. At times it was really hurtful. One night I went to visit a friend. When I got home there was nobody in, the door was locked and I didn't have a key. One of the neighbours went by and told me that he could get me in. I let him prise the door open, it was just an old lock. I thanked him and he dawdled in the doorway. He made me feel uncomfortable and then he started talking suggestively. I did what a lot of women do in that sort of situation; I picked a cloth up and started to do some work. He scarpered. When Don came home I asked him if he would have a word with the neighbour because I hadn't liked what he had been saying to me. Don lowered his paper. There wasn't a hint of sympathy.

'Do you mean to tell me he fancies thee? He must be bloody crackers!'

He lifted his paper up again.

Don had decided he was going to take his redundancy as soon as he could after they got back to work. The pit itself closed within eighteen months of the strike finishing. Don's hobby was fishing, he liked to go to the coast to fish in the sea. After he took his redundancy he decided to set himself up as a fish seller going round pubs and clubs selling what he'd brought back from Whitby. He couldn't drive so he had me taking him in my car all the way to Whitby to pick up crabs and lobsters. As soon as he got home he had every gas ring on the hob boiling shellfish. He stunk the house out and I couldn't move for him because once he'd boiled his crabs he would be sat dressing them on the table. The house started to smell like a fishmonger's shop. Some of the women used to tell me that I should nip his idea in the bud because people visiting would blame me for the stink.

Woman On A Train
Anne

One day I'd been in London to see Arthur and was coming back on the train. On the platform at King's Cross I noticed a woman struggling with a big case. She was elderly so I asked her if I could help. Between us we got the case on the train and I lifted it onto the luggage rack for her. We sat down at a table seat opposite one another. She was a well-dressed, well-spoken woman and I took to her straightaway. She told me that she was going to get off at Leeds as her son was meeting her there. I said that I was getting off at Doncaster but that I would lift her case down for her before I got off. She told me where she lived and talked a bit about her son and daughter-in-law and how she was looking forward to visiting them. She then asked me where I'd been and where I was going. I told her that I lived in an old pit village near Barnsley. She asked me which one. I told her Worsbrough.

'Isn't that where Arthur Scargill lives?'

Here we go, I thought. Then she set off.

'I think that man is a hypocrite, he has led the miners up a garden path and all the time he is living in the lap of luxury.'

I decided not to say anything. I told her that I was going to the buffet bar for a cup of tea and asked her if she would like one. When I came back with the teas, she carried on.

'I've heard that he lives in a huge mansion with a swimming pool.'

'I don't think he does. I live in the same village and there's nobody in Worsbrough with a swimming pool in their garden as far as I know.'

'They say he sent his daughter to private school.'

'I'm not sure that's true either. I believe she went to the local comprehensive.'

I managed to change the subject and talked to her about times gone by. I told her that I'd worked at the Co-op for a lot of years and the changes I had seen. I talked about the changes I had seen in my own community since the pit closures, but every time there was a break in the conversation she fetched it back to Arthur.

'He is a horrible man and he is to blame for what has happened.'

I found it hard to stomach what this lady was saying. On the one hand I could see a kind and friendly person and on the other I could see someone who hadn't got her facts right. I wondered if I ought to say something, but every time I thought about speaking, the subject changed and she said something nice. I decided to keep my counsel.

As the train approached Doncaster, I reached up to get her case down for her. She thanked me.

'Can I just say this has been a lovely journey. It's not every day you meet someone so thoughtful and kind.'

She took my hand and told me her name. I bit my lip and thought, 'Bugger it, I'll tell her.'

The train started to slow down.

'I'm Anne Scargill. I'm Arthur's wife. We live in a small bungalow with three bedrooms. Our daughter lives with us and so does Arthur's dad and we've got a couple of dogs. My husband works really hard for his union and my daughter is training to be a doctor.'

She didn't know what to say. I looked through the window and saw that the train was pulling up to the platform.

'Oh! My goodness! Oh! My goodness dear, you must think me completely awful.'

I told her that I wasn't too offended and that I had to put up with comments about my husband all the time, especially from the newspapers and television. I then asked her how she knew so much about Arthur.

'Well, I suppose I have read it in the newspapers.'

I set off down the carriage to get off.

'Can I just say love, that you shouldn't always believe what you read in the paper.'

I waved to her as the train set off.

There was a lot of deliberate lies and misinformation spread about Arthur which did cause him some bother. Late one night, he had travelled home from an interview in London and pulled up into the drive at our bungalow. As he was walking up the path, I suddenly noticed through the curtains bright blue flashing lights and a huge amount of commotion. I looked out of our bedroom window onto Yews Lane and saw the road filled with police cars, quickly joined by further cars with wailing klaxons. I was petrified as to what was happening and ran out onto the front lawn in my housecoat to see what the commotion was. The bright lights dazzled me and stopped me in my tracks. I was bewildered as to what had happened; with this amount of police presence my immediate thought was there had been a murder. The officers prevented Arthur from coming into the house.

This heavy-handed police presence was because it was alleged that Arthur had been speeding. The speeding charge was dismissed but Arthur didn't leave it at that, he brought an action against the police for wrongful arrest. The court hearing was held in Manchester and Arthur was represented by the barrister Michael Mansfield. Mike was mesmerising to watch in court; he skilfully built arguments and steered the witnesses to fall into the holes they'd dug themselves. I was called as a witness to the fact that Arthur had been unlawfully detained outside his own home. When I took the stand I had a quaking, shaking voice throughout my testimony, plus the judge couldn't understand my accent. When I explained that I had noted the time on the night by looking at the cooker clock, he asked whereabouts in the house was this 'cuckoo clock'?

This was the first time I'd met Mike. During the case and after, Mike became a family friend; he and his wife Yvette and their son Freddie came to stay with us often. He has a formidable presence, both physically and in court, and his considerable success in cases has earned him a reputation as one of the leading human rights barristers in the world. On top of this he is grounded and tolerates me really well; he was foolish enough to give me his personal direct line and said 'call me if you are ever in trouble, Anne'. I suspect he regrets this as call him I did on numerous occasions whenever I was in trouble with authority. If I had some bolshie bobby or officious bloke trying to bully me, I would 'draw his name like a sword' and be able to get live advice from the top bloke. They hated that as they all knew about him and his formidable reputation. I loved it.

Mike was fantastic company, I used to love to have dinner and chats with him. When people ask who would be the top 10 people for an ideal dinner guest list – he would be without doubt my number one choice. He's had a fascinating life and is an excellent raconteur. We might not always agree on things, but he can be very persuasive. We were born on the same day and he always used to ring me on our mutual birthday. Margaret and I joined him and his guests for his 70th birthday at a party in London at the 606 club in Chelsea where Doreen Lawrence was also a guest, the mother of Stephen Lawrence. Unfortunately I didn't get the opportunity to talk to her.

One of Mike's stories, which he tells often, is about a time when he was defending a young miner who had been arrested for calling the policeman 'a name'.

'What was that name?' asked Mike.

'He called me a wanker, sir,' said the bobby.

Mike made the bobby squirm by forcing him to elaborate on what a 'wanker' was.

'Someone who plays with their private parts, sir,' answered the bobby.

'Far from this being an insult, I suggest it was quite a pleasurable activity,' replied Mike, looking to the judge for affirmation. Cue embarrassed shuffles all round from the boys in blue and a sage like nod from the judge.

Leaving Don
Betty

When I first went to Northern College, if there was going to be a social event at the weekend I asked Don if he would like to come. He never once said yes. He was too busy in the ale house and he made it clear that he didn't like the new friendships I was making. Not only had I started to meet men for the first time in my life who were different to the men I had known previously, I also became friends with women who were supportive. Up to then my women neighbours had judged me as a wife and mother; how white my washing was, how well my kids were turned out for school and what I bought off the van when the travelling butcher came. I once had a set-to with a woman in the Barugh Green Club who told me, 'I'm glad you got your knee broken, it might teach you a lesson that it's not a woman's place to be on a picket line.'

One midweek night I came home from college and got into bed for an early night. I woke up when I heard Don coming in from the pub. He came upstairs, dropped his shoes on the floor, got undressed and got into bed. He wanted what he called 'bed work'. Something came over me that night, I realised for the first time that I could say no. I got out of bed, put my coat on and drove myself back to the college. The next morning the police rang the office. Don had reported me missing. I spoke to the policeman on the phone. He told me that I should come home and if I wanted he would be there while Don and I talked things over. I went. I pulled up outside of our house and decided not to go in. The daughter of a neighbour of mine said that I could sit in her house and wait for Don to show up. The policeman in an attempt to comfort me put his arm on my shoulder. I shrugged him off and told him not to touch me. Don didn't turn up. I drove back to college and decided that I must leave.

Once I had made my decision, I started to worry that perhaps I was not a proper wife and mother. I dreaded to even think about what my mother thought. Then another feeling would wash over me; I had tried and tried for years to make my marriage work, I had done what I thought I ought to do for my boys, now with the support of my fellow students and my tutors I had an opportunity for myself. I still worried about Michael. He was seriously epileptic and at the same time drinking heavily and forgetting to take his medication. I tried to persuade him to come and live with me at the college, but he wouldn't. I arranged to visit him on Wednesdays and do his washing and ironing. He kept to this for about ten weeks and then one day I went and he wasn't there. He had gone to the pub with his dad.

Don kept ringing me up. He told me that he would increase my housekeeping to £27 a week and that he would take me on a nice holiday. Even his mates started ringing me. I stayed firm. Now I had made my mind up there was no going back. Don tried every kind of threat, eventually he said he would go and see my mother and tell her how I was treating him. He knew that my mother would side with him. I told Don that if he went to my mother's house, that divorce papers would land on the doormat the very next day. He promised he wouldn't, but he did. He told her that he was having a nervous breakdown with all the stress. I got legal aid. I had to pay some money towards it. It cost me £800. It was the best £800 I ever spent.

I saw Michael occasionally if he was at my mother's house when I visited there. I still loved him a lot but the situation was hard to bear. My mother was annoyed with me and kept telling me that I should go back to my husband. This was the same lady who had gone on her knees and begged me not to marry him in the first place. She told me that Don had been round to see her and that he had cried. I told her that he would never shed anywhere near the amount of tears that he had made me cry. I told Donny. He said, 'Mum, you ought to have left him years ago.' He reassured me that I had done the right thing.

I met a lovely man called Bill at a party. He was studying trade unions. I started to do things with Bill that I'd been missing doing for years. At the drop of a hat we'd go to the Red Beck transport cafe near Wakefield for a fried breakfast in the early hours of the morning. I enjoyed drinking and staying up late talking about politics. Bill, because of his trade union background, was well versed in current affairs. He had recently separated from his wife. He was a bit younger than me, he was kind and he did his own washing and ironing. I suppose it was a bit irresponsible for a woman in her fifties with grown-up children to be behaving in this way, but I had never had the opportunity before so I enjoyed every minute.

Jean McCrindle was looking for somewhere new to live. I talked to Bill and the three of us decided to try and find somewhere together. I met a lady called Doris Clarney who told me that a little old cottage near where she lived had been empty for a while. Jean, Bill and me put in an offer and got it for a small rent. We moved in together and started to do it up.

Bob Fryer, the principal at Northern College, asked Bill and me to undertake a joint project on the history of Houndhill and the vicinity of Northern College. Houndhill is a fortified sixteenth-century farmhouse in Worsbrough. It has been the home of the Elmhirst family for more than twenty generations. Octavius Elmhirst was a lovely old gentleman, the eighth son of his father. He told us the entire history of his family. They were Royalists during the civil war and their home was captured by Parliamentarians under the command of Thomas Fairfax. Octavius's ancestor Richard Elmhirst would have been murdered on the spot by the soldiers, but Fairfax intervened saying, 'Now leave that lad alone, he went to school with me.' Octavius's older brother was Leonard Elmhirst who founded Dartington Hall, the school for progressive education in Devon. Jean McCrindle picked up on the Elmhirst project and eventually she moved on from our cottage and rented one from the Elmhirsts.

Anne and Arthur were neighbours of the Elmhirsts and good friends. Octavius's wife Gwen made beautiful scones for them and at the height of the press persecution of Arthur, when they were sneaking about in the countryside near where they lived, Octavius gave them short shrift and would shout at them, 'Get off my land and leave the lad alone will you.'

When I left Northern College I decided to apply for a place at university. I was offered places at Bradford, Leeds, Edgehill and Sheffield. I wanted to carry on with my studies, but I had to consider family as well. My mother had become increasingly dependent on me as she grew older, plus I was helping my daughter-in-law cope with three young children. I would have loved to have accepted the Bradford offer because it carried with it a social work degree, but that was a four-year course and I didn't know if I could commit to that. Edgehill was too far away for me to keep coming home. A friend called Kath who had been at Northern College with me said, 'Come to Sheffield with me Betty, we'll do social policy together.'

I started at Sheffield in October 1989. I was in my fifties, a very mature student. I wasn't as shy as I had been when I first went back to education. I had the organisational ability that I had gained during the miners' strike and I felt the confidence now to challenge people who I had once thought were cleverer than me. I saw that some of the younger students were academically bullied so I started speaking up for them. They told me, 'We love it when you are in our tutorials Betty, because you stick up for us.'

I found the university experience wearing and tiring. I was nursing my mother as well as trying to concentrate on my learning. I expected to just about pass, but I was thrilled to get a 2.2. I graduated in July 1992. I was fifty-four years old by then. It had taken a long time, but the ambition my mother had for me to achieve a cap and gown finally reached fruition. None of it would have been possible if it hadn't been for the miners' strike and my involvement with Women Against Pit Closures.

Betty's graduation day, Sheffield University, July 1992.

Losses
Anne

In January 1989 I was invited to Australia with Sammy Thompson's wife, Alma. Sammy was a staunch union man and a big ally to Arthur. He was known for making links to other unions both over here and abroad. He spent time during the strike in Australia trying to persuade the workers over there not to send coal to Britain. He was very successful and made a lot of friends in the seamans' and miners' unions. Sammy died young and Alma said she wanted to go back to Australia to thank everybody personally for their kindness and solidarity. She asked me if I would go with her. We stayed with John Maitland, the president of the union in Sydney.

While I was out there I went to visit Norma and Geoff Brown. They were from our village but had emigrated on the £10 Pom deal. They lived in a place called Balgownie near Wollongong on the coast of New South Wales. In their house they had a wall full of photographs of old Barnsley to remind them of home. I looked at the photos and it dawned on me that the one of a little girl riding her bike was me. When I turned the photo over it said on the back, 'Anne Harper riding her bike in Barugh Green.' It was the one taken by Mr Senior all those years ago when I had tried to ride away frightened. They had got it off a bloke on Barnsley market who sold old pictures and books. I went to see him when I got home and bought one for myself.

I had been in Australia less than a week when I got a phone call from Arthur. He told me that his father had died. I discussed it with Alma. She decided to stay and I decided to come home for the funeral. I had known Harold as long as I had known Arthur and I'd had a love and hate relationship with him throughout that time. He was set in his ways and I never knew where I stood with him. I don't know if he even liked me. He loved our Margaret though and it was his patience and teaching that really brought her on when Arthur and me were working all the time. Harold ought to have been somebody, he was so intelligent, but sadly he had been held back by his own life.

Arthur suffered another terrible blow the following year. Jim Parker and his wife Elaine were very close friends to Arthur and me. Jim had been in the Young Communists with Arthur as far back as the 1950s. When the strike started Arthur took Jim on as his driver and, because Jim was a big lad, he helped to watch Arthur's back.

We were inseparable for a lot of years and I count Jim and Elaine as some of the closest friends I've ever had. Jim was a great prankster. One time he and Arthur had been chatting to Margaret about her studies when she had been involved in dissection at the medical school. She had been dissecting the arm and hand and to listen to what the medical students experienced was fascinating. Jim decided to bring home a very realistic amputated plastic hand complete with blood at the end and placed it in the fridge. Jim knew that Arthur was incredibly squeamish and he remarked to him that Margaret had been bringing her work home with her just as Arthur opened the fridge.

As a group we used to go on day trips in Jim's long campervan. We visited Hardcastle Crags, Cow and Calf rocks at Ilkley and went on trips around the Dales. Jim and Elaine were lovely to me and it felt like an extended family. We went to Cornwall on holidays together and stayed with a couple in their bed and breakfast house in Redruth, using this as base as we toured around in Jim's van. I have some really lovely memories of those times.

We were all very close and Jim was so loyal. Then in 1990 Jim agreed to appear on the Roger Cook programme and talked to the *Daily Mirror*. The paper and the television programme claimed that Arthur had paid off our mortgage with money from Libya that was meant for miners struggling with hardships. It was all lies of course, just another attempt to besmirch Arthur, but for reasons known only to himself Jim fell for it and they paid him some money to tell his story. To this day I don't know why he did this after years of friendship and loyalty. All he got out of it was enough money for a new campervan.

Charlie's Angels
Anne & Betty

Betty
From the end of the strike up until 1992, 125 pits had been shut down and over 100,000 men had lost their jobs. Then, in 1992, the Tories decided to do away with British coal mining all together. There was only fifty pits left when Michael Heseltine, who had been appointed as President of the Board of Trade, announced that he was going to shut another 31. It caused a massive public outcry. After a long time wondering what we could do next, the Women Against Pit Closures started to get active again.

Anne
Our visits to Greenham Common gave us a lot of ideas. We decided to set up camps outside some of the pits that still had plenty of coal left in them but were marked for closing down. Aggie Currie from Doncaster got a four-berth caravan off a bloke and started to sleep in it at Markham Main pit. We were picketing at Grimethorpe, but we used to come home at night because we had nowhere to sleep. Norman West, who had been a councillor on the old South Yorkshire County Council before becoming an MEP, organised for us to have a Portakabin fetched to the pit yard. It was alright for getting out of the rain in but you couldn't really sleep in it. Then the bloke who had got the caravan for Aggie came to visit us and said he would get us one too.

We parked the caravan across from the manager's office. Richard Vivian who worked for welfare rights at Barnsley Council organised for us to have a telephone line installed. Then somebody fetched us an old generator to give us electric light and we had that chained to the side of the caravan. It was the noisiest generator in the world.

We were sleeping there in shifts. There was me and Betty; Derek and Maureen Stubbings, who were the caretakers at the union offices

Demonstration outside Barnsley NUM HQ. Front row (L to R) Betty, Anne, Lynn Hathaway, Brenda Nixon and Aggie Currie. Joan Machin is at the back.

Pit camp at Grimethorpe with a visitor from London, 1992.

in Sheffield; Olga Robinson, Karen Dyson and Madeleine; and Jean from the Royston group. I worked Tuesdays, Wednesdays and Thursdays at the Co-op so I stopped in the caravan in the pit yard at weekends. If I was on my own I used to take Che with me, one of our giant schnauzers.

We had a tick account at the local grocer's shop. The lasses went across for provisions and Betty used to go and settle up with them every Monday morning. There was a butcher's shop run by Mrs Fenton. Every day she came across at closing time and whatever she had left in the window she donated to us; pork pies, sausage rolls and sausages. I brought a frying pan from home and we fried the sausage on a Calor gas stove.

We had visitors coming to see us most days. Charlie Williams the old comedian came one day. He said, 'Eeeee! It's Charlie's angels.' The actress Sue Johnston came as well. We had visitors from Hebden Bridge Trades Club, Bradford Labour Party and women's groups in London. We bought a visitor's book for them to sign we were getting that many. It wasn't just a pit camp, it was more like a social centre.

The lasses set up seven pit camps altogether. There was ours at Grimethorpe, Aggie's at Markham Main, Vane Tempest pit in Durham, Seaham in Northumberland, Trentham in Staffordshire, Rufford in Nottinghamshire, and Parkside, the last working pit in Lancashire. Each of us had a navy blue umbrella with the name of a pit camp on each section. They were designed by the partner of John Hendy, who was a barrister and a good friend to us.

We sat in that camp for a year. It was an occupation and an attempt to bring attention to what the Tories were doing to what was left of the mining industry. For me though it was an important visible thing for the lads who were working at the pit, so they could see us when they went in and out of work and know that we hadn't forgotten them.

A young Irish girl called Hari Hyslop turned up one day at the pit camp. She was gentle, kind and genuinely interested in what we were doing. She studied graphic art in London and had built her own home in the wilds. She called it 'The Doll's House'. She had a cross-breed dog that she adored and a campervan. One day we sat round the brazier and talked about having a banner. Hari said that she would make one for us. She made a gorgeous hand-stitched banner in purple and green. It became known as The Grimethorpe Pit Camp Banner.

We made a plan to get down the pit and occupy it. At Grimethorpe there are two different ways down – by the cage or down a drift. We decided to go down the drift. Dot Kelly from Parkside was with me and two young women, one from Greenham Common and the other from the Socialist Workers Party. We watched the security going past with their torches and said to ourselves, 'They won't be back for another hour.' The Greenham lass knew how to cut through fencing with bolt cutters, so we followed her. She made a hole in the fence but just as we were about to go through we were surrounded by security men with their lamps shining. We started to run but one of them caught me by the coat. I was shaking like a leaf but I managed to slip my arms out of my coat and get away. There was a getaway car waiting for us which we'd organised in advance in case anything went wrong.

I phoned Mike Mansfield the next morning. I told him that I had tried to get down the pit and what had happened. He was reassuring. Later in the day I went back to the pit yard. The manager and a security guard came straight up to me. The security man pointed to the fence and said, 'We've got you now Scargill, damaging coal board property.' I told him I hadn't cut his fence. It cost them a fortune for a replacement. I was worried about being charged but nothing more came of it.

Betty
It was a Sunday and I had promised to do a shift at the pit camp. I had been working until 11 o'clock at night and when I got there Elaine Evans was sitting round the brazier. The police were racing up and down everywhere and the village was full of blue flashing lights. I asked Elaine to bring me up to speed with what was going on. She told me that the authorities knew that Anne and some of the lasses had tried to get down the pit to occupy it underground. A policeman came across to us, took out his notebook and said, 'Right, I want you

to tell me what you know.' We told him that we hadn't the faintest idea what he was talking about and that we had just been minding or own business and poking the fire.

'Look here, we have left a serious fight outside a pub in Cudworth to be here.'

Elaine looked up at him through the smoke from our brazier.

'Aye! We started that an'all.'

Occupy Parkside
Anne & Betty

Anne
Two regular visitors to our pit camp were Dot Kelly and Lesley Lomas, both Lancashire lasses. Dot told me that Parkside Colliery liked to take visitors underground to show off their pit. Dot suggested that we could pretend to be visitors and then, when we got down, refuse to come up again. The Easter holiday weekend was approaching and we heard that there was an Open Day on Good Friday. A bloke called Alec McFadden rang the pit up and asked if they had room for a party of four schoolteachers. They had, so we booked. There was Dot, Lesley, me, and Elaine Evans from our camp at Grimethorpe.

Elaine was a lovely woman, she taught at Barnsley College and was so well liked I don't think I ever heard anybody say a wrong word about her. She said to us that she believed it was gossip that had got us caught at Grimethorpe so this time our trip was to be conducted in absolute secrecy. She told me that I would have to disguise myself because I was the most easily recognisable. I darkened my hair. She also said that when we got there I was to keep my gob shut because they might recognise my voice as well.

We set off from Barnsley early doors and it was raining like hell. I left my car in Dot's garage in Bolton. I think sixteen people were booked to go down the pit that day; us four, two other women and the rest were men. We had a cup of tea during a safety briefing and a speech about the history of the pit, then they brought us some equipment and asked us to sign the book. I put Anne Harper down and made up an address in Ilkley. Elaine was elbowing me in case I put Barnsley. In the lamp room there was a young lad looking me up and down as though he knew me. To distract him, Elaine started talking to him and pushed me forward.

We got changed into our pit clothes in the manager's office. We noticed that one of the two other women had heels on. We told her that she couldn't go down a pit like that and she ought to ask for some boots. While she was out of the office we pulled extra clothes out of our holdall and put three or four layers on. We had been told that Parkside was a cold pit. We were last onto the cage; as it set off down Elaine winked at me and whispered, 'I think we have cracked it, kid!'

The pit manager was planning to go away for Easter, so the under-manager was put in charge of conducting the trip for our party. He showed us all the way round the pit and then we got on the Paddy train to come back to the pit bottom. Lesley, who was really pretty, leaned across and complained about one of the miners. 'This bugger here is nearly sitting on my knee.' We told her to grin and bear it and get his big bottle of water off him. At the pit bottom some maintenance men were waiting to go up. One of them recognised Dot, we had to tell him to shush. Then another shouted, 'Hey up Scargill, what's tha doing down here?' Everybody looked at us, including the ones who had been taking the trip round. We were shaking like leaves. I jumped up and shouted.

'We are Women Against Pit Closures. We are occupying your pit, do not try to touch us or force us into the cage. I have rung my barrister Mr Michael Mansfield and he says only the police may fetch us out.'

Everybody was quiet, nobody seemed to know what to say next. The under-manager found his voice and said, 'Don't talk so bloody silly.' I told him we were serious and we intended to occupy his pit. Then pandemonium broke out. They shouted at us and we started laughing for no reason other than we were nervous. When the cage came down, the other guests were ushered in quickly and up it went, leaving us four and the management team glaring at us by the light of their pit lamps. We sat down.

Two blokes were sent down to negotiate with us. They played good cop and bad cop. The bad cop was a rotten little shite.

'What are you going to do?' he asked. 'We won't give you anything to eat, you won't get a drink and there's no toilets down here.'

Elaine was always quick with a reply.

'I've already had a pee, can't you see how shiny my boots are?'

The little shit tried talking to Elaine but quickly realised how intelligent she was. He started to brag to her that he was a member of MENSA. She slow timed him and put him firmly in his place, and that made him madder. Meanwhile, I had laid down and chucked muck over myself. In his anger he lashed out and kicked my legs. I jumped up and said, 'Right, we will run amok in this pit.'

The four of us started to run about. They chased us. We came to a little pit-bottom office, ran in and spragged the door with a lump of wood so they couldn't get at us. It was late afternoon going into evening by now. We sat talking and laughing nervously amongst ourselves before trying to settle down as best we could on the muck on the floor.

Two different blokes were sent down to negotiate with us. They stopped outside all night. At six o'clock in the morning when the lads started coming down on the day shift, I was frozen. I rolled over on the floor and said to Lesley, 'Do you mind if I cuddle you?' The lads started to shout messages of support to us and that lifted our spirits. One great big collier handed us some snap and said, 'Here, my wife's made this for you.' He let me put his lamp inside my coat to feel its warmth.

Later in the morning the manager arrived. He wasn't best pleased because he'd had to cancel his holiday. He tried not to show it.

'Good morning ladies, I'm Mr Ramsey. Can I first say that I am very pleased to meet you all.'

Elaine was as quick as a flash.

'No you're not. We're occupying your bloody pit, how can you be pleased about that?'

He tried reasoning with us.

'Alright ladies, can I ask you then how long do you intend to be here, it's just that I've got press and TV cameras swarming all over my pit yard.'

'How long did Terry Waite do?' Elaine asked him. 'We might have a try at breaking his record.'

He didn't see the funny side of that. We told him that there are people who pay a lot of money to go to health farms where they don't get anything to eat, so if he was thinking about starving us out he would have to wait a long time because we were more then happy to shed a few pounds.

'We would appreciate a drop of water though', said Elaine, 'just for the sake of human rights.'

Mr Ramsey huffed and puffed and said he was going. Elaine shouted after him.

'You know it's customary when you visit someone in their new house to bring some flowers or a plant. If you're not bringing us any water, you'd better make it a cactus.'

As he went out we overheard him ask the two lads guarding the door what our morale had been like. They told him we had never stopped laughing.

Lesley had some clips with prongs on in her hair. We found some old hessian sacks and used the prongs on the clips to unpick them. We then sewed them together to make a big blanket. We sat eating buns that the wife of the big miner had packed for us. When we had done, Elaine suggested a game of I Spy. Lesley went first.

'I spy with my little eye, something beginning with D.'
'Dust.'
'No.'
'Dirt.'
'No.'
'Darkness.'
'No.'
'We give in.'
'No, there's no giving in.'
'Damp.'
'No.'

Easter Sunday came and we still hadn't got Lesley's I Spy and she wouldn't let us give in.

Betty
I was in charge of the phone at Grimethorpe pit camp. I spent a lot of the weekend fielding phone calls from the press. I was also in touch with some women from the camp at the pit top at Parkside. Not all of them were supportive of what Anne and the other three women had

done. There were all sorts of reasons for this. The main one was that the management there had got at the women and persuaded them that the occupation would only bring bad publicity, not just to the pit but to the women's cause. The management tried to egg these women on to persuade Anne and the others to come out. If truth be told there was also a bit of jealousy at the Parkside pit camp that might have stemmed from them not being told what was going to happen. It transpired that a lot of Easter eggs and goodwill messages never got passed on to Anne, Dot, Elaine and Lesley. I had got used to talking to journalists and knew most of their tricks by then, but trying to calm down women who hadn't been told about our plan was another matter entirely.

Anne
On the Sunday afternoon, Dot said that she wasn't feeling very well. She was shivering with the cold and I think she was missing her family. She said, 'I'm going to have to give in.' We had planned to stay down the pit for a week. Dot said that we should try to do that, but she would go up on her own. We put our heads together and agreed that because we had come down together we should go out together. We decided we would do one more night and come up on the Monday morning. That was settled on. Then we set about finishing Lesley's I Spy. After thirty-six hours she relented and told us it.
 'Debris.'
 'Debris!'
 'Yes, debris. What's left.'
 When the men came down on Monday morning we told them we were ready to go up. They made us wait while the afternoon. At the pit top they were having a Bank Holiday rally. People were cheering and singing. Mr Ramsey gave me my bag of clothes that I had left in his office and marched me straight to the pit gates. He told me that he was glad to see the back of me. The press were after me as soon as I came out of the gate. I was wise enough by then to know that they wouldn't put what I said. I came home in my pit muck, boots, helmet, lamp, the lot.

Guarding The Flame
Anne and Betty

Betty
There was a big demonstration in London planned for a Saturday. On the day before we decided to let Michael Heseltine know exactly what a pit camp was all about. We agreed to take our camp to London and set up outside the Department of Trade and Industry building. Hilary Wainwright was our contact in London. We persuaded a bloke with a battered van to drive us down in the early hours of the morning. Brenda Nixon went with us, as did Aggie Currie and Lynn Hathaway. We took the brazier and some foreign coal that we knew burnt with a lot of smoke, a tent, our visitor's book and some old milk crates to sit on. We set up camp next to the front door, got the brazier going, set the tent up and then we put the kettle on. Aggie had some posters so we stuck them with spray glue onto the glass doors and the pillars at the side.

The smoke started billowing in no time. A bobby came round the corner, looked at us and then went back round the corner. Five minutes later he came back with a mate. They both looked at us and then went off again. Finally he came back with a third policeman; they still didn't have a clue what to say or do, but they walked up to us and stood gawping. The smoke got thicker and blacker and it was blowing about on the breeze. Somebody came out and had a word with the bobbies. They asked us to put out our fire because the smoke was blowing through the front door. We started singing. We sang all the verses of 'Women of the Working Class'. By now a fair-sized crowd had formed and Hilary Wainwright was running up and down with her collection bucket shouting 'Support the miners' wives'.

The fire brigade was sent for. As soon as they pulled up, Anne went running over to them. She told the driver that we were an official picket and if they were to turn water on to our brazier they would be crossing a picket line. The driver asked who we were. As soon as Anne told him we were Women Against Pit Closures and that we were protesting against Heseltine's plan to shut more pits, the fire brigade decided to stay in their vehicle. The two policemen then decided to chuck a red bucket filled with sand over the brazier. We all gathered round and put our arms across it to guard the flame. We sang 'We Shall Not Be Moved'. It was worse than being tear gassed. The smoke choked us and what with the spray glue still on our hands we were soon black bright with coal muck. The policemen were coughing and rubbing their eyes too.

Brenda Nixon got a long length of chain out that she'd brought with her. Her and Anne chained themselves together and wrapped the chain round the door handle. The police asked the fire brigade if they had chain cutters. They had, but told the police they didn't want to use them. The police commandeered them and tried to cut the chains. They found the cutters were blunt, so called for another fire engine. In the meantime Aggie was appealing to the crowd to sign our visitor's book, so they were queuing up to write their names down. Word must have gone down the road to parliament. Harry Barnes, the MP for North Derbyshire, came up to see us and say hello. He was the only MP who did. We told him that we'd like to see Mr Heseltine when he had a minute. He laughed. The police weren't laughing by now. The second fire engine came with some sharper chain cutters. The firemen still refused to use them, so the police set about our chains. We were giggling because what the silly buggers didn't realise was we hadn't been able to lock them because we had forgotten the keys to the padlocks, so they just had them wrapped round themselves. Of course Anne was milking it for all it was worth shouting, 'You're hurting me!' and 'Didn't your mother tell you not to run about with sharp scissors?'

When they had done cutting the chains we sat down round our brazier. Inspector Firth of the Metropolitan Police appeared on the scene. He asked us politely to put our fire out. We told him that it wouldn't be a pit camp without a brazier and a lovely fire burning. We also told him that we planned to sleep there that night and would need to keep warm. He handed us each a letter. We will never know what that letters said because we threw them straight on the fire. He tried his best to reason with us. He told us that he was willing to have us taken to Speakers' Corner where we could continue our protest. We told him that we couldn't go without our brazier. He said he was willing to transport that over there as well. We told him our protest concerned Heseltine and until he came out to talk to us we wouldn't be going anywhere.

'I have to tell you now that your actions could lead to you being arrested.'

'Well that's entirely up to you love.'

'I am obliged by law to keep a clear passage for our Lords to attend Parliament.'

'It's Friday love, they've all gone home,' I told him.

He waited a moment or two and then barked at us. 'Move!'

Out of nowhere the arrest wagon turned up. We started screaming that we wanted to be arrested only by female officers. It took another ten minutes for them to arrive. Aggie chucked a bit more coal onto the brazier. Finally they loaded us into the wagon in front of the TV cameras. As we were being driven away we saw some serious-faced men in suits peeling our posters off the walls and windows. They were using fire extinguishers to put out our fire which caused even more smoke to billow up. Aggie was always quick with a line.

'Jammy bugger Heseltine, he'd always wanted smoked glass windows and now he's got them for nowt.'

We got to the police station at dinner time. I think the day shift were ready for knocking off and the afternoon shift were about to start. The desk sergeant was eager to get us booked in. We sat on a long wooden bench opposite his desk. We were covered in coal muck and stunk of smoke. We were laughing and giggling like a gang of kids on bonfire night. Policemen were bringing people they had arrested in through the door and they were looking at us as though to say, 'What the hell have we come to here?'

We knew from previous experience that the police have to write down everything they take off you at the station, so we had filled our bags with stuff. I think they counted out nineteen odd earrings from Aggie's handbag and I had a plastic carrier with all sorts of rubbish in it, from tab ends to bits of paper. It was then they decided that they didn't have enough room in the cells, so they were going

Protesting outside Tory HQ with Dot Kelly, Mary Smith and Aggie Currie.

Anne arrested for demonstrating against pit closures outside the Department of Trade and Industry, February 1993.

to send Anne to another police station. She got angry with the desk sergeant.

'Look here,' she told him. 'Tomorrow there is going to be a massive march through this city. If you don't want 10,000 women laying siege to your police station you want to buck your ideas up a bit.'

They got fed up of dealing with us and put us all in the same cell. I was the first to be called out by the sergeant.

'If you promise to keep the peace I will let you out now with a caution.'

I told him that I was already keeping the peace, my demonstration was perfectly peaceful. I had just been sitting round a brazier minding my own business. He said 'Give me strength' under his breath and told me to wait back in the cell while he did some paperwork. He then said I could go. I told the other lasses not to accept a caution.

We got let out without charge. I came out first. Ken Livingstone was waiting for us with a big box of chocolates. He told us he knew a vicar who said it was alright for us to put our tent up in the church grounds. I told him he must be joking, we wanted a good bath and a bed for the night. As it turned out Anne went to stay with Arthur in his flat at the Barbican and the rest of us were invited out by the fire brigade's union to a meal in a Greek restaurant. We turned up still in our muck.

Anne

The next morning we marched to Hyde Park, thousands of us. It was a sight to see; there were more mothers pushing prams and dads with toddlers on their shoulders than I had ever seen. Of course it was political and some of our best MP's were there, Tony Benn and Dennis Skinner, but in the main it was a lovely family march. It was left to me to welcome everybody. When I looked from the platform into the park I could see working-class people with their banners and children holding up cards with the names of all the 31 pits on the list for closing down. Old men on walking sticks were there, some of them wearing medals from the war, some carrying placards that said 'Sack Major not Miners', but mainly it was miners' wives from across all the coalfields.

Betty
A young Diane Abbott gave a rousing speech. She echoed our own slogan when she started.

'I don't want five pits saving, I don't want ten or even twenty to be saved, I want all 31 pits saving.'

She talked about the madness of what the government were doing in threatening the livelihoods of 100,000 families and said there could be no genuine economic case for what was happening. She got a loud cheer when she said that Arthur Scargill had been vilified by the government, the TV and the press at the time of the strike, but it was now obvious to everyone that he had been right with his predictions of what was going to happen.

'These pit closures are about class politics and vindictiveness, the Tories final campaign to destroy the unions as revenge against the miners for daring to take on Thatcher.'

Arthur spoke well that day. He argued passionately about the devastating affects that further pit closures would have on the lives of hundreds of thousands of families. 'There comes a time when marching up and down with red noses and balloons isn't enough, there comes a time when the talking has to stop and the strikes start.'

He told the gathering that there could be no justification whatsoever for subsidising the nuclear power industry and then turning round to say that coal cannot compete. He reminded them that if the coal industry was given the same sort of subsidy as the nuclear industry got, they would be able to give coal away free of charge, pay the hauliers to deliver it, give £10 apiece to the customers for receiving it and still turn a profit. He turned on the government for importing cheap coal, that we neither wanted nor needed, especially the importation of coal from countries like Colombia where children as young as five were working at the mines. He said it was the economics of the mad house. He also paid tribute to the Women Against Pit Closures movement.

'Don't for one minute believe that this is just their struggle. It's also about a fight to save our health service, our education, local government and social services. Don't be under any illusions. If coalminers suffer, families suffer and ultimately we all suffer.'

Arthur finished his speech with a sentence that must have made everybody think and shudder.

'I don't believe in looking back, except to learn a lesson from history. If the TUC and the Labour Party had got behind us in the strike we wouldn't be where we are now.'

Arthur has never been one for reminding people what would happen in the coal-mining regions if the strike failed. I think that day in London was probably the nearest he ever came to saying, 'I told you so.'

When I got home my mother came to see me.

'I turn my television on for the evening news and I see my daughter being put into a Black Maria, what am I supposed to tell the neighbours?'

I told her that I couldn't warn her what might happen because it was a secret mission. In the end she laughed, she was getting well used to my antics by then.

Anne

We didn't get to see Heseltine in London, but after we got home we discovered that he was coming to Doncaster to open an engineering factory. A protest had been organised by the Socialist Workers Party and the usual suspects. Brenda Nixon and Aggie roped Betty and me in and introduced us to a tall woman from Upton who they knew. She was an expert in making flour bombs. We stopped on the way to Doncaster at a canteen and the woman from Upton showed us how to make them.

The factory had two gates, top and bottom. We stood at the top gate. A policeman came up to me and told me out of the corner of his mouth that we were at the wrong gate and that Heseltine would be coming in at the bottom. We got down to the gate just as they were opening it to let Heseltine's car in. We ran in after him and booed him as he got out of his car. It turned out that the tall woman from Upton was just as good at chucking flour bombs as she was at making them. She threw one at a wall and as it burst it sent flour all over Heseltine's head. Then somebody chucked some eggs at him – if we'd had a drop of milk we'd have turned him into a Yorkshire pudding. Some of the dafter ones started chucking stones. I ended getting my head cut that day after one of the younger end hit me with his stone. Heseltine didn't stay long. Somebody had dusted the flour off him, but he still had a line of it under his long hair when he got back in his car.

With Heseltine making a quick getaway, there was a lovely spread going begging. To their credit, the factory owners invited the protestors in to eat the buffet. We all tucked in. Brenda Nixon noticed a brass plaque on the wall with curtains on a frame round it. It was the one that Heseltine had unveiled in the few minutes he was there. Brenda made a big to-do of drawing the curtains.

International Aid
Anne & Betty

Anne

The Grimethorpe pit camp shut when they closed the pit in May 1993. I watched them chucking all sorts of stuff into skips. I remembered a time when I had been with Arthur as he welcomed some Cuban miners' representatives. They talked about a lack of equipment. It seemed a shame to let all the stuff they were throwing out at Grimethorpe go to waste. I started washing the safety helmets and putting them to one side. I met some people from William Sugden's who made industrial clothing, so I arranged a deal with them to supply some overalls and trousers.

Betty

We launched an appeal and Frank Watters agreed to organise it. We collected toothpaste and toothbrushes, soap and basic medicines like painkillers. Some time after, we were invited to visit Cuba to meet the people who had benefited from our campaign. We arrived at a small mining community. The people in the village had put the items we had sent on display for everybody to see before they were distributed. While we were there we adopted a hospital in Havana, specifically the children's heart unit there. We were able to pay for some medical supplies and stethoscopes. Once the children have undergone their surgeries, they have a period of convalescence with their mothers. The set-up made a big impression on me. Every child's bed had a rocking chair next to it. This enabled mothers to sit and nurse their children to help them with their recovery.

When I was trying to decide what to do for my second year dissertation at Sheffield, Bill's daughter Diane went as a volunteer worker to the Romanian orphanages with The Hesley Foundation. She talked to me about it. I decided that I would write something about childcare in Romania pre- and post-revolution and I would start by visiting the orphanage at Tatari. I had seen reports from there on the television and wanted to experience it for myself. I went on a trip arranged by the same foundation that had organised Diane's trip. The Hesley Foundation was established to raise the profile of child-related issues throughout the world and research into childcare and education.

At my first meeting with the foundation I was told that they planned a convoy but at present they were short of vehicles. I approached the manager of the transport division at Empire Stores. He was very supportive and agreed to lend me one of the company delivery vans. He then went further and suggested that it shouldn't go empty. The company provided mattresses and outfits for every child in the orphanage.

The stipulation of insurance was that I must drive along with a nominated co-driver. I had never driven outside of Britain before, let alone a big van, and I had no idea how I would cope driving on the right-hand side but I was determined to give it a go. It was a long journey. When we finally arrived, I flopped into bed in the hotel that was to be our base for the next fortnight.

The next day at the orphanage I was asked whether I would be prepared to work in what they called 'the worst room'. By that they meant work with the disabled and special needs kids. I told them I was willing to work anywhere that might make a difference for the children. I don't know how anyone could be prepared for the conditions I encountered. It was totally different to what I had experienced while training as an orthopaedic nurse back in the 1950s. The children there needed care of course, but what struck me immediately was that they needed physical contact and love.

They had one residential doctor. I was told he had been sent there as a punishment for failing his medical exams. His only interest it seemed to me was watching endless television. At one point I had to rouse him and insist that he turn his telly off and come to visit the children.

I am glad that I made the trip to the orphanage, but the whole time I was there I was filled with mixed emotions. I loved giving out plenty of hugs and smiles, while at the same time realising it wasn't enough. I was also acutely aware that the material comforts and gifts we had taken weren't always going to where they should go. One day a big lad called Josef came to me. He took my hand and pointed to his shoes and said, 'Adidas.' The tops of his shoes were leaving the soles. In one of the containers we had transported there was a gift from the British Shoe Corporation. There were more than enough pairs of shoes for everybody to have some. I approached the woman in charge. I told her that Josef needed some new shoes.

'But Betty, we have no shoes for him.'

My blood boiled.

'Right, give me the key to the container and send the children ten at a time, they will all have new shoes today.'

It was as difficult to deal with the carers there as anything else. The pre-revolution ideas were ingrained in them, which meant that the needs of the infirm or those with special needs were often overlooked. Josef was always going to be the last in line.

We Will Not Be Budged
Anne

After nearly all the pits had been shut, the government and private mining companies like Budge decided to start open-cast mining in the very districts where thousands of jobs had been lost. It was insult to injury. The mining communities had lost all their heart and now they were going to have to put up with years of muck, pollution and noise without the jobs. Steve Parry who had been active in the students' union and Mick Appleyard who was on the union at Sharlston pit put their heads together to come up with a protest.

Michael Heseltine was the deputy prime minister to John Major at the time. He spent his weekends at his mansion, Thenford House in Northamptonshire. It is said that the view from his balcony is one of the most beautiful views in the whole of England. Steve and Mick decided to put a planning application in to open-cast Heseltine's grounds in front of the house, partly as a protest to what was happening in former pit villages, but also to see if he himself would protest against open-casting. Steve and Mick were deadly serious abut their application; they wanted to test for the depth of any coal deposits on Heseltine's land, the calorific value of the coal and the sulphur content. They had geological maps and all sorts. Mick's wife, Mary, got dressed up in her tweeds and went down to Thenford to do a recce. She took some field glasses to have a peer over Heseltine's wall. The house he lives in is a Grade I listed building and four times a year he opens his private woodlands to the public.

One morning Steve and Mick assembled us for a mission to dig up the garden to test for coal. There were a few ex-colliers, some students and environmental campaigners. A parade of us walked through the village in the early hours as we made our way towards the big house. Mick and some of the others recited Kipling's poem, 'A Smuggler's Song'.

> If you wake at midnight, and hear a horse's feet
> Don't go drawing back the blind, or looking in the street,
> Them that ask no questions isn't told a lie
> Watch the wall, my darling, while the Gentlemen go by.

When we got to the boundary wall round Heseltine's property I couldn't climb it so Mick had to chuck me over. At five o'clock in the morning an electric klaxon like a pit buzzer was sounded and we set off working. We marked an area out and knocked in poles. We taped it round, set out orange flags and put up a sign that said 'Heseltine Open-Cast Mining'. Then the lads set about the grass with pick and shovel. It wasn't long before the police came to see what we were doing. As the sun came up, Heseltine himself appeared on the balcony in his pyjamas with a lavender-coloured dressing gown wrapped round him. He shouted to the police, 'I thought we had laws on trespassing, clear them off.' There were only about eight policemen there and to be fair to them they were friendly. They said to Steve Parry, 'Come on now, you've had plenty of publicity, call it a day now and get yourselves out of this county.' We came in over the wall and went out by the front gate.

We did another protest in the grounds at the Duke of Devonshire's home, Chatsworth House in Derbyshire. He wanted to open-cast mine on part of his estate. We went to his land in protest. It was snowing when we got there. We had a great big lorry with speakers on it and we played tape recordings of the noise that machinery and jackhammers make. The Duke of Devonshire sat on some sort of government quango that monitored the environment. He had been tipped-off that we were coming and was ready for us. He had told his cooks to make some pans full of stew and the staff put a big spread on. One of the protestors kicked one of the stew pans over into the snow but the duke behaved like an old-fashioned diplomat. He came out to see us and fetched another silver tureen full of hot consommé soup with sherry in it. A butler came out with a tray of brandy inviting everybody to a drink. I spoke to the duke for a long time. He was dead straight with me. He admitted he was in it for the money. He said that if he was in my position he might consider protesting as well. I have a copy of *The Times* with his obituary in it.

They mention that he thought I was a charming woman. I don't fall for that sort of flannel, but I couldn't get cross with him. Apart from Octavius Elmhirst, he was the only toff I came across who I liked.

At Doe Hill in Derbyshire there was a massive open-cast mine. I went with Mick Appleyard and Paul Hardman. We crept through the early morning mist up to the site. In all of my years on picket lines and being involved in direct action, that was the day when I became truly frightened when I saw what was going on. The campaign had attracted some aggressive and ill-disciplined young people who seemed intent on doing damage. They were setting fire to machinery and pushing equipment down into the quarry. I said to Mick, 'I don't want to be here.' I knew when and where to draw the line; making mischief and peaceful protest was one thing, but this was very different. I didn't want to be involved with that sort of behaviour so we left.

My last protest against open-casting was when we tried to occupy the grounds at the home of Richard Budge. Budge had bought up most of the last handful of British coal mines and his company RJB Mining was starting to rip up the countryside. I got arrested twice that day. The first time I'd only just nicely arrived and I was taken to the police station after I tried to walk past a police line. They let me out at dinner time and I went back to the protest. I saw the police roughing up a woman so I tried to intervene and they arrested me again. A few days later I was served with an injunction at work at the Co-op. It said that I was banned from going anywhere near a coal mine, an open-cast mine or any land belonging to RJB Mining. Steve Parry got an injunction as well. I haven't seen hide nor hair of him since.

The campaign against open-casting started breaking up after that. A fair few of the hot-headed youngsters were thrown in jail, the older men and women from London who had been with us since the miners' strike joined up with various other environmental groups. Now that the bother started coming to my doorstep at work as well as at home, I had to take a serious look at where I was going.

I wanted to be involved with something that wasn't as destructive as that had become but I still wanted to help folk. I got to know how serious the problem of homelessness was in Barnsley from a man called Peter Mulrooney. Some people at Athersley Church told me about a church hall on Doncaster Road where the homeless could get a hot meal. I asked if I could volunteer.

I started on a Monday just before Christmas. On my first day we had forty-seven clients. They had a cooked breakfast of bacon, egg and tomato and a bag with some fruit and biscuits in it to see them through the day. My first job was filling the bags. I progressed to washing up and eventually I did the cooking. On Thursdays and Fridays we did dinners. When we moved from Doncaster Road Church Hall to a new place opposite Morrisons supermarket I was frying eighty eggs every morning. By the time I left I was preparing food for more than 140 people. I was giving food and clothes to kids who had been thrown out by their parents. That would never have happened at one time in our village, somebody would have taken them in.

When I was a girl, a tramp used to pass by our house on a Wednesday morning on his way from Huddersfield. My mother used to leave tea and toast out for him when she knew he was on his way. Those old tramps were the only homeless people I knew in them days. The homeless now were nothing like the old tramps of yesteryear, they were mostly young lads and lasses with all their lives in front of them.

The problem now is that as soon as people get on the streets they get sucked up into the drug culture. You shouldn't have to say it but I can remember Arthur and other speakers at the time of the miners' strike saying that the government was going to cause all sorts of social problems by robbing people of work and that came true in less than a generation. A lot of these kids on the street were the children of good families whose dads and grandads had never been out of work till the pits started closing.

Always Leave A Hat On The Sideboard
Betty

In her old age, my mother decided to move back to West Melton. She moved into a council bungalow there. It was a sentimental decision; I think she wanted to die in the village that she had grown up in. Her bedroom window faced on to the church hall. No matter what time of day or night it was, if someone had left a light on in the hall, she would phone the vicar to tell him.

It took her a long time, but in her last years she mellowed to the things that I did. For years, my mother thought that I wasn't fit to be a wife and mother and said I was neglecting my husband and children, but eventually she did come round and admit that I was doing something worthwhile. I think that deep down she became proud of me, but she would never have told me that. When I graduated on 9th June 1992 I finally achieved the ambition she'd had for me as a girl.

At the age of 85 she decided she wanted to visit the pit camp in Grimethorpe. I picked her up and drove her there. I can see her now, sitting outside the door of our caravan in front of the brazier with a hat on and her handbag tucked under her arm. She had a thing about hats. One of the first things she told me when I got my first house was 'Always leave a hat on the sideboard near to the front door'. Her theory was that if anybody came visiting who you didn't want in, you could always put your hat on and tell them you were just about to go out. The day my mother came to Grimethorpe happened to be the day that Charlie Williams visited. She adored him and he really tickled her that afternoon. Strange as it seems that proved to be the start of a thawing in her attitude to me. I really felt for the first time in my life she was starting to understand me.

Mother passed away at the age of 87 in 1994. At the funeral, the vicar mentioned that only a few days ago she had phoned him in the middle of the night to say that someone had left the light on in the church hall and it was wasting electricity.

Falls
Anne

George Buckley, the MP for Hemsworth, died while he was still young. Everybody thought that Ken Capstick would get the job. He was the miners' candidate and Hemsworth was still a big mining constituency, so it seemed obvious. The Labour Party in London had a different idea and asked Roy Hattersley to look at finding a moderate. Derek Enright, a former schoolteacher and MEP, got the job. When Tony Blair changed Clause IV of the Labour Party constitution to remove the idea of common ownership, it was the straw that broke the camel's back for Arthur. He left Labour and formed the Socialist Labour Party.

Arthur had been a Labour Party member for most of his adult life. As a young man, he had been a member of the Young Communists. I don't know what happened exactly but I know he was asked to leave. A bloke called Bob Wilkinson from over Leeds way came to the door. I was bathing our Margaret in a little white bath in front of the fire. I don't know what was said but I think that Bob Wilkinson chucked him out of the party that night. What I know for certain is that Arthur didn't renew his card. Harold wasn't best pleased because he'd been a member of the party all of his life.

Derek Enright didn't last long as an MP, he became poorly with cancer and he died young as well. Arthur wanted me to stand at the Hemsworth by-election for his Socialist Labour Party. I really didn't want to do it, but Arthur tried to persuade me. In the end I put my foot down and said no. It might have been the first time I ever said no to him about anything and it was like a hand came off my shoulders. In the end Brenda Nixon, who had been with us at the pit camps, put up for Socialist Labour and she did well, at least she didn't lose the deposit. John Trickett won it for Labour, of course. The comedian Mark Thomas, who had put up as an independent candidate, joked that if they'd had a plate of tripe with a red rosette on it, it would have won. Brenda finished fourth only just behind the Liberal and the Tory.

Shortly afterwards there was a by-election for Barnsley Council in our ward at Worsbrough. Arthur was at me again to put up. I said no again because Jimmy Rae was the Labour candidate and I liked him. He lived at the back of us and I used to see him most days. It was Jimmy who had got me a pair of pit boots during the strike and I always walked beside him when we were picketing. Arthur persuaded me against my better judgement and I let myself be put forward as the Socialist Labour candidate. I finished second behind Jimmy Rae. I'm glad I finished second for two reasons; first because I really liked Jimmy, and second because I knew if I won I'd have had Arthur at the back of me, trying to influence.

After the strike we had moved from Yews Lane to a house at Houndhill. I felt even more isolated and lonely there. The house was bigger and emptier. I didn't see much of Arthur. When I did see him, I used to ask, 'Are you coming home tonight?' At first he would tell me straight whether he was or he wasn't; he usually had something to do, so most of the time he wasn't coming home. Then as time went by he wouldn't tell me whether he was or he wasn't, he'd just shrug his shoulders and say 'I don't know' in that way that tells you somebody can't even be bothered to answer your question.

One day he asked me to sit down with him and he made me a cup of tea, which was a bit of a rarity. He said, 'I think we have come to the end of the road.' I had known in my heart that he hadn't wanted me for a while, but it still came as a shock. When I got over the shock I started to feel stupid and naive and think to myself, 'Have I bloody wasted all these years?'

My mam and dad were getting older. I visited them to help out where I could. My dad fell and broke his knee. They sent for me to come out of work to talk to him because he was lying in pain but refusing to be taken to hospital. There was an ambulance drivers' strike at the time and the police had called for a green army ambulance to take him. When I got there he was shouting and bawling.

'I am not going to hospital in a scab ambulance.'

I tried to calm him down. The police offered to take him in one of their vans. What with the pain he was in and the time that had passed, he started shouting even more.

'That's just as bad, I'm not going with them either. They don't call me bloody Mick Smith!'

He was reeling off the names of all who had scabbed in every strike since 1926. I tried again to get him to go in the army ambulance. He looked me straight in the eye.

'Anne, I am not a scab and I'm not going to start being one at my age. I will not go in that bloody contraption, it looks like Ned Locker's threshing machine.'

He was witty even when he was in agony. I found myself remembering when Jonathan Dimbleby had come to see him. At one of the miners' galas Jonathan told Arthur that he would like to interview some of the old union men, Arthur suggested my dad. Jonathan went off to find him and came back shaking his head.

'I can barely understand a word that he is saying, we would have to use subtitles.'

A few days before my dad fell I had been helping out on the picket line for the ambulance men. I went to them and told them what had happened to my dad and that he wouldn't go to hospital in a scab ambulance. Mr Foster the union man said, 'Don't worry Anne, we can make an exception for Elliott Harper, we'll go and get him.'

My dad never walked right after he broke his knee. He tried to carry on working on his land, he loved his garden so much he was gardening on his hands and knees like a collier down the pit, but even that was getting too much for him. I went to see my mam and dad one Friday and I saw some money on the kitchen table. When I asked what it was doing there, my dad said that Clive Cawthrow had offered him £100 for his land and he had taken it. My dad thought £100 was a lot of money.

Clive Cawthrow went to school with me. He emigrated to Australia in search of his fortune and when he didn't find it he came back to Barnsley. There was a house stood empty on Higham Common Road and when Clive got back from Australia he went to live there like a squatter. My dad still had a piece of land near that house with some greenhouses on it. Clive started being nice to my parents; my mother was nearly ninety at the time and my dad was 86. Clive spent hours with them, being as nice as pie and puffing them up.

I went straight round to Cawthrow's and gave him the money back. He threw it at me and said he wouldn't take it. He told me that he had shaken hands with my dad and made a gentleman's agreement to buy the land. I was livid. I fetched the money back to my mam's and asked her if she had the deeds for the land. The deeds were upstairs so I took them and the £100 and put them safe. I phoned Mike Mansfield and told him what had happened. He laughed and said, 'How long has your father been a gentleman?'

I told Cawthrow that I had been in touch with my solicitor but he wouldn't listen. He started making a boundary round some land at the back of the Co-op and then fenced off my dad's land. It ended up in court at Sheffield. Cawthrow was a cocky bugger who thought he could easily win and decided to conduct his own defence. He made a right mess of it and had the land taken off him. Cawthrow had a spell as Mayor of Barnsley but resigned in October 1995 after being accused of defrauding the DHSS of £653 – stating 'health reasons'. He appeared in court later that year.

My dad died before he knew the land Cawthrow tried to pinch was still his own. He was 87. I felt sad for him. He had worshipped that bit of land all his life, raised animals on it, grown food and nantled there since he was a young man.

My mam had always been argumentative. She loved calling folk and she got worse after my dad died. He used to say to her, 'Harriet, if thy lived in a forest, thy would fall out with the trees.' She could be nasty with me as well. She used to say that I was more interested in helping Arthur's dad Harold than I was in helping her.

My mam had a bad fall. I always say that if she hadn't fallen, she'd still be with us. They took her to Mount Vernon hospital. I'd been on holiday but went to see her as soon as I got back. The first thing she said was, 'Anne bring me a drink of water will you.' They had been refusing to let her drink much water. I fetched her some and the doctor played hell up. I stood my corner and let her drink some.

Our Margaret got her a place at Gawber Hospice. She passed away not long after she got there.

I saw the doctor who I rowed with once or twice after. He looked straight through me, so I looked straight through him as well.

Socialist Christian
Anne & Betty

Anne
My work had changed a lot since I first went to the Co-op. When electronic calculators and computers started coming in the 1970s, the comptometers were phased out. Comptometers were cumbersome clumsy machines, a bit like old-fashioned typewriters were to word processors. I retrained to deal with stolen and bounced cheques and worked there until the Co-op decided they were going to shut the Barnsley offices. We were made redundant and then the bosses approached me and three others to see if we would go to Rochdale to train some new people there. I drove over to Rochdale every day for about three months. Then they decided that they weren't going to shut the Barnsley office after all. They said that if I repaid my redundancy money then I could have a job back at Barnsley.

I told Arthur.

'They can't make you pay redundancy money back,' he said.

'What if they sack me?'

'They can't sack you.'

The other three women decided to give their redundancy money back and got new jobs at Barnsley. I pleaded with Carol my mate not to do that, but she was frightened that they would find a way to get shut of her if she didn't. And that's what they tried to do with me. I was friendly with one of the bosses' secretaries, she tipped me off.

'They're after you Anne. They're planning to get rid of you next Wednesday.'

Arthur talked to John Hendy QC, one of his barrister mates in London. John called me and introduced me to a young lawyer called Damian Brown. Damian decided to challenge the decision to make me redundant in the first place. He argued that the selection procedure was defective. On the Tuesday there was a hearing in

Leeds. The Co-op put somebody in front of the judge who said that I wasn't wanted back at Barnsley because I was disruptive and didn't get on with my colleagues, which was a pack of lies. I'd never heard any of that before. After that first hearing Damian said to me, 'Don't worry, they haven't a leg to stand on.' In the end I kept my redundancy money and I got my job back at Barnsley. I stayed at the Co-op until I became a pensioner.

Betty
I retired from work at Empire Stores in 1999. I was already a pensioner by that time so it made sense to take my redundancy when they offered it. I had tried once before for redundancy and they turned me down. This time I thought I deserved it.

I hadn't been retired for long when I started to get bored. I had worked hard all of my life and for the previous few years I had been caring for Bill as his health declined. He was on dialysis by then. It sounds selfish but I was a reluctant carer, I suppose it was because I'd done more than my fair share of it over the years. Now I wanted something for myself.

When Michael was diagnosed with epilepsy in 1962 I looked after him right through to 1988, by which time his drinking was a major concern. It got to the stage where I couldn't handle him anymore. I saw him occasionally at my mother's after that. Michael died at the age of 38. He had one last big seizure in the living room at home. By the time his dad came in from the kitchen he was gone. Michael was my first born. When he was a boy my sense of caring was strong, but when he became a man I struggled. When Michael's drinking was out of control I sought advice from the GP. I needed to know what I could do to ensure that Michael was taking his medication. The doctor told me that at the end of the day Michael knew what he had to do and the consequences of his heavy drinking.

Michael would not work with me. He just wanted to be in the pub all the time. I still feel guilt about what happened, but I had a life to live as well. I think back to the time when I finally broke free from my marriage and all that entailed. Don's mates used to say, 'Do you know what you are doing? He is in tears all the time.' I got to the stage where I used to say, 'Tough! I am sitting in the pub now, like he was when I was in tears.'

When Bill developed diabetes, I cared for him at Woodbine Cottage, the little place we got together when I was still at college. I started to feel a need to go to church. I don't know how it came over me, but I felt a need to find something or at least somewhere to be. I'd been a Sunday school teacher when I was fifteen, but since my wedding I hadn't been much to church. I tried a Methodist chapel at Mapplewell but stopped going after a few weeks because I didn't find anything. I then started going to Pilley Methodist Chapel just up the hill from where I lived. It's a very small chapel, the type where a lot of lay preachers come to lead the service. I made a lot of friends there and I found that I was able to give positive support to the chapel in return.

One of the ladies, Norma, also went to the Salvation Army. We became close and I used to take her for days out in my car. One day I dropped her off at the Salvation Army in Hoyland Common. Before I could drive away a woman called Barbara Sabin came out and asked me if I would like to join them. I liked Barbara immediately. I joined there and then. They did luncheon clubs on Sundays and I became a regular.

I still carried on going to the Methodist chapel. One Sunday a young minister came. Before he started he said he would like us to think of a particular group or person who we ought to pray for. I said 'Homeless people'. A woman's voice behind me said, loud enough for all to hear, 'A lot of them are homeless because they want to be.' I couldn't believe I was hearing that inside a Christian building. I knew that I had to move on. From that moment I committed myself to the Salvation Army. I became an adherent, though I don't wear the uniform. The army encourages its soldiers to live an alcohol-free life and I still like a drink. I'm there when I am needed though and I help out with the luncheon group, the over sixties, and I have worked with special needs groups. My faith has held me up over more recent years. Now when I find myself in a situation I ask myself, 'What would Jesus do?'

Anne

I first started going to church with my mother who took me to St Thomas's in Gawber. I was confirmed and married to Arthur there, my mother and father are buried there, and I suppose when my time comes I will be too. I occasionally went while I was married, but when Arthur and me divorced I started going again.

It was Father Rodney Marshall and his wife Marilyn who encouraged me back to the fold. Rodney had been on the picket lines with us. He was a socialist Christian and believed in putting others before himself. He arrived in Goldthorpe from Manchester just before the strike. He understood what it was about and did more to help people in the struggle than anybody. He was golden. I went to his church St Helen's at Athersley until he retired, at which point I moved back to Gawber. I came full circle. I even bumped into my first boyfriend who I had met at that church just after the war. It was a pleasant surprise to find that Paul was still involved in church life and singing in the choir going on for seventy years later. I like going to church, I find friendship and company there. I can't bear the thought of loneliness and as I've got older that comes over me.

Rent A Mob, Rent A Gob
Betty

Two women came to interview us at a Women Against Pit Closures meeting in Stoke-on-Trent. During the conversation they mentioned that there might be an opportunity for some women to go to a big international conference in Mumbai. The World Social Forum is an attempt to bring voluntary groups, humanitarian activists and social groups together on an international scale to find alternative answers to the world's problems. It had started in Brazil a few years before and this was the first time it was going to be in India. All the lasses that were at the meeting in Stoke were enthusiastic as soon as it was mentioned, but our faces dropped when we realised that we had to raise our own funds.

Anne and I met up with Hilary Wainwright and told her we'd like to go. Hilary found some money in a trust that she knew of to get us started. She also commissioned me to write a piece for *Red Pepper* magazine. Both Anne and I were asked to make speeches at the conference; Anne to talk about the affects the miners' strike had on coal-mining villages, and I was down to talk about technology at call centres, drawing on my experience at Empire Stores as the team leader of thirty-odd workers taking catalogue orders over the phone.

Mumbai was a culture shock to us. We saw poverty like we had never seen before; folk begging with babies on their arms and workers living on the pavement trying to make a few coppers a day. The conference was in a series of huge marquee tents that had been erected on fields. We travelled there each day by taxi from our hotel. On the first day we noticed a lot of people on the grass verge between the lanes on the dual carriageway and saw them again on the way back. The next morning when we drove past the penny dropped; they were living there.

After a few days we began to find the whole event disconcerting. We heard stories at the conference about people in struggle at every meeting we went to, yet when we looked round all we saw was delegates tip-tapping on their laptops and walking about with their thumbs on the latest mobile phones. They seemed to be just talking whereas Anne and I were used to doing something; neither of us are any good at talking shop.

The food didn't suit as either. The cooking was done in big pots in one of the tents with flies swarming about and it didn't look too appetising. We had taken some tea bags with us and I found a shop that sold Laughing Cow processed cheese, so I lived for nearly a week on that with crackers. Anne found a bloke on the market selling grapes. She picked a pair of scissors up off his stall and snipped some off the bunch. Every time we passed him after that he waved his grapes and scissors at her.

At one of the seminars we heard about a nearby Coca Cola plant that was drawing all the fresh water and not leaving any for the local people to drink. I said to Anne, 'Why are they just talking about this? We ought to be outside the factory gates picketing.' We really didn't like it.

Things came to a head on the last morning when they wouldn't let us in. The security had been next to useless all week. There were three gates, one at the top of the site, one at the bottom and one in the middle. We had been going in at the top gate, but we realised we would be nearer to where we wanted to be if we went in at the middle. The security there wouldn't let us in and told us to go back to the top gate. It was a very long walk between gates. When we got to the top gate we were told we needed an armed guard to go in with us, and he was at the middle gate. We did the long walk back to the middle gate only to be refused again. Some cotton workers were having the same problem so we persuaded them to join the Barnsley Women Against Pit Closures and cause a fuss. We decided to form a picket line. It was very funny, we were singing miners' strike picket songs and the cotton workers were rattling the gates. For the first time in our lives we were demanding that the gates were opened rather than shut. The arrest wagon turned up.

'Go steady here,' I said to Anne, 'we don't want to be getting arrested and put into prison in India.'

Rodney Bickerstaff, the former president of the TUC, was stood across the road with a delegation representing pensioners. He didn't come over, he must have thought, 'They're here again: rent a mob, rent a gob.'

Some women from an Irish trade union were staying in the same hotel as us. They remembered Anne from the time she spent on the picket lines outside Dunnes supermarket in Dublin. They told us that they were going to do yoga because it was relaxing and asked us to join them. We had never done anything like that before but we tagged along. The yoga class took place in a Catholic church hall. When we got there a little bow-legged fellow who looked like he'd just got off his horse greeted us. He gave us each a brick, a small chair and a mat. The man beckoned to us with his finger, so we followed him. He told us to put our foreheads on a window sill and then left us to it. After about ten minutes he hadn't come back so I said to Anne that we must be in the naughty corner.

'I think I've had enough now,' Anne said. 'Shall we give it up as a bad job?'

We both decided to escape and ran out into the street to flag down a taxi. At a traffic light a beautiful woman came up and put her hand through the open window asking for money. We were going to give her some but the taxi driver shot off as soon as the light started to change. He shouted over his shoulder to us.

'No money, no money, not man not woman, not nice, number six.'

To this day we don't know what a number six is.

We decided to treat ourselves to breakfast at the Taj Mahal Palace Hotel. We then went to look at the harbour and the Gate of India. A lad started following us wanting to clean our shoes. I had a pair of sandals on but Anne let him clean hers. A policeman came up and tried to hit him with a stick. We had to stand in the road to stop him. We saw too much of that there, poor people getting hit for no reason. It happened in a cafe we went in. A young lad was setting the table and he must have done it wrong because a bloke came running at him and swiped him across the head. Anne went mad. She shouted, 'Hey! That's enough.' Everybody was looking at us. Then she took the young waiter to one side and told him the best cure for a bully like that was to hit him back. She probably said, 'Sithee, if he bullies thee ageean, make sure tha gives him some back.' I don't know if he understood a word that she said, but he knew we were on his side.

The bloke who owned our hotel wanted to take us to a gymkhana club. It felt like something from the days of the Raj, so we declined. Anne told me that when she came down to make us a cup of tea on a morning the staff were asleep in the corridors. She said she had to step over sleeping bodies just to get to the kettle. We had an English newspaper shoved under our door every day. I was laid on the bed reading it one afternoon when we got back from the conference and I noticed an advert.

'Hey Anne, guess what. They've got a Marks & Spencer's here and they've got a sale on.'

She jumped up. 'Take me to it now.'

We went but it was only as big as a corner shop and the prices even in the sale were twice as dear as the Marks & Spencer's in Queen Street in Barnsley. Anne was disappointed. She likes Marks. Arthur used to say to her, 'I wish you knew your Marx as well as you know your Marks & Spencer.' I liked the shoe shops there and I came home with eight pairs of beautiful shoes.

There was a laundry shop opposite our hotel so we decided to have our washing done and pressed to save us doing it when we got home. We left our laundry and went for a pedicure. The bloke in the pedicure shop told us that he was a hair stylist to the film stars in Bollywood and showed us his portfolio. He wouldn't leave us alone until we agreed to let him do our hair. He couldn't stop touching Anne's blonde hair and fetched some of his mates to have a touch. We both ended up with a hairstyle as flat as a pancake on top of our heads and we had to do it again ourselves. When we fetched our clothes back from the laundry they had wrapped them in old newspapers tied up with string. We unwrapped them to find our clothes were still wet through and black with newsprint, so we'd that to do again as well.

The Price Of Coal
Anne & Betty

Betty

My son Donny remained a coalminer after the strike and through the years of closures. When Woolley pit shut down he was transferred to Riccall, a pit in the new Selby coalfield. He moved to a house just on the edge of Selby town itself. The sense of camaraderie and community spirit was different there and he couldn't get used to it. Donny had grown up in a village where everybody knew everybody else. He said to me, 'Do you know Mum, I don't even know where my next-door neighbour works.'

Donny was born in a hurry, I was in labour for less than half an hour. From the time he could crawl, he was a mischievous little monkey with the most infectious giggle when he laughed. When he was about three, one of Don's relatives bought him a push-along-toy, a dog on wheels. He would trot alongside it down through the woods to Woolley Colliery. When he got there, a neighbour would turn the dog round and off he'd trot back home again. He loved nature and was always up in the woods. When I undressed him on a night to wash him before he went to bed I had to check his pockets for frogs, worms or beetles. In his bedroom there was an old sideboard that he had turned into a nature table. He brought things to it that he collected and made his own notes. I looked at it one day when I was cleaning his room, he had written 'Or Forn' next to some hawthorn leaves.

Donny also had a great humanitarian streak. If he heard that other children were being bullied or unjustly treated, he was the first to stick up for them. When he left school he wanted to go to art college. His career advisor tried to put him off. He went anyway but only lasted three months before he was back home. Then he decided he was going to join the army. It seemed to suit him. We went to see him at Catterick. He had only been joined up what seemed like two minutes when he went to Blackpool for his holidays and met three girls from the Falls Road in Belfast who told him stories about the troubles. He made good friends with these girls and invited them to stay with us one New Year. He said he had changed his mind about the army because if ever he was sent to Northern Ireland, he might have to shoot people like those girls. Donny had a strong sense of social justice, but it was left to me to buy him out of the army.

His next step was to get himself a job at Woolley pit. He knocked about with some lads who were the sons of a woman I knew on the Coniston estate. She had three lads similar ages to my three. She also had a daughter who was at teacher training college at Scarborough. One time, Donny went with his mate Brian to visit his sister Jennifer at the college. While he was there he met Jennifer's mate, Sue. Not long after Donny said to me, 'I've been asked to go to Hull to meet Sue's parents.' My first reaction was 'You've not got her pregnant have you?' He laughed and said, 'No. It's just that her dad is a bank manager and her mother is a headmistress.' I told him not to worry, they were no better then us.

They got married in 1980 at a Methodist church in Hull and had their reception at the university. It was a posh do with a toastmaster and everything. They bought a house in Barnsley first. Sue got a job teaching at St Agnes School. Donny supported the strike with a passion and stayed solid all the way to the end. I was so proud of him for that. It helped of course that his wife had a good job and no children at that point, so they managed well. He had a mate who had a girlfriend and seven kids between them and they were struggling to keep a fire going. Donny went with him every day to the woods of his childhood to chop trees down and saw them into logs. I liked it because he came to see me most mornings and had a bacon sandwich.

Donny and Sue had their children when they moved to Selby after the strike. Andrew was born just before Christmas in 1988 and Emma was born three years later. They planned to retire early. Then, UK Coal, the private company that had taken over from the coal board, announced that the whole of the Selby coal complex would be closing down, less than forty years after it started producing coal. Donny thought about applying to work on the railways but decided that he would miss the camaraderie of the pit so instead he opted for a transfer to Kellingley Colliery.

Anne

It was a Wednesday morning. I got a phone call at about half past eight from Chris Kitchen, the General Secretary of the NUM who had previously been the branch secretary at Kellingley.
   'Have you seen Betty?' he asked.
   I told him that I'd seen her at the weekend.
   'Will you pass on our condolences.'
   I didn't know what he was talking about. He must have realised.
   'I'm sorry, but Donny was killed at work last night.'
   I put the phone down and didn't know whether I was coming or going. Then it dawned on me that Betty would be on her own so I jumped into my car and drove over to her house. I banged on Betty's front door. When she answered she could see I was crying. She smiled at first.
   'Whatever's the matter love?'
   I looked at her.
   'You don't know yet do you? Your Donny has been killed in the pit.'

Betty

I couldn't believe what Anne was telling me. I have never been a good sleeper at night and often drop off when it's nearly time to be getting up. I had some missed calls from Donny's number on my phone and had intended ringing him after my breakfast. It turned out that Sue's father had been trying to call me from Donny and Sue's house. I just kept walking backwards and forwards refusing to believe it. Anne had to go back home to sort her dogs out. At that time she was looking after peoples' dogs when they were away. My next-door-but-one neighbour came and sat with me.
   The news of what had happened started to come to me. There'd been a roof fall. Donny's mates had managed to dig him out and at first he was conscious but in a lot of pain. The lads had to transfer him from the site of the fall in agony. They gave him morphine on the way to the pit bottom. A team of paramedics were waiting at the top when they brought him up. They got him out and rushed him to Pontefract Infirmary where a specialist crash team had raced

over from Pinderfields Hospital. Donny was pronounced dead and was moved to a hospital mortuary at York. He had just celebrated his 50th birthday.

Donny is buried at Brayton cemetery near Selby, in a part that looks over a farm. I like it when I go there and see the hens clucking about. I remember Donny as a little lad being mischievous with a woman called Mrs Chalkley who lived just down from us at Woolley. Mrs Chalkley kept hens. Now and again I'd hear Donny's voice, 'Mrs Chalky,' he couldn't say Chalkley, 'Mrs Chalky, your bloody hens are out.' Then she would come running out and say, 'Oh dear! My bloody hens are out again.' Donny would then run down the yard and shout, 'Mrs Chalky, I let your bloody hens out.'

Donny was a well-known miner and a popular lad at Kellingley. The lads made a big collection and decided to build a memorial garden. The Barnsley sculptor Graham Ibbeson made a beautiful piece of a miner striking with his pick. The piece became a memorial to all of the miners who had lost their lives at Kellingley. It was put up in the pit yard.

The week before Christmas in 2015, Kellingley became the last deep coal mine in Britain to close. That was on a Friday and on the Saturday thousands of people gathered at Knottingley Town Hall to march to the social club. The media were there in numbers; the same media who had portrayed the miners as the scum of the earth during the strike were now doing sympathetic sob stories about the sad decline of a once proud workforce. There was even a documentary made for television called *The Last Miners*. I sat in that social club and thought about my Donny and what it had all come to.

When they demolished the pit and cleared the yard they moved the memorial to the coal-mining museum at Caphouse. I go there a lot. I find comfort and peace there, but it still hurts. You don't expect to outlive your children. I have lost two of my boys. I miss my Donny so much. He was a proud collier, a loyal man to his union and a great comrade to his mining family. My darling boy, he paid the price of coal. When I lost my Donny it was my faith that pulled me through.

Speaking Engagements
Anne & Betty

Betty
Over the years Anne and I have been invited to speak at many different events. Since I lost Donny I have been making a speech about health and safety in the workplace and was asked to give it at University College, London. Neil Kinnock was on the same platform, the Labour leader who refused to support the miners in the strike, so I didn't feel like doing it. Neither Anne nor I liked him but in the end we went.

Anne
Kinnock was due to speak before lunch. Betty and me planned to stand up and walk out when he started; make a big show of it. At the last minute they made a change to the running order and decided to put us on before lunch and Kinnock on after. While we were waiting to go on stage, Betty got up to speak to Ian Lavery. Ian had been the president of the NUM after Arthur and had just been elected MP for Wansbeck in Northumberland. I was sitting there on my own and who should come walking up but a smiling Neil Kinnock. He tried to soft soap me.

'Ooooh! Hello Anne love, I haven't seen you for ages.'

I set about him.

'I don't speak to people like you. You are a traitor of the first degree. You ought to come and have a look at my village now!'

'Well it's the same where I live Anne.'

'Aye, and you were one of the people that caused half of that by not getting behind us. And to think I paid to come and see you that night in Sheffield.'

He went off to the back of the room. One of the journalists told me later that he had been very upset by what I'd said to him. I told the journalist that he could never be as upset as I was about what had happened to us in the strike.

Betty

Anne and I got a call to ask us if we could sit on a panel at Ilkley Literature Festival. Two journalists, David Hencke and Francis Beckett, had written a book called *Marching to the Fault Line* which they said was the history of the miners' strike. These two were invited to talk about their book and I think they asked us two so that we could give some first-hand experiences of the picket lines and soup kitchens. Just before we set off we got a phone call from a journalist friend called Peter Lazenby. He told us to be wary of Hencke and Beckett because they had misquoted us in their book.

It was like a pantomime when we got there. I turned up on crutches because I'd just had a hip replacement. The two journalists spoke first. One of their mobile phones kept ringing and he had the bad manners to answer it. I think it happened three times. After that Anne was to speak. Before she started she looked up the table and referred to the journalists quoting her in the book.

'I'm sorry love,' she said, 'I don't know you and I can't ever remember speaking to you about the strike.'

The journalists weren't best pleased.

'Oh yes you did.'

Anne came straight back with, 'Oh no I didn't.'

It went back and forwards a bit before the chair intervened and asked us to tell our stories. When it came to my turn I told the journalists that I hadn't read their book as it was too dear for me. I then referred to a passage in the book that I'd seen that said we were petrified on the picket line. I told the journalists and the audience that I was never petrified, sometimes downhearted, but never petrified. I then asked Anne to join me in our song, 'Women of the Working Class'. We brought the house down. Afterwards we set our stall out to sell our badges and stuff. I don't know how many books the two journalists sold, but we nearly sold up.

Effigy
Anne

When Thatcher died a lot of people in former mining communities couldn't shed a tear or even bring themselves to feel sorrow. When they announced she was to have a state funeral with her coffin draped in a union flag and carried on a gun carriage to St Paul's Cathedral, it upset a lot of people. Mick Wood from Goldthorpe decided to organise his own event. He borrowed a horse and dray and had a cardboard coffin and effigy of Thatcher made with shoes, handbag, blue outfit, the lot. He told the local bobbies what he intended to do on the day of the funeral and asked them not to interfere. He told them that people in the local village would self-police 'Thatcher's funeral' and it wouldn't cost the tax payer a penny.

I had an official invite from Mick and went with Georgina Chapman. On the day thousands turned up in Goldthorpe to watch a procession set off from the Union Jack club. The horse had a black plume on its head and a lone Scots piper played 'Scotland the Brave'. They fetched the effigy of Thatcher out of the club tap room, placed her into the coffin and loaded her on the horse and cart. The procession toured the village and ended up at The Rusty Dudley pub. At the appointed time, to coincide what was going on in London, they set a bonfire alight on some waste ground and chucked the coffin on. We went for a funeral tea in the pub and when we had done with that we came out and danced on the ashes opposite some boarded-up houses. I was back home by 5 o'clock.

Of course the press were there wanting to know why we were doing what we were doing. They pretended that somehow they had sympathy for us, but really they just wanted to say we were showing disrespect. One bloke from Goldthorpe got plenty off his chest when the local news asked him for his thoughts.

'Why are you asking me what I'm joining in with this for? Just look round you, you can see with your own eyes what's happened here. I'm proud to come from this village, but look at the state of it and that woman caused it. That's why I'm here today.'

The press pestered Betty and me constantly when Thatcher died and at the time of her funeral. They couldn't wait for us to say we were glad she was dead. I gave them what they wanted. I told them I was glad because I hoped we could now move on and repair our ruined communities, sort out some of the social problems and create some jobs. Of course they just used the clip of me saying I was glad. They just wanted me showing disrespect. If I had shown half of the disrespect that Thatcher had shown for good, hard-working people and their families, I'd still be nowhere near her on that score.

The Daughters Of Mother Jones
Anne & Betty

Betty
Anne and I have a lot of adventures and sometimes it's an adventure just getting to where we want to be. We were invited to take part in a coalfields reunion conference in America and we'd booked the midnight coach from Meadowhall shopping centre outside Sheffield to Heathrow airport. I used to go to London a fair bit then and I thought I knew where to stand to wait for the bus. We waited and waited and then somebody told us that the bus had gone. We had to be at the airport first thing in the morning but there wasn't another bus. We decided to take a taxi and chase the bus to its next stopping point which was Chesterfield. The taxi driver wondered what the hell was going on. He told us he was going to phone his wife and tell her that two crazy women from Barnsley had kidnapped him. We didn't catch the bus before Chesterfield but spotted it on the road to Nottingham so we made the driver follow it right into the city to the bus station. The taxi driver turned round and said that he wasn't allowed into the station. We made him go in, then we jumped out of the taxi and ran across to the coach. Anne jumped on and gave the driver a right rollocking.

'Hey you! We were waiting at Meadowhall to get on this bus and you have driven straight past us and left us stranded. We have had to follow you for forty bloody miles in that taxi. You better let us on here now or there will be some right bother.'

The driver shook his head and didn't know what to say back. We realised that we had left our tickets back at Meadowhall but thankfully the driver just let us get on and never asked for our tickets.

Anne and I flew to Knoxville in Tennessee for the big reunion. We hadn't seen our American sisters for over twenty years and most of them were now in their retirement years, so it was an emotional meeting. June Rostin met us with her friend Carol, a union organiser who had lost part of her leg in an accident underground. The gathering was organised by our friend Marat Moore and took place in Jonesborough, a town in the Appalachian Mountains. Jonesborough is the oldest town in Tennessee and the locals are proud of their history. They have protected and listed most of their old buildings so the whole place has a timelessness to it. Every year they have a storytelling festival that attracts people from around the world to tell real stories about ordinary lives. Jonesborough also prides itself on being the first place to print a newspaper that campaigned for the abolition of slavery. It was the perfect place for a gathering of women who campaign on behalf of coal-mining community and culture.

We received a rapturous welcome when we arrived. The Americans seemed thrilled that two women from England had travelled all that way. The first evening was a very moving one. There was a memorial service for women miners who had lost their lives in the pit and for those who were no longer with us. As names were read out we were invited to place a sprig of green in a large wicker basket and say a few words. I spoke about my Donny. Anne placed her sprig in memory of Betty Heathfield who had been with us when we first visited America.

On the Saturday we left in what the Americans call 'a caravan of cars' to visit the archives of Appalachian culture at East Tennessee University. They have a wonderful history of women and mining there, plus there was an exhibition of drawings and paintings that children had done of their mothers in pit clothes. We listened to tapes of old women miners talking about their work and life experiences. We had taken some cassette tapes of songs from our strike and they let us play them. They liked them so much we had to do an encore. Anne and I were asked to record interviews about our strike for the social studies department. We told them about how the strike had changed a lot of attitudes amongst women in the Barnsley area.

In the evening we went to Jonesborough Theatre to listen to some old Appalachian music. The main singer was Sue Massek, a singer and banjo player, who for forty years was a leading member of the feminist hillbilly group Reel World String Band. She told us the story of Sarah Ogan Gunning, a ballad singer and miner's wife who helped organise the Kentucky coalfields in the 1930s. Sarah had married a coalminer when she was just fifteen and was a heroine for the women of the coalfields. Anne and I were persuaded to sing, so we sang Mal Finch's famous song 'Women of the Working Class'.

On that night we discussed how we could strengthen the ties between the UMWA and Barnsley Women Against Pit Closures. We decided to become The Daughters of Mother Jones and that we would meet up the following year at the Spirit of Mother Jones Festival in Cork, Ireland. Mother Jones was born in Cork and emigrated first to Canada and then to America. Not a lot of folk in England know much about her, but in America she is a heroine of working-class people and those in struggle. She dedicated much of her life to persuading workers in the mining districts to join a union and was sent to jail many times. The authorities despised her and she was known for a time as 'the most dangerous woman in America', which was an achievement for a tiny woman who wore round glasses and a bonnet and traipsed about in a dress that swept the floor.

We got back to Knoxville early the next day and had a bit of time to look round. In the marketplace we saw the bronze statue to the memory of three suffragettes; Tennessee was the last state to allow women to vote. Anne and I had never known anything like it and we both agreed it was the most beautiful tribute to women either of us had seen. There is an inscription on the bottom that says 'All honor to women, the first disenfranchised class in history who unaided by any political party, won enfranchisement by its own effort alone'. The sad thing was, when we asked people round and about to tell us something about the statue, nobody seemed to know anything about it. It was the same when we went to the tourist information place. They didn't have any leaflets to give us.

We kept our promise and travelled to our first Mother Jones Festival in Cork the following year to speak about our experiences in the miners' strike. We learnt a lot about Mother Jones on that trip and became enamoured with her story. Mary Harris Jones was born in 1837. Her family emigrated to America because of the potato famine. She had a heart-breaking life. Her husband and four children died in a yellow fever outbreak. She made a fresh start as a dressmaker in Chicago, making clothes for the upper classes, but then she lost everything when her shop burned down in the Great Chicago Fire in 1871. She was a committed Christian and an early socialist who helped to organise some of the first trade unions. She campaigned especially on behalf of the coalminers and encouraged strikes for better pay and conditions. She became known as Mother Jones for her habit of calling striking miners 'my boys'. The US senate denounced her as 'the grandmother of all agitators' and in response she said that she hoped to live long enough to be 'the great grandmother of all agitators'. She lived to be 93.

The Mother Jones Festival is fantastic. On that first trip there was a strike by dustbin men. Of course we went straight to the picket line. There was a binman there and he'd brought his thirteen-year-old daughter out of school so that she could be on the picket with him. He told us, 'This is an important part of her education.' We were ever so proud of him. We go every year now.

Joan Lazenby made us a Daughters of Mother Jones banner. There was nothing on the reverse of it so we got in touch with Emma Shanklin at Durham Bannermakers to finish it off. Anne and I are painted on it, but we also wanted to feature women that inspire us. Kipp Dawson is on there. Kipp is one of the most inspirational women miners in America. Then there's Betty Jean Hall, a lawyer and union organiser who became a judge, and Marat Moore who spent a lot of time travelling across America interviewing women miners. We also wanted to feature our own personal heroines, so two famous suffragettes appear on our banner: Emily Davison and Annie Kenney. Annie Kenney is my heroine because she is one of only a few working-class women who rose up to prominence in the suffragette movement. It's well known that most of the women in the movement were well-educated and middle class, but Annie was different. She had been born in Oldham, one of twelve children, and by the age of ten she was working in the mills. She was a Christian and became a trade unionist with a keen interest in self-education through reading, campaigning for literacy amongst working folk. Annie joined the suffragettes after hearing Christabel Pankhurst speak at a club in Oldham. When she was imprisoned for

Anne and Betty at the Mother Jones Memorial in Ireland.

Party at Margaret's house with some of the cast and crew to celebrate the success of Maxine Peake's radio play *Queens of the Coal Age*.

her activism, she was one of the women who had to undergo the horror of being force-fed after going on hunger strike. Her ashes were scattered on Saddleworth Moor.

Anne

I grew up listening to the story of how Emily Davison was trampled under the king's horse Anmer at the Epsom Derby in 1913. I admire her because she did a brave thing for all women to get the vote. I have been to the polling station every election – council or parliamentary – since I was old enough at 21 to cast my vote. I don't always put my cross on. There have been times when I have spoiled my paper. If I don't like any of the list of candidates I generally write, 'I am not voting for any of the above, but I have come because of Emily Davison.'

Some people will tell you that Emily committed suicide by deliberately throwing herself under the king's horse. I don't believe that. I have studied the old film and it is clear to see that she was trying to put a banner onto the horse so that when it finished there would be publicity for the cause.

Betty

We met a producer called David Thacker. He was doing a film for the television called *Faith* set in the strike. It was about two sisters. One was married to a miner and the other one to a policeman. David asked us if we would go to a meeting at Doncaster to share our experiences. We spoke to the two actresses who were playing the sisters. One was Christine Tremarco and the other was Maxine Peake. They did a lot of filming at Hatfield Main. I was involved in a crowd scene at the pit gates.

The film was shown at the independent cinema opposite the railway station at Sheffield. We met Maxine again that night and we got on well with her. She came to see us afterwards because she wanted to research a play about the sit-in at Parkside pit. She ended up writing one for the radio called *Queens of the Coal Age*, which was later adapted for the theatre. We loved it and we are very fond of Maxine too.

A Memorial
Anne

My sister Joan developed motor-neurone disease and ended up in an hospice. She started to say that she felt like she was walking on clouds. Joan was always in bother. Whatever happened, our poor Joan seemed to get the blame. When I married Arthur, she came to live with us for a while because my mam and her were struggling to get on. She married a bloke called Geoff Bland. He worked at Stocksbridge in the steelworks offices. Joan worked hard all of her life, first at Brook Motors like me and then as a home help for the elderly. She still found time to come and volunteer for the soup kitchen after work. Everybody in Kendray where she went to live knew her. She was well-known and well-liked. She was full of fun. Joan was not a fan of Christmastime, but she always made an effort for the sake of others. We once went to a party and she came as a Christmas tree all lit up. Every year she bought holly and sat in her garage making wreaths to raise money for the hospice, the same hospice that she ended her days in.

I went to see her on the Saturday. I said, 'Come on Joan, love.' She couldn't speak to me, so I gave her a piece of paper and a pencil. She wrote on it, 'Nobody wants to live like this.' On the Sunday morning, Margaret met me coming out of church. She took me to the hospice. She told me as we were going in that my sister had died at 6 o'clock. Joan had always had a fear of being buried alive. When she took poorly she asked Margaret to check her when she passed just to make sure. Margaret examined her and confirmed that she had passed away. I lost not only my sister, but also a dear friend that morning.

When Dougie Stables died I ended up with his ashes. I liked Dougie, he was a good man for the community and a good friend to a lot of people. He must have been the secretary at the Swaithe club for fifty years or more. Me and my friend Georgina were going to Ireland, so we asked him if he'd like to come with us. When we got to the airport they asked him for his passport.

'Nay lad, I'm 82 and I've not bothered with one.'

They asked if he had any kind of identification. It turned out that he had a bus pass in his wallet. They let him through, but asked him to take his shoes off while he went through security. Poor old Dougie, he'd no idea what was going on.

'What have I got to take my shoes off for to go to Ireland?'

He was a comical old bugger, dry as a stick, you couldn't help but take to him.

At the time of his death they were building a memorial to the industrial heritage of Worsbrough on the road to Sheffield, near The Red Lion pub. I wrote to the council and asked if I could bury Dougie's ashes under it. The council turned me down. The night before they laid the concrete, a good friend of mine helped me to dig a hole. I fetched the ashes and placed them into the hole with a message saying, 'Douglas Stables. He did a lot of work and should be recognised.' Then we filled it back over. The next day the council workers came and put the concrete down and not long after that erected their monument. I always think of Dougie when I go past.

Orgreave Truth And Justice
Anne

As the thirtieth anniversary of the Battle of Orgreave approached, Bridget Bell decided that we shouldn't let it go past without some sort of commemoration. She suggested that we should have a picnic there. She wanted to bring the story of Orgreave and what happened back to the top of the agenda. It's well known now that the so-called Battle of Orgreave was co-ordinated by the police and they deliberately set about our lads and tried to blame them for the violence. It was the same police force who were supposed to be looking after the crowd at the Hillsborough football match and then tried to blame the innocent fans when things went wrong through bad policing. We knew about the burning injustice, but it always needs somebody to spearhead the movement and Bridget was second to none at doing that, she was a brilliant organiser.

We first knew Bridget when she worked at a refuge for women who had escaped from violent relationships. When the strike started she was one of the people who got the North Staffordshire women organised. North Staffs was only a small coalfield and everybody seemed to know one another but it was Bridget who pulled them together. Rose Hunter, one of the Staffordshire miners' wives, once said to me, 'She had made us even closer than sisters.' Bridget was a good singer and she taught the women a lot of songs, she even showed them how to do breathing exercises, it was all very professional. The Staffordshire women became known for their singing which they used to raise funds; Bridget took them to London a lot. Whenever you saw her she had plans. I used to say to her, 'Can we afford to do all these things?' She never blinked, 'Of course we can afford it! Just turn up, it will happen.' She was full of enthusiasm and energy and seemed to know everybody. In 2004 when we had a twentieth anniversary of Women Against Pit Closures Conference at Wortley Hall, she arranged for Bernadette McAliskey to come and speak to us. Bernadette Devlin – as she had been known – was the youngest woman ever to be elected to parliament when she won a Northern Irish by-election in 1969.

At the Orgreave picnic we put our gazebo up and fetched some cheese and bread from Morrisons supermarket. We blew up coloured balloons and let them go; a lot of them got caught in the trees. The mayor of Rotherham turned up in the mayor's limousine. I had to laugh when the chauffeur got out in his uniform. He came up to Betty and me in the gazebo.

'Can I introduce you to the mayor of…'

'Hold on a minute love, we know her. She used to be in Women Against Pit Closures with us.'

The television people wanted to interview us. The man who did the interview said that he had been a young reporter at the time. On the day of the Battle of Orgreave, 18th June 1984, he told us that he had been sent to cover the picketing and had thought it was going to be just another routine day. When he saw what was going on he got onto his bosses back at the office and said, 'You better get some more cameras and reporters down here, the police are rioting.' The news sent a helicopter. The reporter told us that they took the door of the helicopter off to film better. When they went back to collect the door from the field where they had left it, there was no sign of it. Betty used to joke that somebody had taken it to make a door for a pigeon loft.

The Orgreave Truth and Justice Campaign grew out of the picnic. Betty and me pray that we will live long enough to see some compensation for those families who were affected by police brutality at Orgreave.

Pride
Anne & Betty

Betty

At the end of 2003, I kept seeing an advert in the *Barnsley Chronicle* for call centre operators. I phoned up and asked if they had any policy on employing older workers. When they confirmed that they were not ageist, I applied. I got an interview at the Barnsley Innovation Centre, a place that had been built after the strike with European Union money to try to attract investment and jobs back to the areas ruined by pit closures. They told me I could start on Monday. I worked from two until six every day. My job was to call the parents of children who had missed registration at school. I phoned families the length and breadth of England and Scotland. When I was a girl, most schools had a bobby who would go round knocking on doors rounding up kids who weren't where they should be, now I was phoning people from far away and sending reports to schools I had never heard of. Most of the time it was just a case of teachers not noticing that kids had come in late, or a parent forgetting to let the school know that their child was going to be away. Occasionally there would be a case where a child had gone missing and the police were involved.

I can remember vividly during the time we spent at the pit camp in Grimethorpe, the reporters were constantly pestering us about why we were doing what we were doing. GMTV came to the pit yard to interview us. They kept asking 'Why are you doing this?' Every time we gave them the answer, they would ask the question in a different way, 'What is the future for this dirty, dangerous industry?' We tried to explain that we wanted future generations to have worthwhile jobs in a safer environment and some hope. We knew what was coming if they closed all the pits, but the media people just didn't get it or didn't want to.

In the past a lot of men and boys didn't have a choice about whether they worked in the pit or not. When my Donny marched back to the pit after a year on strike with his head up and chest out, I swelled up too. When he decided to carry on working at the pit I was prouder still. Some might say 'What an ambition for a mother to have for her son' but my Donny was not forced down the hole. He wanted to do it and made his own choice. At least at the pit the lads looked after one another's backs. They were a society that worked. Not like now where a lot of working-class people are against one another.

I worked at the call centre until I finally retired at the age of 81 in 2019. By then I was doing work for Conexions, an organisation that deals with 'NEETS' – short for young people not in education, employment or training. I think 'NEETS' is an awful word. It labels young people who haven't had much of a chance to start with.

When I told them I was ready for my retirement, they said I could come back in September and retrain for a new job. I told them I had done my share of working and now fully intended to be an official retiree. I want to spend more time with my family. I still try to make it up to my lad Glyn for the times I wasn't there. My family have been long enough without a mother, a granny, a great-granny and in five cases a great-great granny. My grandson married a woman who already had grown-up children and they now have had kids of their own. I still volunteer at The Salvation Army and I'm still available for picket lines, demonstrations and direct action – that will never stop.

Anne

I am a woman who stood up and I'm still standing. I am still a bit uncomfortable at calling myself a feminist. I believe I can make my own mind up about what's right and wrong. One thing that I have learned over years of protesting is that actions speak a lot louder than words. Both Betty and me are socialists, we are also Christians, but neither of us believe that you can subscribe to socialism or Christianity and then sit on your arse without doing anything useful. When I worked with the homeless I did it because I felt very sorry for the predicament they were in, but mainly because I wanted to make a difference to the society we had ended up with. I did that for twelve years but had to stop because my arthritis got the better of me. I had a knee replacement and I couldn't bend down to put stuff in and out of the oven. When our Joan died in the hospice, I wanted to do something to help them, so I volunteered at their office across from our church. I sort the donated clothes out and check to see they are clean and in good repair before they are sent out to the charity shops. The lads and lasses there are like my new family; good and kind people who are also interested in making society better.

I haven't given up on picketing. Anybody who needs help on a picket line only has to pick the phone up and I'll be there. I still believe in direct action. I was talking to a woman recently. She is one of a group who are trying to save a piece of green land in Barnsley called Penny Pie Park. There are plans to build a new road system straight over it. Some of the locals have banded together to try and stop it. I asked her what she planned to do. She told me that they want to tie some ribbons around the trees. I told her that she can tie as many ribbons as she wants but it won't make a blind bit of difference. Sometimes you need to get laid down in front of the bulldozers.

Margaret qualified as a doctor in 1992 and took a job as a junior house officer at Leeds General Infirmary. She was there just six months when the opportunity to work at Barnsley General came up. She became a GP in 1996 and joined a partnership based in Kendray, an estate in Barnsley where a lot of coal-mining families had once lived. The practice manager at the Kendray surgery was Jim Logan. Jim had once been the under-manager at Grimethorpe Colliery, the very place where we made the pit camp protests.

I'll never forget the night I found out that Margaret was going out with Jim. She said to me that she had a new partner and she wanted to invite me to tea to meet him. I walked through the door. He was sitting there. I said, 'I know you! You worked at Grimethorpe pit.' Jim said he knew who I was too. Of course he was well aware of what I had got up to at the pit.

We had Jim and Margaret over to celebrate the New Year in 1997, along with some local friends plus the rail union leader Bob Crow and his wife Nicola. We played Trivial Pursuit, boys versus girls. It was a laugh a minute. Because Margaret was the captain of the girls' team, Arthur tried to suggest we took out any medical questions.

Then when some questions on politics came up, Arthur and Bob Crow wanted to debate everything. There was one question about the history of the Labour Party; Jim knew it straightaway but the lads argued for at least a quarter of an hour before giving a different answer to the one Jim said. Margaret was laughing her head off when she declared that the answer Arthur and Bob gave was wrong and that Jim had been right in the first place. Then there was another debate when they were so confident in their own answer that they declared the question setters must have got it wrong. In the end the card was ripped up and thrown away like confetti, but Margaret was adamant that they didn't get a point. Before we finished the lads got another politics question and the answer was Arthur Scargill. At least they got that right.

Jim and Margaret got married at the registry office at Barnsley Town Hall. Afterwards they had a separate ceremony at their house. They ordered a big marquee and put it up in the garden. Father Marshall came and gave a blessing and her Uncle Geoff gave Margaret away. Arthur had been invited but chose not to attend. Rod Bickerstaffe gave the father-of-the-bride speech. It was really kind of him to make the effort to come from London as he felt sorry for Margaret.

The night that I had my tea with Jim and Margaret wasn't the most comfortable of evenings, but I came to like Jim a lot. I love him today. He's a smashing son-in-law, a good husband, a great father to his boys and a good worker. His forward-thinking health practice in Kendray is inspired by ideas from Cuba. When Luis Enrique Marcano Sanz, a notable Cuban paediatric heart surgeon from the William Soler Hospital in Havana, came to visit England he stayed with us. Luis Enrique was a well-grounded, friendly and driven man with a huge passion for his work. When he was over here he made friends with the local cardiologist Walter Rhoden. Walter and Jim went for a memorable trip to Cuba to look at their health system and create contacts at the hospital. Jim studied their polyclinic healthcare system – the idea that all services could be under one roof in a 'one stop shop' – and adopted its principle for his medical project in Kendray.

Anne with grandsons Harry and Tom at the unveiling of Oaks Disaster Memorial in the grounds of Oaks Park Primary Care Centre, 2016.

Kellingley Miners Memorial at the National Coal Mining Museum.

Betty and Anne in the Kellingley Memorial Garden, National Coal Mining Museum.

Jim and Margaret have twins, Harry and Thomas. I couldn't wish for better grandchildren. Every time I see them I tell them I love them all the world. And the reason I do that is because my mother never told me she loved me and it hurts me when I think about it. The lads have just gone to university. Thomas has gone to Keele to study politics and Harry has gone to St Andrews to do chemistry. Tom wants to be a politician and Harry wants to be a lecturer and research chemist based in a university. It's a long way from Barugh Green and me growing up, but I couldn't be prouder.

Acknowledgements

Anne and Betty would like to thank:

Ian Clayton
Ian Daley
Paul Darlow
Margaret Scargill
Jim Logan
Mick and Mary Appleyard
Bobby Graham
Barry and Margaret Swan
Norma and Geoffrey Brown
Geoff Bland
Peter and Joan Lazenby for kindness and emotional support
Women Against Pit Closures
Daughters of Mother Jones
Mother Jones Festival Committee
Durham Miners' Association
Durham Women's Banner Group
With Banners Held High
The National Coal Mining Museum
Orgreave Truth and Justice Campaign
Past Pixels
The Trade Union and Labour Movement

And for financial support
USDAW
ASLEF and ASLEF branches
PCS
NUM National
NUM Yorkshire
UNITE
GMB North West and Irish Region
GMB Yorkshire and N Derbyshire Region
FBU
Sheffield Women Against Pit Closures

Authors

Anne Scargill has devoted much of her life to direct acti
days of the coal miners' strike, through to helping the
volunteering for the local hospice, she believes actions a ..ys speak
louder than words.

Betty Cook is a proud daughter of the coalfields. She learned all she knows about community and activism on her journey from Brick Row in the pit village of Woolley.

Ian Clayton is an author, broadcaster and storyteller from Featherstone, West Yorkshire. His stories are about making sense of where we come from. His books include *Bringing It All Back Home*, a bestselling book about music; *Song For My Father* about his lifelong search for a father figure; *Our Billie* about loss; *It's The Beer Talking*, about adventures in public houses; *In Search of Plainsong* tells the story of a folk-rock group.

For more on this book, please visit:

www.route-online.com

Printed in Great Britain
by Amazon